Liberty under Law

THE AMERICAN MOMENT

Stanley I. Kutler, *Consulting Editor*

The Twentieth-Century American City
Jon C. Teaford

American Workers, American Unions, 1920–1985
Robert H. Zieger

The House Divided: Sectionalism and Civil War, 1848–1865
Richard H. Sewell

Liberty under Law: The Supreme Court in American Life
William M. Wiecek

LIBERTY UNDER LAW

The Supreme Court in American Life

WILLIAM M. WIECEK

The Johns Hopkins University Press
Baltimore and London

The Johns Hopkins University Press
701 West 40th Street
Baltimore, Maryland 21211
The Johns Hopkins Press Ltd., London

The paper used in this publication meets the minimum requirements of American National Standard for Information Sciences—Permanence of Paper for Printed Library Materials, ANSI Z39.48-1984.

Library of Congress Cataloging-in-Publication Data

Wiecek, William M., 1938–
Liberty under law.

(The American moment)
Bibliography: p.
Includes index.
1. United States. Supreme Court. 2. Judicial review—United States. I. Title. II. Series.
KF8742.W52 1988 347.73′26 87–31139
ISBN 0-8018-3595-X (alk. paper) 347.30735
ISBN 0-8018-3596-8 (pbk. : alk. paper)

This book is for Kristen
carissimae filiae

CONTENTS

FOREWORD

William Wiecek has written with great distinction on numerous aspects of our constitutional history. Here he offers a fresh synthesis of the Supreme Court's history, one keyed to understanding its place at the juncture of law and politics. His assessments of the Court's special functions are shrewd and carefully measured within a historical framework. Wiecek's chronological overview is sprinkled with rich, considered reflections, from the Court's origins through the key formative work of Chief Justices John Marshall and Roger B. Taney and into its pivotal role in arbitrating political, social, and economic controversies in the twentieth century. That work, and the reactions it provoked through the years, is a vital component of the American experience in law and governance. *Liberty under Law* provides both a useful introduction and an essential foundation for understanding the Supreme Court.

The Supreme Court's role in the American governmental apparatus reflects the rich variety of our political, social, economic, and cultural history. The Court's history has generated parallel streams of controversy and public reverence, largely dependent on reactions to particular lines of decisions in various historical periods. The justices periodically have shaped new meanings for the Constitution and repudiated old ones; as such, they have alternately pleased and provoked deeply-vested interests. The Supreme Court has expressed, for better and sometimes for worse, the values and ideals of American life. Thus, the Court has rationalized the "constitutionality" of separate but equal facilities based on racial differences but a half century later found such notions inherently "unconstitutional." What had changed was not the Constitution but the society, its experiences, and its discovery of newer, more appropriate values.

The Constitution is an everyday experience in American life. It uniquely blends words written in 1787 with the leavening of experience. We have by a combination of accident and design chosen to rely largely on the Supreme Court to peacefully make the necessary adjustments that have enabled the

Constitution and the nation to persist for two centuries. In *Liberty under Law*, William M. Wiecek has imaginatively captured this inextricable bond between the nation, the Constitution, and the Supreme Court.

The American Moment is designed to offer a series of narrative and analytical discussions on a variety of topics in American history. Books in the series are both topical and chronological. Some volumes survey familiar subjects—such as Puritanism, the American Revolution, the Civil War, the New Deal, and the Cold War—and blend necessary factual background with thoughtful, provocative interpretations. Other volumes such as those on women and reform movements, urban affairs, ethnicity, sports, and popular culture chart new or less familiar terrain. All provide narrative and interpretation to open significant new dimensions and perspectives on the American past.

Stanley I. Kutler
The University of Wisconsin
Madison, Wisconsin

ACKNOWLEDGMENTS

The title of this book is taken from a passage in the Supreme Court's holding in *Bolling* v. *Sharpe* (1954), the companion case to *Brown* v. *Board of Education*, which mandated desegregation of the public schools of the District of Columbia: "Liberty under law extends to the full range of conduct which the individual is free to pursue, and it cannot be restricted except for a proper governmental objective."

The titles of each of the chapters are phrases from Chief Justice John Marshall's greatest opinions, *Marbury* v. *Madison* (1803) and *McCulloch* v. *Maryland* (1819).

Liberty under Law was written while I was associated with two different institutions, the University of Missouri—Columbia and Syracuse University. I am indebted to the law libraries and librarians of both, especially Professor Susan Csaky at Missouri and David Naylor and Louise Lantzy at Syracuse. William D. Karchner and Robert Faulkner, research assistants at Syracuse University College of Law, made valuable contributions. Professor Norman Rosenberg of Macalester College provided an extraordinarily thorough review of the book in manuscript, and it is much improved for his suggestions. Stanley I. Kutler similarly provided valuable recommendations for revision, which I have gratefully followed. Though I gladly share credit for the book's strengths, I alone am responsible for its deficiencies.

Liberty under Law

Introduction

THE UNITED STATES SUPREME COURT AND AMERICAN CONSTITUTIONALISM

An interpretive history of the Supreme Court written on the occasion of the Constitution's bicentennial celebration must address the issues raised by the past century of constitutional theory. Ever since James Bradley Thayer's seminal essay, "The Origin and Scope of the American Doctrine of Constitutional Law," appeared in 1893, constitutional theory in the United States has been dominated by the problem of the legitimacy of judicial review. Put simply, this problem is: how can an institution that is not at all democratic in its composition and methods legitimately exercise the power of holding void the laws enacted by the democratically elected branch of government, the people's representatives? This question of legitimacy has provoked another: can Supreme Court adjudication be objective? That is to say, when the Court holds a statute or an action of the executive branch unconstitutional, can its decision be defended by reference to criteria of judgment external to the judges' personal political, social, economic, religious, and ideological preferences? Or is appellate judging really nothing more, in the end, than the judges substituting their own views about desirable social policy for those of the people's representatives?

The problem of objectivity has most often been tackled by asking what values the judges select and use as the basis of their decisions. "What values?" may be stated in another way: where do judges turn for the substantive content of the values they impose on the legislative and executive branches? More than a century and a half ago, Chief Justice John Marshall set down the basic framework within which we ponder these questions. In *Marbury* v. *Madison* (1803), Marshall centered American constitutional theory around two fundamental propositions. First, the Constitution is law. As law, it is therefore something judges can interpret and impose while they are doing the usual customary work of judges, namely, applying the law. Second, law is something radically different from politics. Law is the product of reasoned judgment; politics is the child of arbitrary will and power. Law, therefore, is the domain of judges and courts; politics is the province of legislatures. No one has ever challenged Marshall's first point; only rarely has anyone rejected the second, and in those few instances contemporaries have howled down the critic as a heretic who threatens the very rule of law itself.

From these questions and axioms, we derive the content of the debate about constitutionalism in the past century. The current state of that debate, which has posed the questions addressed in this book, can be crudely polarized around two positions. In the current state of the controversy, these antagonistic positions go by the unfortunate names of "interpretivism" and "noninterpretivism," two multisyllabic mouthfuls that say nothing about what they purport to describe. The first pole of this debate (interpretivism), which I will call here constitutional literalism, demands that the Court find its values exclusively in one of three sources: the text of the Constitution, the Framers' intent, and the historical situation of the Framers. Within this narrowly defined quarry of values, some useful mining might take place. For example, we can learn much about the eighteenth-century Framers' vision of their place in history, and of their sense of the direction in which the Republic was heading. They considered themselves Englishmen (until 1776) and therefore heirs of the British constitutional tradition. To them, this tradition was of supreme importance for defining their values. In it, therefore, we can see much of what they desired and of what they feared. Similarly, their conception of a republic, its possibilities and its weaknesses, runs throughout the constitutions they created.

But rich as these sources are for illuminating the beginnings of the Constitution, they are stultifying as exclusive guides to constitutional interpretation; hence the second pole of modern constitutional debate, which I will call here the fundamental values approach. This position derives from a view of judging espoused successively by Justices Oliver Wendell Holmes, Jr., Benjamin N. Cardozo, Felix Frankfurter, and John M. Harlan. Its content and development can best be conveyed by letting these giants of the twentieth century speak for themselves.

In his often-cited dissent in *Lochner* v. *New York* (1905), Holmes summed up his objection to the doctrine of substantive due process:

> The word liberty in the 14th Amendment is perverted when it is held to prevent the natural outcome of a dominant opinion, unless it can be said that a rational and fair man necessarily would admit that the statute

> proposed would infringe fundamental principles as they have been understood by the traditions of our people and our law.

Later, he amplified this theme of historical traditions in *Gompers* v. *United States* (1914):

> The provisions of the Constitution are not mathematical formulas having their essence in their form; they are organic, living institutions transplanted from English soil. Their significance is vital, not formal; it is to be gathered not simply by taking the words and a dictionary, but by considering their origin and the line of their growth.

And then a few years later, in *Missouri* v. *Holland* (1920), Holmes made explicit what he meant by the line-of-growth metaphor:

> When we are dealing with words that also are a constituent act, like the Constitution of the United States, we must realize that they have called into life a being the development of which could not have been foreseen completely by the most gifted of its begetters. It was enough for them to realize or to hope that they had created an organism; it has taken a century and has cost their successors much sweat and blood to prove that they created a nation. The case before us must be considered in the light of our whole experience and not merely in that of what was said a hundred years ago.

Holmes's seat on the Court was filled, after his retirement in 1932, by Cardozo, and Cardozo, in his turn, was succeeded by Frankfurter in 1939. Both successors elaborated Holmes's historical traditions point. In *Palko* v. *Connecticut* (1937), Cardozo referred to a "principle of justice so rooted in the traditions and conscience of our people as to be ranked as fundamental"; "fundamental principles of liberty and justice which lie at the base of all our civil and political institutions"; principles that are "of the very essence of a scheme of ordered liberty," so essential "that neither liberty nor justice would exist if they were sacrificed." After Cardozo's death, Frankfurter became custodian of the tradition, extolling "those canons of decency and fairness which express the notions of justice of English-speaking peoples" (*Adamson* v. *California,* 1947).

But this fundamental values tradition ran into formidable criticism from Justice Hugo Black, who derided it as a resuscitation of long-abandoned "natural law principles." Frankfurter attempted to rebut the idea that judges were free to concoct their own biases into law under the name of fundamental principles. In *Rochin* v. *California* (1952), he insisted that constitutional provisions, such as the due process clause,

> may be indefinite and vague, but the mode of ascertainment is not self-willed [by judges]. In each case "due process of law" requires an evalua-

> tion based on a disinterested inquiry pursued in the spirit of science, on a balanced order of facts exactly and fairly stated, on the detached consideration of conflicting claims, on a judgment not ad hoc and episodic but duly mindful of reconciling the needs both of continuity and change in a progressive society.

Black remained unpersuaded. He carried on the debate with Justice John M. Harlan in *Duncan* v. *Louisiana* (1968): "The 'fundamental fairness' test is one on a par with that of shocking the conscience of the Court. Each of such tests depends entirely on the particular judge's idea of ethics and morals instead of requiring him to depend on the boundaries fixed by the written words of the Constitution."

In recent years, conservatives have shifted the polarities of the debate by claiming that the meaning of the Constitution is fixed and unchanging. Justice William H. Rehnquist conceded that the terms of the Constitution could be applied to new circumstances not anticipated by the Framers but that its meaning does not change and cannot be tampered with in the name of keeping the document relevant to the times. Professor Richard Epstein condemns "the idea that constitutions must evolve to meet changing circumstances [a]s an invitation to destroy the rule of law" (Richard A. Epstein, *Takings: Private Property and the Power of Eminent Domain* [Cambridge, Mass., 1985], 24). Such ideas are a throwback to the notice of an immutable Constitution for which Chief Justice Roger B. Taney contended in the disaster of his *Dred Scott* opinion (1857).

In the bicentennial period, constitutional theory seems adrift. Nearly all judges and commentators (including conservatives) have rejected judicial intervention in policymaking typified in the 1905 *Lochner* decision. But even though activism of the *Lochner* sort has been discredited, nothing has appeared to take its place. Since the constitutional revolution of 1937, the United States Supreme Court has given little succor to the claims of property that discredited the *Lochner* era, instead spending its efforts in protecting civil liberties and civil rights. But this new emphasis has not resolved the debate over legitimacy and objectivity. On the contrary, that debate has flared with undiminishing force ever since *Brown* v. *Board of Education* (1954). The literalist–fundamental values division persists as contentiously as ever today. United States Attorney General Edwin Meese has fanned the fires of the controversy by adopting an extreme version of the literalist approach, which he calls a "Jurisprudence of Original Intention." Meese's simplistic position has had one beneficial effect: it has refocused debate on the era of the Framers and on the question of how the Supreme Court has used history and been affected by history.

This book is a contribution to that renewed inquiry.

Chapter 1

"The province and duty of the judicial department"

THE ORIGINS OF AMERICAN CONSTITUTIONALISM

THE UNITED STATES Supreme Court is heir to a constitutional tradition now some eight hundred years old. This tradition is summed up in the word constitutionalism. Its essence is limited government, the belief that the government itself must function under the rule of law. Our constitutional order is dedicated, as Justice Robert H. Jackson insisted, to "the principle that ours is a government of laws, not of men, and that we submit ourselves to rulers only if under rules" (*Youngstown Sheet & Tube* v. *Sawyer,* 1952, concurring opinion). Governmental power is limited in order to protect the rights of the individual person. The Anglo-American tradition does not pursue the ideal of limited government for its own sake, simply because we think such a government is more attractive, or works better, or is morally superior. Rather, it links these ideas together because each is necessary to give meaning to the other.

For five hundred years after Magna Carta (1215), the English strove to bring government under the rule of law. This long struggle climaxed in the turbulent seventeenth century, as the Stuart kings tried to free themselves from the nuisance of having to submit to laws, while Parliaments and judges sought to impose that restriction on them. Lord Chancellor Ellesmere expressed the Stuart attitude in *Calvin's Case* (1608): "The monarch *is* the law; the king is the law speaking." The monarch at that time, James I, a domineering man with a violent temper, reacted indignantly when Sir Edward Coke, chief justice of the Court of Common Pleas, rejected that view by insisting that the king was under law. This insistence produced a dramatic confrontation between the two men in the autumn of 1608.

Coke had been issuing writs of prohibition from his court to halt proceedings in another court, High Commission, a prerogative court controlled by the king.* James called Coke and representatives of the prerogative courts to a meeting of the Privy Council to settle the matter. Coke insisted that the king was *sub Deo et Lege:* under God and under the law. This idea was not new, by any means. Bracton had written precisely the same words in the thirteenth century: the king is under God and under the law, because the law makes the king. James did not see it that way and was not impressed by an idea already three centuries old. He exploded with rage. A bystander tells us: "His Majesty fell into that high indignation as the like was never knowne in him, looking and speaking fiercely with bended fist, offering to strike [Coke]. Which the Lo[rd] Coke perceaving fell flatt on all fower; humbly beseeching his Majestie to take compassion on him and to pardon him" (quoted in Catherine D. Bowen, *The Lion and the Throne: The Life and Times of Sir Edward Coke* [Boston, 1956], 305). Lawyers and English Whigs, describing this incident, invented a different tradition: the other judges of Common Pleas groveled on their hands and knees before the king, whereas Coke stood upright, stiff-necked and defiant. Whatever happened, Coke's view prevailed in the long run, but only after a civil war and two revolutions.

James's son, Charles I, was beheaded by the Parliamentary party in 1649; Charles's sons, Charles II and James II, clung to their father's absolutist idea that he could ignore or suspend the law. To rid themselves of this notion and its royal adherents for good, the Parliamentary party in 1688 deposed James II in what has become known as the Glorious Revolution. They imposed a constitutional settlement on the new monarchs, William and Mary, partly embodied in the Bill of Rights of 1689, which declared that the "pretended power of dispensing with laws or the execution of laws by regal authority as it hath been assumed and exercised of late is illegal." Ever since then the rule of law has gone unchallenged in England and has been at the heart of our shared constitutional tradition.

The English Bill of Rights contained other provisions that ratified the idea of limited government. Each passed into our tradition intact, but they are more important collectively as an assertion of the rule of law and the rights of the individual. They include provisions prohibiting the king from raising standing armies in peacetime without the consent of Parliament, abolishing High Commission and other ecclesiastical prerogative courts that short-circuited the rule of law, prohibiting the king from raising taxes without Parliament's grant, guaranteeing English people the right to petition without fear of being thrown in jail for doing so,

*In order to avoid cluttering the bottoms of pages with footnotes defining technical terms such as "writs of prohibition" and "prerogative courts," I have defined all such terms in a glossary at the back of this book.

freedom of debate in Parliament, and freedom from excessive fines, bail, and cruel and unusual punishments.

Another pillar of constitutionalism long predates the Glorious Revolution. Magna Carta's celebrated thirty-ninth chapter provided that "no freeman shall be captured or imprisoned . . . nor will we go against him or send against him, except by the lawful judgment of his peers and [or] by the law of the land." The last provision embodies the Anglo-American ideal of the rule of law. Government cannot act except through law; arbitrary rules are forbidden, whether they be the will of the president or the actions of the military. The law-of-the-land provisions were rephrased and significantly extended by Parliament in a 1354 act that provided that "no Man of what Estate or Condition that he be, shall be put out of Land or Tenement, nor taken, nor imprisoned, nor disinherited, nor put to Death, without being brought in Answer by due Process of the Law."

In the nineteenth and twentieth centuries, American courts have held the two phrases, law of the land and due process, to be synonymous, but there is an important difference between them. "Law of the land" implies that the law*making* body—Parliament or Congress—can declare what the law of the land shall be and that its will in the matter is supreme. "Due process," on the other hand, suggests a source of law superior to legislation, a law whose process is supreme. "Due process of law," Alexander Hamilton maintained in the 1787 debates in the New York Assembly, can refer only to the actions of courts; "they can never be referred to an act of the legislature." Due process suggests a greater role for courts, the law-*declaring* body, seeing to it that all government acts by process of law, applying established judicial procedures that protect individuals from arbitrary legislative and executive action. The United States opted for the second emphasis, whereas the mother country was content to retain a government of legislative superiority. Hence the role of the Supreme Court is far more extensive here; it has no true counterpart in Great Britain.

Despite the tradition of parliamentary supremacy confirmed by the Glorious Revolution, English constitutional experience passed on to Americans the idea of the balanced constitution. In the seventeenth century, English writers thought of government as being layered in estates, which, in the English constitution, coincided with classical forms; thus:

King:	monarchy
Lords:	aristocracy
Commons:	democracy

The great virtue of the English constitution, as Englishmen saw it in the eighteenth century, was that historical experience had contrived a balance among these estates and principles, so that the body that governed England, the king-in-Parliament, functioned in a state of healthy, dynamic tension. Each of the principles of government had its characteristic virtue and its corresponding characteristic tendency to degenerate into an extreme:

monarchy: power—tyranny
aristocracy: wisdom—oligarchy
democracy: liberty—anarchy

In a well-governed state, no single principle predominated, and the state enjoyed the benefit of each, while keeping in check its tendency to degenerate.

This conception must appear too pat today, too much a matter of self-congratulatory rationalization, and so it was. But Americans distilled from it the idea of constitutional balance, to which they added a distinctly American innovation: the concept of embedding that balance in contrived structural forms, such as a bicameral legislature. They also derived from the idea of the balanced constitution a fear of what would happen as a result of *im*balance. Too much power in the hands of the executive part of government, the seat of power, would result in the oppression of the people and the destruction of their liberty. Too much power in the people would cause the government to degenerate into anarchy. Some predicted that the state of anarchy would prove so intolerable that the people would clamor for a military dictator, with the resulting annihilation of liberty. They thought they saw something of the sort prefigured in the failure of the English Commonwealth in the 1650s, and in any event, their fears would soon be confirmed by the events of the French Revolution and the rise of Napoleon. Hence the notion of dynamic balance took on a special intensity for Americans of the revolutionary generation; it was a problem that urgently required some sort of solution. A large part of that solution was to be found in their courts.

In the struggle with Great Britain during the 1760s and 1770s, Americans considered themselves the heirs of the common law and repeatedly reminded the mother country of that fact. English legal authority supported this claim, to an extent. For example, Sir Bartholomew Shower observed in the 1693 case of *Dutton* v. *Howell* that, when "certain Subjects of England . . . go and possess an uninhabited desert Country; the Common Law must be supposed to be their Rule, as 'twas their Birthright." Seeing things in that light, Americans insisted in the "Declaration and Resolves of the First Constitutional Congress" (1774), one of the most important constitutional statements to emerge in the course of the American Revolution, that the "colonies are intitled to the common law of England, and more especially to the great and inestimable privilege of being tried by their peers . . . according to the course of that law."

At first glance, it might seem perverse that Americans so exalted the common law, because they well knew that English law was a smorgasbord of differing legal systems, of which the common law was only one among several. When it suited their needs, Americans did not hesitate to adopt some of these other systems, such as admiralty or equity. But Americans gloried in the common law, opportunistically seeing in it certain guarantees of rights they claimed in their disputes with the mother country—above all the right of trial by jury (an institution unknown to other bodies of law). Americans considered the common law so integral a part of the British constitution that, in moments of rhetorical excess, they sometimes claimed that it *was* the British constitution. Once independent, they took great care to establish the common law as the basis of their new commonwealths.

The claim of the common law as the English people's birthright is significant because, obviously, only a court can administer the common law. By making the common law central to their constitutional experience, Americans guaranteed an equally central role for their courts in the day-to-day administration of their public law.

We inherited from England not only a libertarian constitutional tradition but also institutions. The most important of these were courts. In the Anglo-American tradition, courts have a peculiarly political function that distinguishes them from the court systems of non–common law jurisdictions. An English or American court must take some existing body of law and apply it in a way that will affect the rights of an individual. Because the English libertarian tradition placed such a high premium on protecting these rights, courts found themselves, in their ordinary, day-to-day functioning, balancing law on the one hand with personal liberty on the other. Eventually this tradition led courts to limit the actions of government, sometimes by upholding individual rights in the face of government oppression, sometimes by holding the laws themselves void as a violation of some higher standard of justice.

English judicial experience at the time of America's early settlement provides examples of both sorts of the courts' emergent functions. The renowned *Seven Bishops Case* of 1688, which did much to precipitate the Glorious Revolution, was a prosecution of seven bishops of the Church of England for seditious libel. The bishops had petitioned James II, objecting both to his Declaration of Indulgence, which would have eased the disabilities on Dissenters and Roman Catholics, and to an Order in Council requiring the Declaration to be read at church services. The

Court of King's Bench provided a forum where the law of seditious libel could be argued by prosecution and defense counsel and debated by the judges. It also gave a jury, that sensitive political instrument, an opportunity to reject either a principle of law or its application in a particular case—in this instance, the idea that a petition to the king could constitute a seditious libel. The court also proved to be the matrix in which a constitutional principle took form. Despite severe pressures to convict, the jury acquitted the defendant bishops. The principle implicit in this verdict was written into the Bill of Rights the next year, and from thence a century later into the First Amendment: the guarantee that a citizen may petition the government for a redress of grievances.

The second example shows an English judge—none other than Chief Justice Coke of Common Pleas again—calling into question the validity of a statute of Parliament. *Dr. Bonham's Case* (1610) was a prosecution of a physician for violating a statute that permitted the College of Physicians of London to punish physicians who practiced without a license from the College and to keep half the fines exacted. Coke found for Bonham, stating that "in many cases, the common law will control Acts of Parliament, and sometimes adjudge them to be utterly void: for when an Act of Parliament is against common right and reason, or repugnant, or impossible to be performed, the common law will control it and adjudge such Act to be void." We should not read into these lines more than Coke himself would have seen in them. He was not saying that a court would hold a statute "unconstitutional," or, more accurately, void because of internal contradiction. He did not, in other words, claim that English courts would exercise the power of judicial review as we know it in America. Such a doctrine has never been part of the British constitution. He asserted, however, that despite Parliament's supremacy in the English political system, statutory law might be invalid because of its clash with some superior source of law.

The words of *Bonham's Case* remain ambiguous; not so the assertion of Chief Justice Henry Hobart of King's Bench in the 1614 case of *Day* v. *Savadge*. In that case Hobart boldly proclaimed that "even an Act of Parliament, made against natural equity, as to make a man judge in his own case, is void in itself, for jura naturae sunt immutabilia and they are leges legum." (The Latin phrases mean, respectively: "the laws of nature are unchanging" and "the laws of laws.") In this case, too, Hobart was not saying that a court would hold a parliamentary statute unconstitutional, but rather that the law was simply void. Even allowing this to be so, it is not clear what consequences followed for Hobart, Coke, and other seventeenth-century common law judges. Their significance for American constitutional development lies in their assumption of a fundamental or higher law, a source of laws superior to ordinary human enactments. Such a law, in Coke's words, would "control" an ordinary statutory law and determine that it would be void. English jurists derived this higher law from many sources. Hobart found it in the laws of nature; Coke thought it was the common law, seen as the embodiment of reason; more conventionally pious judges sought it in the word of God, the Bible, or the teachings of the Christian religion.

The ambiguity of Coke and Hobart suggests that English judges were ambivalent about whether there might be some superior authority that could hold a statute void. This ambivalence is strikingly demonstrated in the great summation of English law written on the eve of the American Revolution, Sir William Blackstone's *Commentaries on the Laws of England* (first edition, 1765). Blackstone wrote on both sides of the issue. The distinguished American legal historian Julius Goebel suggested that this peculiar self-contradiction resulted from several English judges' reading the manuscript before publication and editing it or suggesting revisions, with the consequent inconsistencies predictable when a committee tries to write or revise a document. Whatever the cause, on the question whether a parliamentary enactment would be void because of a conflict with a higher law, Blackstone perhaps inadvertently tried to have it both ways. First, he suggested the absolutely binding character of higher law: the "law of nature, being co-eval with mankind, and dictated by God himself, is of course superior in obligation to any other. It is binding all over the globe, in all countries, and at all times: no human laws are of any validity, if contrary to this" (William Blackstone, *Commentaries on the Laws of England* [Oxford, 1765], 41). But then some fifty pages later, he wrote that if Parliament "positively enact a thing to be done that is unreasonable, I know of no power that can control it." If judges could disregard legislation merely because it was inherently contradictory, "that were to set the judicial power above that of the legislature, which would be subversive of all government" (Blackstone, *Commentaries,* 91).

Blackstone was not alone in this difficulty. His American contemporary, James Otis, argued as counsel in the *Writs of Assistance Cases* of 1761 that "an Act [of Parliament] against the Constitution is void" (quoted in John Adams, "Abstract of the Argument," in L. Kinvin Wroth and Hiler B. Zobel, eds., *Legal Papers of John Adams* [Cambridge, Mass., 1965], 2:144). And in his 1764 tract, *The Rights of the British Colonies,* he maintained that, "should an act of Parliament be against any of [God's] natural laws . . . their declaration would be contrary to eternal truth, equity and justice, and consequently void" (James Otis, "The Rights of the British Colonies Asserted and Proved," 1764, reprinted in Bernard Bailyn, ed., *Pamphlets of the American Revolution, 1750–1776* [Cambridge,

Mass., 1965], 1:454). But, on the other hand, "the power of parliament is uncontrollable, but by themselves, and we must obey" (Otis, "Rights of the British Colonies," in Bailyn, *Pamphlets,* 1:448). Such confusion was pardonable in an American such as Otis, who with his countrymen was caught in a transition from one constitutional system (of legislative omnipotence) to another (marked by judicial review).

Blackstone's difficulty suggests that the English legal system has not yet worked its way through to a solution of one of the oldest problems of government in the western world. About a century after Christ, the Roman satiric poet Juvenal posed the issue thus: who is to guard the guardians? That is, how is a government to be effectively restrained? The ideals of the rule of law and of constitutional limitations on government can only be realized by some institution or mechanism capable of continuously holding government in check. To Blackstone and most of his English contemporaries, it was a contradiction in terms to suggest that such an institution would be part of the government itself, something like expecting a dog to leash itself. Americans resolved this dilemma creatively through their republican ideology.

The new American republics inherited not only a judicial tradition but also working courts. By Independence, each of the colonies had developed a court system. These judiciaries were served by a professional bar, and operated under mature and sophisticated procedural systems. Several characteristics of the colonial courts influenced the creation of the United States Supreme Court. All were common law courts. Some of them also administered two non–common law bodies of law: equity and admiralty. The first state constitutions, like the pre-1776 constitutional documents, all claimed the benefits of the common law, and assured that the legal systems of the new republics would be common law courts.

Colonial courts were also hierarchical, having defined jurisdictional limitations and lines of appellate authority. Most of the colonies had a fairly simple two-level system of trial courts and appellate bodies. Generalization is difficult because no two colonies had the same structure and because each colony's judicial system was constantly evolving. But in all the colonies, British Americans were familiar, by reason of their own experience, with a court system in which a higher appellate authority exercised some supervision over the working of lower courts. In most colonies, the appellate courts consisted of the governor and council, not a body of full-time judges who did only judicial business. Judicial supervision took place at two levels. Within each colony, an appellate court oversaw courts of more limited jurisdiction. Within the empire, appeals lay from courts in the colonies to the Privy Council in England. Thus Americans by 1776 were accustomed to thinking of a judicial system having different levels of courts and having certain bodies, both within and outside each colony, act as appellate courts.

That a case would be appealed outside the colony also gave Americans some experience with the workings of a "federal" system. The British Empire before American Independence was in no sense a true federation. Yet in broad outline, it operated somewhat in that way. Americans thought in terms of a pattern in which a central authority exercised some superintendence over the legislation and the judicial workings of individual colonies. Here, too, they were being conditioned to the creation of a Supreme Court.

To understand this pre-1776 proto-federal structure, it would be helpful to think in terms of an "Imperial Constitution": an evolving, unwritten collection of precedents, customs, and institutions that provided the rules for the governance of the British Empire. The constitutive documents of the colonies, such as charters, enabled the governing body of the colony to make laws, provided they were not repugnant to the laws of England. If this limitation was to be anything more than an unenforceable exhortation, some sort of machinery would have to assure conformity. This goal was accomplished in two ways. After 1696, an administrative body in London known as the Board of Trade reviewed all colonial legislation, scrutinizing it for conflicts with English law, as well as with policies of the mother country. And the Privy Council, a body of advisors to the Crown, exercised ultimate appellate authority over all colonial civil litigation in which the amount in controversy was more than £300. Though the Privy Council heard only a tiny fraction of all such cases, the mere existence of its power to review colonial appeals accustomed Americans to the notion of an ultimate review tribunal in a de facto federal system.

By Independence, Americans had evolved a constitutional tradition that gave them a firm sense of collective self-identity. They considered themselves and their colonial governments as having rights that neither Parliament nor king could impair—rights to jury trial, security of property, self-government. They thought of the governments that held sway over them as being limited in their power by constitutional restraints. They had well-developed court systems in their colonies, and had gained practical experience in working within an imperial federation. In their Revolution, they transformed all these inheritances into republican institutions.

Though the United States Supreme Court was not organized until thirteen years after Independence, important precedents established in the period 1776–89 influenced its creation and functioning. In the court systems of the states, the practice of judicial review emerged: the power of courts to hold a statute unconstitutional. At the national level, predecessors of the Supreme Court were created under the Articles of Confederation. Their existence demonstrated that a national judiciary was feasible; their limitations proved that one was necessary.

The courts continued to function after Independence, though they were reorganized by the new state constitutions. The constitutions also established legislative supremacy, an odd outcome considering that the Americans had been struggling for more than a decade to rebut claims of parliamentary supremacy. In any event, the new legislatures asserted their primacy in state government. Governors were everywhere weak and limited in their powers. Separation of powers, as a principle, proved a feeble barrier against the encroachment of the legislatures on the rights of individuals and the powers of courts. In the decade after Independence, two kinds of statutes regularly brought the legislatures into conflict with the state courts. These were statutes confiscating Loyalist and British property (including debts owed them), and legislation providing various kinds of relief to debtors in the postwar depression of the 1780s. State courts were hostile to both and established a beachhead for the principle of judicial review.

By 1787, some eight or nine cases in eight states may have claimed for judges the power to hold statutes unconstitutional. In only one of them did a court flatly and unequivocally determine that a statute violated the state constitution; but in all of them we can see judges moving toward that end. The judges of the Virginia Court of Appeals stated in 1788 the early rationale for this innovation: if the state constitution and a statute are inconsistent with each other, the judges must decide in favor of the constitution. In doing so, they do only what judges have traditionally done: "declaring what the law is, and not making a new law." Three of these cases were on the minds of the Framers of the Constitution: *Rutgers* v. *Waddington,* a 1784 New York case involving wartime confiscation or occupation of property; *Trevett* v. *Weeden,* a 1786 Rhode Island case involving one of the state's debtor-backed paper money laws; and *Bayard* v. *Singleton,* a North Carolina case voiding a Loyalist confiscation act. *Bayard* was decided while the Philadelphia Convention was meeting in 1787 and was the first explicitly to declare a statute unconstitutional.

These early judicial review cases were controversial in their time because they challenged the assumption of legislative supremacy. Legislators and supporters of the laws sharply condemned the judges, who in turn just as vehemently defended themselves. The legitimacy of judicial review was not definitively settled at the time, but it was raised. That Americans were thinking of a role for the courts in keeping their legislatures under constitutional restraint was to have great significance for the United States Supreme Court over the next century.

America's first national Constitution was the Articles of Confederation, a document strikingly different from the Constitution of 1787. One of the major differences was its lack of a real national judiciary. Although judicial experience under the Articles affected the creation of the Supreme Court in 1787, that influence was largely negative. The Articles revealed the problems facing efforts to create a national court and provided some experience in how not to go about doing so. The Articles provided for three types of national "courts." The first, a court for the trial of piracies and felonies on the high seas, never became a national court as such. Rather, the Continental Congress authorized such trials in existing state superior or admiralty courts. The second type actually did become a functioning court: the Court of Appeals in cases of capture. Growing out of a congressional standing committee that heard appeals from state courts in prize cases, the Court of Appeals constituted America's only real national court, and one of severely limited jurisdiction at that. The third body consisted of a panel of five "commissioners or judges," appointed ad hoc by a complicated procedure. It was to be "the last resort on appeal" in cases of state boundary disputes, the related problems of private land titles growing out of conflicting state grants, and, ambiguously, "any other cause whatever." This body never became a true court; it was an arbitration panel. It served a real need, because of the troublesome and sometimes bloody disputes between states over boundary regions.

America's brief experience with these national proto-courts, like that under the Articles as a whole, convinced many anxious nationalists such as Alexander Hamilton and James Madison of the need for a true national judicial authority, one capable of functioning independently of the states, having effective powers of command over individuals, deriving its authority not from the league of sovereign states that existed under the Articles of Confederation but from the sovereignty of the American people as a whole. Meanwhile, as this practical need made itself felt more urgently every day in the 1780s, Americans' republican ideology was also developing in a direction that would clear the way for creation of true national courts.

The United States Supreme Court and the entire national court system were products of a rapid and intense ideological development that occurred between Independence and 1790. In creating a national judicial system capped by a supreme tribunal, Americans amplified on constitutional themes they inherited from England, and originated new doctrines appropriate to the "New Order of the Ages."* In some matters, they simply reaffirmed the English heritage with little substantive change. They saw themselves heirs of the seventeenth-century libertarian constitutional tradition that culminated in the Glorious Revolution. So seriously did they take this heritage that they revolted when they came to believe that the mother country was betraying the principles of that Revolution. Thus they insisted on maintaining the rule of law, which they thought could be achieved only under a regime of constitutionalism. This they defined in terms of limited government whose principal end was to secure the rights of individuals.

America approached these questions with an important difference of emphasis and with assumptions that made them Americans rather than simply English people who happened to live outside England for a time. They were the disciples of John Locke, as well as of James Harrington, Montesquieu, and lesser-known early eighteenth-century English Whig and radical writers. Thus to the common stock of ideas they shared with English people, they added distinctively American and republican elements. Foremost was the American refinement of the idea of fundamental law. Americans shared a generalized belief that there was a higher law than the statutes enacted by Parliament or their provincial assemblies. During the American Revolution they tried to demonstrate to Parliament that its errors were obvious, only to be met with forcible repression. Americans therefore determined to embody *their* fundamental laws in written constitutions.

The constitutions of the revolutionary era typically had two components—a "frame of government," which detailed the structure and procedures of government, and a "declaration of rights," an enumeration of the rights of the people and consequent limitations on government. In this way, Americans hoped, all generations would have a criterion against which they could measure the legitimacy of government's actions. James Iredell, a future justice of the United States Supreme Court, argued that a state constitution was not "a mere imaginary thing, about which ten thousand different opinions may be formed, but a written document to which all may have recourse" (quoted in Gordon S. Wood, *The Creation of the American Republic, 1776–1787* [Chapel Hill, N.C., 1969], 461), especially judges. The existence of written constitutions made it possible for the early courts to justify judicial review by saying that a judge merely laid the text of the constitution next to the statute and checked them for compatibility.

*This phrase is the translation of *Novus Ordo Seclorum,* a bit of late-eighteenth-century iconography that appears on the reverse of the current one-dollar bill as part of the Great Seal of the United States.

The new American republics proudly embraced a concept the English spurned: popular sovereignty. Having rejected the idea that sovereignty lay in Parliament or the Crown, Americans relocated it in the people. This doctrine, too, had a profound impact on the power of courts. Taking sovereignty out of one of the institutions of government and placing it outside government altogether, in the whole body of the people, made it possible for Americans to entertain the idea from time to time that government could act without legitimacy. Government and all its agencies—executive, legislature, courts—existed as a servant of the people and had only the powers delegated to it by its true masters. Hence when it acted inimically to the welfare of the people, its actions lost legitimacy. In his arguments on the unconstitutionality of the Rhode Island statute in *Trevett* v. *Weeden,* James Varnum put this argument to practical use, insisting that "the powers of legislation . . . are derived from the people at large, are altogether fiduciary, and subordinate to the association [of the people] by which they are formed." "Consequently," he concluded, "the Legislature cannot intermeddle with the retained rights of the people." Courts must "reject all acts of the Legislature that are contrary to the trust reposed in them by the people."

Their revolutionary experience had taught Americans to fear power. In their thinking, power, an attribute of government, and liberty, an attribute of the people, were two parts of a zero-sum game. If power expanded, it did so at the expense of liberty. Power had a constant tendency to increase, and its increase diminished popular liberty. Hence one of the most stubborn challenges of the Revolution was to limit power yet at the same time endow government with sufficient force to permit it to accomplish its essential functions, such as maintaining order. The dilemma of power was especially troublesome in a large federation, in which power had to be not only checked within states but also apportioned between state and nation. Power was like a dangerous but necessary beast: caged too effectively, it could not serve its purpose; allowed to roam freely, it might devour its master.

The republican solution to this dilemma was partly structural. Power could be bestowed on government if it was divided and checked. Hence the related doctrines of separation of powers and checks and balances. As Americans deployed these devices to leash power, they discovered a role for courts they had not previously perceived. Restraints on power could be built into the structure of government itself, in the form of courts that had the ability to check legislative excesses in the interest of protecting the liberty of the people. But the complete resolution of this challenge had to await the creation of national courts.

The constitutional debates of 1787–88 raised another ideological concern, the problem of majority rule and minority rights. Both because it was ideologically compelling in a government of popular sovereignty and because it was an essential mode of proceeding if anything was ever to get done in the legislatures, Americans accepted the idea of majority rule. But they also saw that majorities could threaten the rights of minorities. Yet how to secure the position of minorities without letting minorities control the majority? A solution to this problem, too, emerged when Americans thought through the place of courts in a republic. As long as the majorities-minorities problem was confined to the legislatures, it had no solution. But because the rights of minorities were grounded in the Constitution, they could be protected in courts.

These ideological considerations were on the minds of the fifty-five men who at one time or another participated in the Philadelphia Convention of 1787. They partly explain the surprising unanimity in support of the audacious proposal to create a judicial system for the nation as a whole. National courts are comprehensible only in the larger context of the Framers' determination to create an effective national government.

The national courts created under the Constitution were based on the existing models of the colonial/state court systems, which consisted of inferior and superior courts, with lines of appellate authority between the two based on writs of error or appeal. Also, for better or worse, the Framers drew on their experience as British colonists to envision how national courts would function, looking back to both the Privy Council and to the development of the common law courts at Westminster. The common law courts' experience taught them that national courts tend to expand their jurisdiction and aggrandize their authority. Their experience with the Privy Council admonished them that local jurisdictions regard a central appellate authority with jealous animosity, ceaselessly suspicious of its centripetal tendency and stubbornly hostile to every encroachment on their jurisdiction.

The various proposals offered at Philadelphia for the jurisdiction of the national courts indicate that the Framers projected a two-part agenda for the new national judiciary. First, looking backward, they saw that certain tasks had to be performed by national courts. These included such things as admiralty and interstate territorial disputes. Looking forward, the Framers projected their vision of a central authority that would exercise some sort of a veto on state policies that clashed with national authority or that disturbed interstate harmony. The decision to entrust this authority to courts, rather than to the legislature, provided the central source of controversy surrounding the national judiciary during the next half century.

In 1787, suggestions that a national court would exercise the power of judicial review drew a mixed reaction. Several delegates at Philadelphia offhandedly assumed that federal courts would hold state and/or national legislation unconstitutional; among them were Elbridge Gerry of Massachusetts, James Wilson of Pennsylvania (a future justice of the Supreme Court), and Alexander Hamilton of New York. Making the same assumption were some opponents of the Constitution: Luther Martin of Maryland and Patrick Henry of Virginia. Others, particularly the Virginians, were doubtful. Thomas Jefferson, who was in France during the convention, was uneasy at the prospect of judicial discretion in construing laws; James Monroe warned that judicial review would "create heats and animosities"; Madison flatly rejected judicial review, which, he said, "makes the Judiciary Department paramount in fact to the Legislature, which was never intended and can never be proper" (quoted in Wood, *Creation of the American Republic,* 304). Perhaps because it feared the "heats and animosities" predicted by Monroe, the Philadelphia Convention compromised or procrastinated the issue by the simple expedient of remaining silent about it in the Constitution.

The Framers did, however, provide an explicit catalog of the jurisdiction of the federal courts. Articles III and VI of the Constitution, read together, created a powerful national court system. The Constitution itself created the United States Supreme Court; Congress had discretion in establishing lower federal courts. In keeping with emergent theories of separation of powers, Articles I, II, and III of the Constitution distinguished and distributed "All legislative Powers herein granted" to Congress, the "executive Power" to the president, and the "judicial Power of the United States" to the Supreme Court and any inferior courts that Congress might create. All Article III federal judges hold their office by "good Behaviour" tenure, and are guaranteed that their salaries will be paid regularly and will not be diminished while they hold office. (Both tenure and salary had been sources of contention between Britain and America during the Revolution. The Framers here expressed their determination that the federal judiciary should be independent of the political branches.)

Under Article III, the Supreme Court has appellate jurisdiction, "both as to Law and Fact" over all cases arising under the "judicial Power." But the Framers immediately added a proviso that has been the source of controversy in the past and that has returned to prominence in the late twentieth century: the Supreme Court's appellate jurisdiction is subject to "such Exceptions, and under such Regulations as the Congress shall make." The exceptions and regulations clause is, in a sense, the reverse of the problem of judicial review. If the essential problem of judicial review that troubled Madison and the other Virginians is the

Court's interference in the authority of the legislature, the exceptions clause introduces the possibility of the legislature's interference in the rightful authority of the Court.

The jurisdiction of the federal courts extends to both law and equity, as well as admiralty, and is defined in two ways: by subject matter and by parties. The parties to whom the judicial power extends include ambassadors and similar foreign officials, the states, the United States itself, and, most important of all, "Citizens of different States." The last is known as "diversity jurisdiction" because the citizenship of the parties is "diverse." In terms of sheer volume of cases coming before the federal courts today, diversity jurisdiction is the most fecund source of judicial business. This importance conforms to the Framers' expectations; they were determined to provide a system of national courts that would be unaffected by the parochial outlook they believed regularly influenced state courts. Diversity jurisdiction has proved to be comparable, as a source of judicial power, to the way that the commerce clause of Article I, section 8, has proved to be a source of legislative power.

The other type of federal jurisdiction is that over subject matter. Aside from the now unimportant problem of conflicting states' land grants, the sole source of federal subject matter jurisdiction consists of what lawyers call "federal questions," which, in the language of Article III, are "Cases . . . arising under this Constitution, the Laws of the United States, and Treaties made, or which shall be made, under their Authority." The Framers regarded this federal question jurisdiction as an essential grant of power to the national courts. They recognized that, no matter how powerful a national government they might create, if its laws were to be interpreted only by state courts, it would be a Gulliver staked to the ground by Lilliputians. To coordinate state court adjudication with national policy, the Framers provided in Article VI that the federal Constitution, laws, and treaties "shall be the supreme Law of the Land" and reinforced that determination by requiring that all state judges "shall be bound thereby," even in the face of contrary provisions in the state constitutions or laws. For good measure, the Framers also required all state officers, including judges, to take an oath "to support this Constitution." They thus created a comprehensive, powerful national judiciary that would enforce federal authority and protect the national market.

In the course of the ratification debates in 1787 and 1788, opponents of the Constitution raised many objections to federal courts and their powers. They complained that the federal courts would deprive the state judiciaries of some or all of their power; that a uniform body of national law would threaten the diversity of local laws; that the implicit power of judicial review would make courts superior to the legislatures; that the grant of equity jurisdiction would give the United States Supreme Court an uncontrollable discretion in construing laws, to the point that the Court would substitute its own policy judgments for those of Congress; that the federal courts would be expensive to suitor and taxpayer alike, and would be remote from most litigants; that the federal courts would not be controlled by a Bill of Rights, as most state courts were; and, generally, that the federal courts were a part of the machinery of consolidation, whereby the federal government would aggrandize all powers to itself.

Supporters of the Constitution had to rebut these arguments. None did so more brilliantly than Alexander Hamilton in the *Federalist Papers,* numbers 78 through 84. He had little trouble on the points of life tenure, salary, mode of appointment, separation of powers, structure, original jurisdiction, and even appellate authority (though it required separate essays, numbers 83 and 84 respectively, to refute the arguments centering on jury trial and a bill of rights). His frank avowal of the power of judicial review produced one of the most influential and subtly reasoned of the *Federalist* essays.

The argument against judicial review that Hamilton had to refute is simplistic, but for that reason it is superficially persuasive. Its basic premise is that whichever body, legislature or court, has the final say on the validity of a law will in effect be the supreme law-giving organ of the state. That was precisely the issue troubling Madison when he maintained that judicial review would make "the judiciary Department paramount in fact to the Legislature." This argument against judicial review is ultimately premised on popular sovereignty, the most potent of American revolutionary talismans. Hamilton took the popular sovereignty argument and inverted it. He began with the axiom that in republican America sovereignty resides in the people, not in the legislature. By their constitutions, the people delegated power to the legislature, and circumscribed its use with safeguards to protect personal liberty. The will of the people is expressed in the Constitution, and is superior to the will of the legislature, which can be expressed only in statutory law. Consequently, when judges find themselves confronted with a statute that conflicts with the Constitution, they must prefer the Constitution over the statute. Hamilton denied that this observation implied the supremacy of the courts; "it only supposes that the power of the people is superior to both" (*Federalist,* number 78). Hamilton thus drew on the tradition of fundamental law, tied it to the new ideological imperative of popular sovereignty, and called upon the national courts to preserve both. It was a tour de force of reasoning that disarmed his Antifederalist opponents.

The ideas Hamilton expressed in number 78 are among the most frequently cited from the *Federalist.* In arguing for the necessity of both good behavior tenure and the separation of powers, Hamilton wrote that the judiciary would be the "least dangerous" of the three branches of government. Noting that the president is commander in chief and the legislature the lawmaker, he went on: "The judiciary on the contrary has no influence over either the sword or the purse. . . . It may truly be said to have neither Force nor Will, but merely judgement." Hamilton's insight here was to be borne out repeatedly in various constitutional crises during the next two hundred years.

These ideas were not original with Hamilton. He merely put into unusually lucid prose some precepts that were emerging in the state courts and became widely accepted within a decade. In the generation after *Bayard* v. *Singleton* (North Carolina Supreme Court, 1787), the courts of Georgia, New Jersey, Virginia, Ohio, Maryland, Tennessee, Pennsylvania, and South Carolina adopted one or another element of Hamilton's rationale. They also elaborated on a point Hamilton did not make: courts in exercising judicial review do not substitute their policy preferences for those of the legislature. Much less do they make laws or displace the lawmaking authority of the legislature. Rather, they stand in an intermediary or refereeing position between the legislature and the people, protecting the latter from the carelessness or perfidy of the former.

The judiciary provisions of the Constitution were not self-executing. Ratification of the Constitution did not of itself create the Supreme Court or the lower federal courts, or specify their jurisdiction. That work has to be accomplished by statute. The First Congress immediately turned to it, and produced the Judiciary Act of 1789, which remains today, with modifications, the basis of the federal judicial system. Because it made the working federal system a reality, not just a possibility, Justice Henry B. Brown in 1911 lauded it as "the most important and the most satisfactory Act ever passed by Congress."

The first Judiciary Act created the Supreme Court, which originally consisted of six justices. Below it was a two-tiered system of federal courts, the United States district courts—at first, one in each state—and circuit courts, composed originally of two justices of the Supreme Court plus one district judge.

The Judiciary Act was a compromise among nationalists, led by its principal draftsman, the Connecticut Federalist Oliver Ellsworth, and a large faction in Congress who favored a greater measure of state autonomy. Its compromise character was most apparent in those sections of the act that bestowed jurisdiction on the federal courts. The federal courts might have been given exclusive jurisdiction of all cases arising under the federal Constitution, statutes, or treaties, and of all diversity suits. But fears that the federal courts would obscure or dominate state courts prevailed, and the exclusive jurisdiction of the federal courts was much more limited, being confined to such things as admiralty and violations of federal criminal statutes. Most subject matter jurisdiction of the federal courts was concurrent with the states; that is, a plaintiff had the option of bringing suit in a federal or a state court. For example, diversity jurisdiction in common law suits (above a specified minimum dollar amount in controversy) was of that sort. Jury trial was required in all civil suits.

The renowned section 25 was a triumph for the nationalist faction and long the source of attack by state court partisans; section 34, on the other hand, represented a major concession to the states' advocates. Justice Oliver Wendell Holmes, Jr., had section 25 in mind when he wrote in 1913 that "I do not think the United States would come to an end if we lost our power to declare an Act of Congress void [i.e., the power of judicial review]. I do think the Union would be imperiled if we could not make that declaration as to the laws of the several states." Section 25 permitted the Supreme Court to hear appeals from three kinds of state supreme court decisions: (1) those holding a federal statute or treaty invalid; (2) those upholding a state statute challenged as repugnant to the federal Constitution, statutes, or treaties; and (3) those adverse to a right claimed under the federal Constitution, laws, or treaties. It also implied the power of judicial review in cases in which the Supreme Court could sustain a state court decision holding a federal statute unconstitutional.

Section 25 recognized the shared authority of the state courts for construing the United States Constitution and statutes, but it made the construction of the United States Supreme Court decisive and final. Without section 25, state courts, in a worst-case scenario, would have been able to construe away federal authority and deprive the United States of the power to enforce national policy and the supremacy of the federal Constitution. Section 34, on the other hand, mollified the supporters of state power, because it made state law the "rule of decision" in common law litigation in federal courts, thus obliging federal judges to look to the states for their substantive law.

The earliest years of the United States Supreme Court have always been eclipsed, as if nothing significant happened before John Marshall became chief justice in 1801. In part this disregard is because the Court lacked strong and continuous leadership. The first chief justice of the United States, John Jay, served from 1790 to 1794, when he left the Court first to conduct negotiations with Great Britain that led to the 1794 treaty bearing his name and then became governor of New York. His successor, John Rutledge, opposed the Jay treaty so vehemently that the Senate refused to confirm him, and he was reduced to the humiliating position of being forced to send back his commission. The chief justiceship of Oliver Ellsworth, Rutledge's successor, was interrupted by ill health. Several of their associates were men of impenetrable obscurity. Who today remembers Thomas Johnson, John Blair, Alfred Moore? Contemporaries treated the position as being of no account. Patrick Henry refused Washington's offer of a seat on the Court. Hamilton declined appointment to it in order to pursue private law practice in New York City. Robert Harrison rejected an appointment because he preferred to serve instead as chancellor of Maryland. The Court lacked a permanent home, sitting for its first terms in New York (as did the rest of the federal establishment), then spending the remainder of the decade in Philadelphia before moving to Washington. When it did finally move to the new national capital, its members discovered to their chagrin that no one had bothered to provide a chamber for them there. They had to do with a makeshift, cramped basement room. More important, a mill requires grist in order to grind, and relatively few significant cases came before it in its first decade.

Yet the early Court did settle some basic questions of American public law, precedents that John Marshall and his successors expanded into landmarks of the Constitution. The Court's earliest accomplishment was to confirm the reality of the separation of powers. In doing so, it asserted for itself a distinct place in the federal government, providing an indispensable base from which it would soon develop the broad doctrines of judicial review and national supremacy. The Court accomplished this in two ways. First, in *Hayburn's Case* (1792), five of the justices, sitting in various circuit courts, held that Congress could not constitutionally require them to pass on the validity of veterans' pension claims, partly because they viewed these duties as nonjudicial, and partly because their decisions were subject to revision by the secretary of war. The judges smoothly avoided a collision with Congress in the matter, however, by holding that the statute required them to act as commissioners, not judges; they volunteered to accept this extrajudicial duty. Their refusal was widely misinterpreted in Congress and in the newspapers of the day to have held an act of Congress unconstitutional, though technically it did not go that far.

Chief Justice Jay reaffirmed the Court's adherence to separation principles a year later when Secretary of State Thomas Jefferson, at the behest of President George Washington, requested the Court to render advisory opinions on presidential regulations enforcing the Neutrality Proclamation of 1793. In tactful language, Jay declined to do so, pointing out that the doctrine of separation of powers required each department to act as a check on the other, a function that could not be properly fulfilled if judges stepped outside their judicial role to serve formally as presidential advisers. (However, as did many subsequent members of the Court, Jay acted extensively as a presidential adviser in an informal, behind-the-scenes capacity. It was he, ironically, who had prepared the first draft of the Neutrality Proclamation for Washington.) Taken together, the results of *Hayburn's Case* and the advisory-opinions correspondence set a fundamental precedent. Federal courts can adjudicate only the "Cases" and "Controversies" specified in Article III, section 2. This limitation usually keeps fraudulent, made-up, or contrived test cases out of the federal courts.

Perhaps encouraged by the warm reception accorded its tentative venture into the domain of judicial review, the Court and its judges on circuit between 1792 and 1798 began exploring their authority to hold federal and state statutes void because they conflicted with the federal Constitution. In the case of state statutes, such decisions were risky. Not only did they raise a basic challenge to state sovereignty; often, as it happened, they involved the politically sensitive subjects of debtor relief or the states' anti-Loyalist measures. Nevertheless, the judges boldly spoke out in such cases. In the 1792 case of *Champion* v. *Casey*, the United States Circuit Court for Rhode Island held unconstitutional a statute of that state giving a specific debtor an extension of three years on the payment of his debts. The judges held that the statute violated the contracts clause of Article I, section 10. This was the first time that a federal court voided a state law for conflict with a provision of the federal Constitution.

Justice William Paterson, sitting on circuit in Pennsylvania three years later, went considerably further in *Vanhorne's Lessee* v. *Dorrance* (1795). The Pennsylvania statute in question attempted to settle the old and vexed problem of what was known locally as the "Connecticut Gore": the land claims of Connecticut to a region of what is now northern Pennsylvania, derived from Connecticut's original seventeenth-century charter grant of lands to the Western Sea. This grant produced, among other things, the Wyoming Valley of Pennsylvania boundary dispute, which had occasioned the provision in the Articles of Confederation making the Confederation Congress an arbitral tribunal to settle such conflicting land claims. Pennsylvania first granted the disputed lands to A; then it vested title to the same lands in B; then it reversed itself by repealing the latter act. Appellee Dorrance claimed title under the original grant. Paterson held the repealer conflicted with the contracts clause of the federal Constitution, but he took a momentous step further by charging the jury that the statute was void on the additional ground that it violated natural law principles not explicitly stated in the Constitution.

Paterson declared that the right to own property "is one of the natural inherent and unalienable rights of man." It therefore followed that a divestiture statute without compensation "is inconsistent with the principles of reason, justice, and moral rectitude [and] contrary to the principles of social alliance in every free government."

Justice Paterson relied on assumptions that few persons accept today but were prevalent in his time. Americans and Europeans in the eighteenth century believed in the existence of natural laws universally valid and binding on all people. Moreover, they believed that these natural laws could be discovered by human reason. The religiously inclined found their source in the will of God, disclosed to humanity through God's revelation as recorded in the Bible. It was this vision of higher law that Blackstone drew on in his declaration that "the law of nature . . . dictated by God himself is binding all over the globe, in all countries, and at all times." (Blackstone, *Commentaries,* 41).

This concept of natural law was not necessarily grounded in a Christian theological base, however. In its secular form, appealing to children of the Enlightenment such as Benjamin Franklin and Thomas Jefferson, the law of nature was just that: a pattern discovered in nature by the exercise of human reason, no less universal for being secular rather than divine. In either form, secular or Christian, natural law created and protected fundamental rights. George Mason set forth the substance of these rights in language more lawyerlike than Jefferson's better-known paraphrase. Article I of the 1776 Virginia Declaration of Rights (which Mason drafted) states that "all men . . . have certain inherent rights . . . namely, the enjoyment of life and liberty, with the means of acquiring and possessing property, and pursuing and obtaining happiness and safety." It was these rights, grounded in natural law, that Paterson strove to protect in *Vanhorne's Lessee.*

A chasm separates our intellectual and social world from Justice Paterson's, and makes his premises seem alien today. In the *Vanhorne's Lessee* opinion, he actually foresaw the dominant assumptions of the twentieth century, and rejected them as a basis for a constitutional order founded on justice, when he charged the jury: "The constitution of a state is stable and permanent, not to be worked upon by the temper of the times nor to rise and fall with the tide of events: notwithstanding the competition of opposing interests, . . . it remains firm and immovable." How different from the world of the late twentieth century in which we assume that the basic dynamic of politics is interest group rivalry, which we accept as inevitable and probably healthy, with the consequent necessity of the Constitution growing and remaining flexible so as to accord with the values of its time.

Vanhorne's Lessee stood on two feet: one an express clause of the United States Constitution, the other a vague unwritten prescript of natural law. How would judges react when they had to decide a case only by standing on the latter foot? That was the problem coming before the United States Supreme Court in *Calder* v. *Bull* (1798), and it produced a classic jurisprudential confrontation between two radically different views of the judge's function in a republic. Before John Marshall put an end to it, the Supreme Court followed the practice of English courts of sometimes having individual justices deliver their opinions *seriatim* (a Latin word meaning "separately"). When opinions were delivered seriatim, no one justice spoke for the Court, and the bar was left to determine for itself which opinion if any was authoritative. Thus the very form of the decision in *Calder* v. *Bull* provided a perfect format for a dichotomous conflict over the role of judges.

The Connecticut legislature set aside a decree of a probate court by statute and granted a new hearing. (This was a common practice left over from the years of early Independence, when legislatures functioned under a regime of legislative supremacy.) The losing party challenged this ruling as an ex post facto law prohibited by Article I, section 10, of the Constitution, and was disappointed by the decision of the Supreme Court, which held that that clause applied only to criminal, not civil, laws. In his *Calder* v. *Bull* opinion, Justice Samuel Chase vigorously condemned the Connecticut act, despite his inability to cite a specific provision of the Constitution with which it conflicted. His arguments have become so classic that the great twentieth-century constitutional authority Edward S. Corwin termed their content the "Basic Doctrine of American Constitutional Law." Chase wrote:

> I cannot subscribe to the omnipotence of a state legislature, or that it is absolute and without control. . . . There are acts which the federal or state legislature cannot do, without exceeding their authority. There are certain vital principles in our free republican governments, which will determine and override an apparent and flagrant abuse of legislative power.

Chase then provided some general examples of such prohibited acts, such as the lawyer's staple: taking the property of A and giving it to B. He concluded: "The genius, the nature, and the spirit of our state governments amount to a prohibition of such acts of legislation; and the general principles of law and reason forbid them."

All this was too much for his colleague James Iredell, who rejected Chase's reliance on general principles of free governments. Iredell stated flatly that, if Congress or a state legislature acting within the general scope of their authority enacts a statute that does not run afoul of some specific Constitution provision, "the court cannot pronounce it to be void, merely because it is, in their judgment, contrary to the principle of natural justice." Courts lack such power because "the ideas of natural justice are regulated by no fixed standard; the ablest and the purest men have differed upon the subject." To the contention that this argument would permit a regime of legislative supremacy, Iredell shrugged: "We must be content to limit power where we can; and where we cannot, we must be content to repose a salutary confidence" in the democratic process.

So prevalent was the belief in natural law of the Blackstonian sort that the *Vanhorne's Lessee* jury charge and Chase's *Calder* opinion provoked surprisingly little criticism. Not so the 1790s cases that subordinated state policy-making authority to the supremacy of federal laws, Constitution, and treaties. The broad questions of federalism raised in these cases proved so divisive that they resulted in the first constitutional amendment in our history that reversed a decision of the Supreme Court.

The Court's confrontation with state sovereignty advocates began with *Chisholm* v. *Georgia* (1793), a routine contracts case in which the South Carolina executors of a man who supplied Georgia with cloth during the War of Independence sued for its value. The whole issue in the Supreme Court turned on the question whether a state could be sued against its wishes by citizens of another state, a jurisdiction clearly conferred on the federal courts under that clause of Article III, section 2, extending the judicial power to cases "between a State and Citizens of another State." Georgia angrily refused even to appear by counsel at arguments. Four of the then five justices of the Court held that the state could be sued.

Chief Justice Jay wrote an incautiously nationalistic opinion that alarmed Georgia and other southern states. States' rights advocates feared that *Chisholm* would open the doors of federal courts to a vast amount of litigation. Suits challenging the constitutionality of numberless wartime and postwar statutes that in one way or another confiscated the property of British subjects or American Loyalists were a doubly controversial subject because they rekindled wartime passions and threatened the security of land titles. Consequently the states reacted with a vehemence difficult to comprehend at this remote date. State political leaders indulged themselves in extravagant rhetoric about the danger of federal judges annihilating state sovereignty and consolidating all America into a single government—a bugaboo that has enjoyed a long life in American political discourse. Congress quickly approved the Eleventh Amendment, withdrawing the judicial power from suits against a state begun by citizens of another state or by foreigners. Then, curiously, the amendment languished in the ratification process, despite the fervor backing it, and was not ratified until 1798.

Closely related to the problem of higher law was the Supreme Court's decision in *Ware* v. *Hylton* (1796), subordinating legislation of the states to the authority of federal treaties. This was the first case vindicating the letter and spirit of the supremacy clause of Article VI. The Court's action in doing so upheld the intentions of the Framers concerning the role of law and courts in maintaining federal supremacy. The issue in the case was politically sensitive. It involved a Virginia statute that confiscated and sequestered debts owed by Americans to British subjects. The Treaty of Paris (1783) terminating the War for American Independence provided that no impediments would be thrown in the way of British creditors seeking to recover prewar debts. The southern states flouted this provision by a variety of statutes that either canceled the indebtedness outright, or required the debts to be paid into the state treasury (thus confiscating them to the use of the state), or permitted them to be repaid in depreciated currency (a partial confiscation). The generic validity of all these statutes was at issue in *Ware.* A curious feature of the case is that John Marshall, then a Virginia attorney, appeared for the debtors, arguing—quite inconsistently with his position after elevation to the chief justiceship—for the superiority of Virginia law to federal treaty. The case was further complicated by the formation of political parties. On the question of the British debt, Federalists favored good-faith repayment in full, whereas Jeffersonian Republicans supported the state legislation.

The Court by a 4–1 vote upheld the supremacy of the federal treaty in a nationalistic opinion by Justice Chase. The decision should have been much more unpopular than it was, and the curious lack of denunciation of the Supreme Court is probably best explained by the political fact that the widely unpopular Jay treaty was under consideration in the Senate, and thus served as a lightning rod deflecting the bolts of states' rights wrath from the Court.

In the same term, the Court demonstrated that it was quite as willing to hold a federal statute unconstitutional as it was a state law. Its decision in *Hylton* v. *United States* (1796) sustained the validity of a federal tax on carriages, as against the claim that such a tax was a direct tax and therefore had to be apportioned among the states. This case, too, was politically sensitive, and was marked by unique circumstances. One was that Alexander Hamilton appeared for the first time at the bar of the Court, and based his argument on economic rather than legal analysis, citing Adam Smith at length. Also, like the *Income Tax Cases* of exactly a century later, *Hylton* was a fabricated case, presenting no authentic controversy as required by Article III of the Constitution, but fabricated solely to test the constitutionality of a statute. It was politically sensitive because any case that dealt with federal taxation would implicate the complex compromises of the Constitutional Convention that prohibited the federal government from taxing slaves or the products of their labor.

But *Hylton* v. *United States* remains significant for us not so much for these reasons. Rather, each of the three justices who participated in the decision assumed the power to hold a federal statute void as a violation of the Constitution. None did so, but the power was there implicitly. This assumption either escaped popular attention or passed by without controversy.

The early Court became as entangled in political controversy as any later Court, not for its politically controversial decisions such as *Ware* v. *Hylton,* but because it could not avoid the intense party conflicts of the era. Its first source of problems was the farsighted but politically motivated Judiciary Act of 1801. Defects in the 1789 Judiciary Act had become apparent almost immediately after its enactment. Most vexing was the requirement that Supreme Court justices ride circuit nine months of the year in an era when land travel was either on horseback or in a carriage that got mired in wet weather, choked its occupants with dust in dry weather, froze them in winter, and at all seasons of the year jounced them mercilessly on hard seats. A Supreme Court justice had to be as much an athlete as an attorney to perform his duties.

After the Jeffersonian triumph in the 1800 elections, Federalists, out of a mixture of unscrupulous partisanship and statesmanlike nationalism, enacted the Judiciary Act of 1801, which created a new tier of circuit courts with their own judges (thus relieving the Supreme Court justices of much of their circuit-riding responsibilities), and which extended to federal courts the full jurisdiction authorized by the Constitution in federal cases. It opened the doors of federal courts to more land title litigation (a move certain to outrage Virginians and Kentuckians, where such litigation was a claimant's nightmare and a lawyer's dream), made it easier to remove cases from state to federal courts, and broadened diversity jurisdiction. The statute was too politically provocative to survive the Jeffersonian Triumph of 1800. The Jeffersonian Republican party repealed it and replaced it with some necessary but minor modifications in the federal circuit court system. The full realization of federal judicial power was thereby postponed until 1875.

The controversy over the 1801 Judiciary Act demonstrated that the Supreme Court had emerged from its first decade of relative obscurity to take a prominent and controversial place in national political life. The early Court stands in the shadow of John Marshall's great achievements, but it deserves better of historians, who have neglected its accomplishments. It sustained limited government by holding that the power of state legislatures was limited both by the United States Constitution and by the principles of republican government. It subordinated state policy-making to the primacy of federal treaties. The Court claimed the power of judicial review over congressional enactments. And it began to define precisely the nature of the federal judicial function, together with the place of the judiciary in the federal government. The Court made an impressive showing for a mere decade and provided a base from which later courts would expand judicial power.

Chapter 2

"*It is a* constitution *we are expounding*"

THE COURT UNDER CHIEF JUSTICE MARSHALL

JOHN MARSHALL remains, without dissent, *the* great chief justice. Few individuals have by themselves redirected the course of American history solely by the force of their thought. Marshall was one of these, and the results of his influence were almost wholly benign. To generations of lawyers and judges, Marshall has been the embodiment of the public law. Justice Felix Frankfurter considered him "the one alone to be chosen if American law were to be represented by a single figure."

Marshall's greatness is partly attributable to his leadership of the Supreme Court. He ascended the bench in 1801 determined that the Court should speak with one voice. He promptly abolished the practice of seriatim opinions. Insofar as he could, he suppressed dissents and concurrences with a firm hand, even to the point of muting his own strongly held views in the interests of collegial unanimity. To forge a consensus among the judges, he took advantage of the circumstance that until 1820 all the justices shared living quarters in the Washington boardinghouse. At the dinner table, Marshall wielded the considerable force of his personality to form a single-minded Court. He could be heavy-handed. His colleague Justice William Johnson of South Carolina complained to Thomas Jefferson: "During the rest of the session I heard nothing but lectures [from Marshall] on the indecency of judges cutting each other. . . . At length I found that I must either submit to circumstances or become such a cypher in our consultations as to effect no good at all." Marshall also used the authority of his office to assign nearly all opinions in major constitutional cases to himself.

Marshall wrote his opinions in the grand style. Indifferent to precedent (or a lack of it), he wove doctrine from the warp of constitutional structure and the woof of dogma. David Currie writes of Marshall's technique of judging: "He reduced the applicable [constitutional] text to an afterthought. . . . He succeeded in *Marbury* in persuading us not so much that judicial review could be found in the constitution, but that it ought to have been put there; time and again he seems to have been writing a brief for a conclusion reached independently of the Constitution" (David P. Currie, *The Constitution in the Supreme Court: The First Hundred Years,* 1789–1888 [Chicago, 1985], 197). The opinions of Justice Joseph Story, his intellectual peer on the Court, provide a striking contrast. Invariably learned, tightly reasoned, amply grounded in English and American precedent, Story's elegant opinions are miniatures of his great treatises. Marshall, in contrast, was impatient with the lawyerly apparatus that adorned Story's opinions; his contained almost no citations to authorities. An apocryphal story illustrates the judicial styles of the two. Marshall supposedly said to his associate: "Now, Story, that is the law; you find the precedents for it." Andrew C. McLaughlin once observed that if Marshall had been a better lawyer, he would not have been so great a judge. A jurist more bound to precedent might have been constrained by the past. Marshall saw issues with a vision unencumbered by reverence for precedent and not confined within the calfskin covers of the English reporters. When Marshall came onto the Court, there were almost no printed American reports. Because there was no system of official reporting of English and American decisions, Marshall wrote on a clean slate. He could have found private reports if he had dug diligently, as Story loved to do, but his vision was directed elsewhere.

Ultimately, however, the measure of the Marshall Court is not the chief justice's penetrating mind, lofty vision, or administrative talent. The basis of the Court's greatness is its achievements. In 1801, John Marshall confronted a threefold challenge, which he met magnificently. First, he had to secure the independence of the judiciary within the federal system. The federal courts had to be placed beyond the routine control and oversight of the political processes: their judges had to be shielded from political pressures that followed unpopular decisions; and their jurisdiction and decisions had to be immune from political modification by Congress or the president. In return, Marshall was happy to concede that the courts' decision making would be outside and above the political process. Cases would be decided solely on the basis of law and not as an exercise of political policymaking.

His second task was to establish the power of courts to hold that acts of the legislative and executive branches violated the Constitution, and for that reason to refuse to enforce them. This, the power of judicial review, had already been asserted in the states, and had been implicit in a few decisions of the federal courts before 1803. But it had not yet been explicitly asserted by the United States Supreme Court, and its theoretical basis in the axioms of republican ideology had not yet been satisfactorily demonstrated by a court. The power to void laws was essential to everything else.

Third, Marshall had to vindicate the supremacy of the national government over the states. He had to transform the supremacy clause of Article VI from a parchment claim into a daily operating principle of American government, and federal courts had to secure for themselves a role in making that principle a working reality. Correlatively, the pretensions of the states to independence, autonomy, and sovereignty had to be suppressed.

In his great decisions, from *Marbury* v. *Madison* in 1803, through *McCulloch* v. *Maryland* in 1819, to *Gibbons* v. *Ogden* in 1824, Marshall accomplished all these goals. Stated flatly in this way, his achievements may seem obvious because we take them for granted today, in the same way that we take the Constitution itself for granted. We do so partly because of a misleading assumption that, when Marshall became chief justice, the United States entered into an era of a youthful optimism and solid national cohesion. In reality, America in 1801 was so beset with danger from without and disintegration from within that we might properly consider the first two decades of the nineteenth century the second "critical period" in American history.

The unity achieved in 1787 threatened to come undone less than fifteen years later because of sectionalism, state autonomy, the emergence of political parties, and resistance to federal authority. The Marshall Court could not hope to dispel all of these, but it successfully suppressed some, leaving other branches of the federal government to deal with the rest.

Sectionalism flared throughout the second critical period and centrifugal, secessionist tendencies appeared at America's geographical extremes. Both North-South and coastal-frontier divisions began to make their influence felt. George Washington worriedly cautioned in his Farewell Address (1796) against "geographical discriminations—Northern and Southern, Atlantic and Western—whence designing men may endeavor to excite a belief that there is a real difference of local interests and views." But by then it was already too late to try to persuade Americans that their sectional divisions were not real. Sectional animosities had appeared as early as 1790 when southerners opposed Treasury Secretary Alexander Hamilton's plan to assume the state war debts. After Virginians denounced the plan on constitutional grounds, Hamilton responded that "this is the first symptom of a spirit which must either be killed, or will kill the Constitution." The sharp controversy over the Jay Treaty in 1795 kept sectional hostilities alive. Virginians resented the provisions negotiated by Jay that looked to eventual payment of prerevolutionary debts owed to British creditors. The Treaty of San Lorenzo (1795) did not succeed in soothing southern fears that a foreign power, Spain or France, might strangle western development by closing the mouth of the Mississippi River to American trade. The fear of losing the right of deposit in New Orleans kept settlers of the American Southwest in a continual secessionist ferment, their loyalties always oriented to whichever power controlled New Orleans, rather than to the distant and ineffectual government in Washington.

Hamilton's whiskey excise added northern frontier settlers to the growing list of the sectionally disaffected because it deprived them of their only cash "crop" and tie to the national market. Their grievances erupted in the Whiskey Rebellion of 1794, and nationalists drew a comparison with Shays's Rebellion, which had been the undoing of government under the Articles of Confederation in the winter of 1786–87. Washington and Hamilton accordingly suppressed the insurrection heavy-handedly, but western resentment lingered.

When Jefferson's administration purchased Louisiana in 1803 and thereby acquired New Orleans, it removed the principal source of western discontent, but only at the cost of rekindling New England secessionist fires. Massachusetts Federalist extremists, who had been hatching separatist schemes since the early 1780s, now proposed to secede and form what they called a "northern Confederacy" composed of New England, New York, and New Jersey. The plan came to naught, but it served as an alarming reminder of how deep sectional animosities ran.

State autonomy reinforced sectionalism. After 1789, the states had never really abandoned their assumption that they could behave as sovereigns when they chose to, Constitution or no. Despite the many prohibitions against economic Balkanization in the Constitution, the states continued to pursue their own mercantilist economic programs, resulting in such shortsightedly parochial projects as New York's monopoly grant of navigation rights across the Hudson River that was to be challenged in *Gibbons* v. *Ogden*. States continued to ignore federal authority almost as freely as they had under the Articles.

State resistance to federal authority was elevated to the level of constitutional theory in the Virginia and Kentucky Resolutions of 1798–9. Jefferson and Madison expressed a theory of union in those Resolves premised on the idea that, as Jefferson put it in the Kentucky Resolution of 1799, "the several states who formed [the Constitution are] sovereign and independent." The federal government was nothing more than a compact, formed by the states as parties and not by the whole people of the United States. Only the states, not the federal government, could determine whether the federal government had exceeded its authority. Jefferson suggested something he called "nullification" as the "rightful remedy" should the federal government usurp power. Though he would soon repudiate that idea when he came into power, the idea itself persisted in full vigor in the states throughout the Marshall years as a troublesome counterweight to federal judicial authority.

The Federalist and Jeffersonian years were a time of extraordinarily divisive party competition, which only deepened sectional rancor. Hamilton's financial program, his vision of political economy expressed in the "Report on Manufactures" (1791), the impact of the French Revolution, Jay's treaty, and the generally strained relations with Britain and France, all contributed to the emergence of parties around 1795. The Framers had feared that parties were a destructive force in society, dividing people into unnatural factions, eroding the unity of purpose essential to a republic's existence. Their fears seemed to be confirmed by the scurrility and excesses of party competition in the 1790s.

The times thus hardly seemed auspicious for wielding judicial authority creatively when Marshall took the oath of office. He faced massive limitations on the use of judicial power, both inherent and potential. To begin with, most Americans held the Court itself in low esteem. So negligible did it appear to John Jay in 1800 that, when President Adams offered him reappointment as chief justice of the United States, Jay refused, saying the Court "would not obtain the energy, weight and dignity which are essential to its affording due support to the national government, nor acquire the public confidence and respect which . . . it should possess" (Jay to Adams, Jan. 2, 1801, in Henry P. Johnston, ed., *The Correspondence and Public Papers of John Jay,* 1763–1826 [New York, 1890–93], 4:284). It was symptomatic of this low esteem and prospects that, when the entire national government establishment moved from Philadelphia to the federal District in 1801, nobody bothered to reserve space for the Court's chambers anywhere. As an afterthought, and with no apparent embarrassment for the oversight, Congress at the last moment assigned the Court a basement committee room in the north wing of the Capitol. Benjamin Latrobe, the architect of the Capitol, described the chambers as "meanly furnished, very inconvenient." The first convening of the Court in the new capital and under its new chief justice could scarcely have been less impressive: only one justice, William Cushing, even bothered to show up for the occasion, and the Court had to be adjourned twice until, on a cold and rainy February morning, a quorum had assembled and John Marshall was sworn in as the third chief justice of the United States.

In this inhospitable environment, Marshall moved circumspectly. The

Court undertook no major initiatives for almost two years, while political storms swirled around it. The Jeffersonian Republican party repealed the broad jurisdictional grants of the 1801 Judiciary Act, a direct blow at the Court's power, and they undertook impeachment proceedings against Judge John Pickering of New Hampshire and Justice Samuel Chase. Yet as the political atmosphere grew dark and foreboding, in 1803, Marshall handed down the first of his great opinions, *Marbury* v. *Madison,* which boldly asserted the doctrine of judicial review in the federal court system. *Marbury* remains today at the heart of the debate over judicial power because Marshall established the terms of that debate. Whether we endorse or reject his result, we argue within the framework that *Marbury* imposed.

Marshall began by holding that the appellants had a right to their commissions as justices of the peace for the District of Columbia, that Secretary of State James Madison violated that right by refusing to deliver the commissions, and that some portion of American law afforded a remedy for this violation. (This part of the opinion infuriated Thomas Jefferson, who for the rest of his life considered it a gratuitous obiter dictum, a demeaning lecture by the chief justice of the United States to the president, motivated by partisan malice and lust for power.) But Marshall went on to hold that a portion of section 13 of the Judiciary Act of 1789, which he construed as permitting the Supreme Court to issue writs of mandamus in its original jurisdiction, was unconstitutional because Congress had no power thus to expand the Court's constitutionally specified original jurisdiction.

To reach this point, Marshall made a sleight-of-hand assertion of judicial review. He began by anticipating what later came to be known as the doctrine of political questions: "Questions, in their nature political, or which are, by the constitution and laws, submitted to the executive, can never be made in this court." He then drew another distinction, which also was to have a long life in American constitutional law, between "political" or discretionary powers on the one hand and ministerial duties on the other, with only the latter being the kind that a court can compel the president or one of his executive subordinates to perform. From there he went on to determine that Congress did not have authority to enable the Court to compel an executive act by writ of mandamus in its original jurisdiction. In order to reach that position, he held that courts could declare actions of the legislative or executive branches unconstitutional and refuse to give them legal effect.

Marshall grounded his reasoning on the bedrock of popular sovereignty and the written Constitution, those two fundamental innovations of the American Revolution's ideology. Because the people are sovereign, they may establish fundamental and permanent principles for their constitutional order, and embed these principles in a written constitution. The authority of the legislature must therefore be wielded in subordination to these principles, because it is merely the temporary representative of the sovereign people. From this reasoning it follows that "the constitution controls any legislative act repugnant to it."

Up to this point, Marshall had not gone beyond the basic premise of *Dr. Bonham's Case;* all he had done was adapt it to the American constitutional order. Then he leapt off into the distinctively American doctrine of judicial review. "It is emphatically the province and duty of the judicial department to say what the law is," he observed, an instance of his ability to use a seemingly harmless truism to clinch an argument. He did so by drawing a simplistic deduction from his premise, in a bit of what twentieth-century scholars would call "mechanical jurisprudence": all a court does when confronted with a challenge to the constitutionality of a statute is to compare the statute with the Constitution, and, in case it finds a conflict, to uphold the superior authority, the Constitution, as against the inferior, the statute. Anything else, he concluded in a piece of question-begging anticlimax, would result in legislative sovereignty. One hundred and thirty-three years later, Justice Owen Roberts repeated Marshall's point: "When an act of Congress is appropriately challenged in the courts as not conforming to the constitutional mandate the judicial branch of the Government has only one duty; to lay the article of the Constitution which is invoked beside the statute which is challenged and to decide whether the latter squares with the former" (*United States* v. *Butler,* 1936).

The perspective of nearly two centuries can distort for us the place of *Marbury* in its own time. Lawyers and laypeople consider the case the foundation of judicial review as we know it in the late twentieth century. In its day, *Marbury* had a much narrower scope. Political scientists have referred to that scope as the "departmental theory of judicial review" or "concurrent review." The phrase refers to an idea, commonplace in the early nineteenth century, that each department of government (legislative, executive, judicial) is responsible for constitutional interpretation within its own sphere, and, presumably, its decision is definitive for the other branches of government. A corollary is that its interpretation on matters outside its realm is not binding on the other branches, and is only as persuasive as the innate force of its cogency.

Viewed in this light, *Marbury* was not a radical or ambitious grab for power on Marshall's part. The case dealt with a subject quintessentially judicial: the jurisdiction and processes of courts. Unlike other memorable cases—*Dred Scott* or *Brown* v. *Board of Education,* for example—Marshall made no broad economic or social policy decision, and he did not intrude into the legislative or executive domains of policy making. Marshall himself remained to the end of his career devoted to the idea that the Court declares only law, and does not hand down policy or political decisions. Under the departmental theory, judicial review was only a means by which courts protected their sphere and powers from legislative intrusions. Its simple formula declared that law was the business of courts, and politics the business of legislatures and the executive branch. Throughout the following century, judges repeatedly professed their faithfulness to the dogma that the function of courts was *jus dicere non jus dare:* to declare the law, not to give it. Giving the law was exclusively within the legislative province; the president executed the law, and the courts interpreted it. The fabric of this neat and simple theory became ever more frayed, until by 1860 it was rapidly becoming a threadbare fiction. But as in so many articles of faith, its simplicity was the basis of its persuasive power.

Marbury was creatively ambiguous in its claim of judicial review power. The pivotal point of Marshall's opinion was his treatment of the Constitution as a law, followed by his insistence that it is the particular function of courts to interpret that law. Thus judicial review is based wholly on the courts' case-deciding, law-interpreting power. It is unclear from the words of the opinion whether Marshall envisioned merely an incidental role for courts in interpreting the Constitution, or a special one. If constitutional interpretation is merely an incident of the Court's going about its usual business of interpreting laws, then the potential role of judicial review will be comparatively limited and congenial to demands for judicial self-restraint. On the other hand, if the Court's constitutional-interpretive role is special, then its function will be unique, activist, exclusive, and supreme.

In its more activist moments, the modern Court has claimed for itself the special, rather than incidental, role implicit in *Marbury.* Charles Evans Hughes incautiously claimed in 1907 that "the Constitution is what the judges say it is." To combat the challenge of massive resistance in the late 1950s, the Court, quoting Marshall's assertion that "it is emphatically the province and duty of the judicial department to say what the law is," insisted that "the federal judiciary is supreme in the exposition of the law of the Constitution"; its interpretation of the Constitution "*is* the supreme law of the land" (*Cooper* v. *Aaron,* 1958; emphasis added). In both the first reapportionment case, *Baker* v. *Carr* (1962) and in Adam Clayton Powell's exclusion case, *Powell* v. *McCormack* (1969), the Court claimed for itself the responsibility, derived directly from *Marbury* of being the "ultimate interpreter of the Constitution." Most recently and dramatically, Chief Justice Warren Burger found it necessary to repeat the hallowed Marshall formula in *United States* v. *Nixon* (1974) as a means of refuting the president's argument that his determination of the scope of executive privilege was binding on the courts.

Marshall's reasoning in *Marbury* was vulnerable, and within a generation one of his peers in the American judiciary, Chief Judge John Bannister Gibson of the Pennsylvania Supreme Court, dissected *Marbury*'s premises in a dissent in *Eakin* v. *Raub* (1825). He concurred with Marshall's logic through Marshall's argument that an unconstitutional law was void. But he diverged on the pivotal question as to whether a court can make that determination, and on that account refused to give effect to the law. Gibson argued that courts possessed no such power, ironically by relying on the distinction between judicial and political questions that Marshall had drawn in *Marbury*.

Despite its weaknesses, *Marbury* v. *Madison* provoked almost no resistance in its own time, partly because of Marshall's circumspection and political tact, which he displayed with particular effect in *Stuart* v. *Laird* (1803). Federalists hoped that this case would be a vehicle for holding the repeal of the 1801 Judiciary Act unconstitutional, partly on the grounds that the successor statute's requirement that Supreme Court justices sit as circuit judges conferred original jurisdiction not authorized by the Constitution (precisely the holding of *Marbury*). Marshall, though sympathetic to this argument, smoothly accepted the constitutionality of the later act on the grounds that the justices' practice of accepting circuit duty since 1790 had settled the constitutionality of the assignment. In a political vacuum, *Marbury* would have authorized, even dictated, the opposite result, but Marshall shrewdly used *Stuart* to reinforce a much more momentous point: the separation of law from politics. The result in *Stuart* signaled the rejection of a politically partisan role for federal judges.

Marshall had cleverly deprived Jefferson of an opportunity to retaliate politically, and the president could only fume impotently at the implied rebuke to him contained in *Marbury*. His frustration became all the more galling when Marshall, serving as chief judge of the Circuit Court of Virginia, again provoked and thwarted him in the conduct of Aaron Burr's treason trial in 1807. Marshall not only issued a subpoena *duces tecum* to the president to compel production of documents, but also construed the treason clause of Article III of the Constitution in a way that erected an extremely high threshold for treason prosecutions.

The inherent structural tensions between the president and the courts, derived from the separation of powers principle, were soon transformed into a federalism issue, that is, a struggle for power between the states and the federal judiciary. In this new form, Marshall's claims for judicial authority proved to be politically explosive and gave Jefferson an opportunity to vent what Henry Cabot Lodge later called his "feline hostility" toward Marshall by the "creeping methods" so typical of him.

The struggle between the United States Supreme Court and the states began with Virginia's seizure of lands in its Northern Neck belonging to an absentee English landowner, Lord Fairfax, under a statute providing for confiscation of land owned by Loyalists. Virginia courts upheld the legitimacy of Virginia's seizure of the lands. The United States Supreme Court reversed that holding in 1813 (*Fairfax's Devisee* v. *Hunter's Lessee*) and instructed the Virginia courts to enter judgment for the person claiming title under Fairfax. The Virginia Court of Appeals refused to do so, and the case went back up to the Supreme Court. Thus Justice Story was given an opportunity for a showdown not only with Virginia but with Congress as well on Supreme Court appellate authority and the scope of the federal courts' jurisdiction over federal questions. (Story got to write the opinion because Marshall had to recuse himself; he was personally interested in the outcome financially and had appeared as counsel in an earlier stage of the litigation before his appointment as chief justice.)

Story began his opinion in *Martin* v. *Hunter's Lessee* (1816) with a gratuitous advisory lecture to Congress, instructing it that not only was it constitutionally obliged to enact section 25's grant of appellate authority over federal questions, but it must go further and provide for federal judicial authority commensurate with the full range of jurisdiction over persons and subject matter specified in Article III of the Constitution, something that it had done in the Judiciary Act of 1801 but then immediately repealed. (Congress did not comply with Story's demand until 1875.) Then, turning to the Virginia challenge, Story warned that if the United States Supreme Court did not have final appellate authority over state court decisions construing questions under the federal Constitution, the Constitution would be subject to varying and inconsistent interpretation by the different states. As to Virginia's contention that this view was inconsistent with the sovereignty and independence of the states, Story belligerently denied state sovereignty when questions arising under Article VI's supremacy clause were involved.

This seemingly technical and arcane subject of the federal courts' jurisdiction played a prominent role in the political debates of the day, so much so that it was the single most controversial subject to come up on the floor of Congress, excepting only the protective tariff, until the 1850s. A group of Virginia state sovereignty ideologues that included Chief Judge Spencer Roane of the Supreme Court of Appeals (Virginia's highest court); Thomas Ritchie, editor of the Richmond *Enquirer;* the state legislative leadership clique known as the Richmond Junto; and Thomas Jefferson himself reacted angrily. Roane, writing in the *Enquirer* under the pen name "Hampden" in 1819, sharply criticized the judicial nationalism of Story and of Marshall's opinion in *McCulloch* v. *Maryland* (1819). Roane called for a return to the state sovereignty principles of the Virginia and Kentucky Resolutions. Marshall refused to retreat in the face of this opposition, though. On the contrary, he resumed the offensive in *Cohens* v. *Virginia* (1821), repelling another Virginia attack on the constitutionality of section 25 and the United States Supreme Court's appellate review powers over state courts. As Story had in *Martin,* Marshall insisted that federal appellate jurisdiction was based on the nature of the suit rather than the character of the parties, thus plowing a major inroad into the immunities that the states thought they had erected around themselves by the Eleventh Amendment.

This succession of cases—*Martin, McCulloch, Cohens*—led opponents of the Supreme Court to begin a decade-long struggle to repeal section 25, modify it substantially, or weaken the Supreme Court's appellate review power in some other way. In part, this attack was purely opportunistic, with those states whose ox had been gored by a Supreme Court decision seeking to strip the Court of authority. But an ideological dimension of enduring significance remains. State sovereignty enthusiasts correctly saw section 25 as the linchpin of the federal system. John C. Calhoun speculated in 1827 that "if the appellate power from the State courts to the U. States court provided for by the 25th Sec. did not exist, the practical consequence would be, that each government would have a negative on the other, and thus possess the most effectual remedy, that can be conceived against encroachment."

Virginians and Carolinians who thought the way Calhoun did warned of a danger they called "consolidation": the tendency of power in the American Union to move by centripetal force from the states to the federal government. This tendency would lead to a destruction of the limitations on the national government and a loss of self-government by the people of the states. Thomas Ritchie warned in the Richmond *Enquirer* that "the Judiciary power, with a foot as noiseless as time and a spirit as greedy as the grave, is sweeping to their destruction the rights of the States." Already, anxious southerners believed, they saw the inexorable march of consolidation in proposals to use federal funds for internal improvements, to create a national bank that would exercise a centralized stranglehold on the expansion of credit in the specie-hungry southern and western states, and to provide the revenues to carry on this unconstitutional activity by a protective tariff. The panacea that they thought would crush consolidation was repeal of section 25, which, Calhoun believed, "would make an entire change in the operation of our system." But the repeal movement dwindled after 1831, and the Court's authority under *Martin* and *Cohens* remained intact.

As the federalism-based attack on section 25 was noisily sputtering out, President Andrew Jackson returned debate to the separation of powers challenge. The presidents, from Jefferson through Abraham Lincoln, clung to a departmental theory approach to the problem. In his bank veto message of 1832, Jackson insisted that "the Congress, the Executive, and the Court must each for itself be guided by its own opinion of the Constitution." Consequently, "the opinion of the judges has no more authority over Congress than the opinion of Congress has over the judges, and on that point the President is independent of both." In his resistance to the *Dred Scott* decision, Lincoln contended that a Court opinion was of no authority as a "political rule." Otherwise, "if the policy of the Government upon vital questions affecting the whole people is to be irrevocably fixed by decisions of the Supreme Court, . . . the people will have ceased to be their own rulers, having to that extent practically resigned their Government into the hands of that eminent tribunal."

Marbury and *Martin* were primarily concerned with establishing judicial authority in general; it was left to other cases to apply the power staked out in those cases to the substance of policy making by the state legislatures. Marshall, who could move cautiously when he had to, did not hand down any provocative opinions for six years after *Marbury*. But when he chose to take on a controversial project again, he did so in circumstances that would have daunted a lesser judge.

Fletcher v. *Peck* (1810) protected speculators' rights to Mississippi lands acquired in the notorious Yazoo bribery scheme. *Fletcher* gave Marshall an opportunity to display his genius for tactical improvisation. He began by tossing a decoy, judicial restraint, in the water, saying a court should be reluctant to hold a legislative act unconstitutional except in clear circumstances. From that deceptive posture, he went on to uphold the validity of the original state land grant. He disarmingly insisted that it would be improper for judges to go behind the face of the statute to inquire into legislative motivation or to impugn the morals of public servants. It followed that persons who took from the original grantees were bona fide purchasers, that is, innocent bystanders as it were, who should not be punished for the legislative corruption that may have tainted their title. Next, Marshall held that the original grant was a contract within the meaning of the contracts clause of Article I, section 10. There were two innovations in this holding: Marshall extended the clause to public contracts, in which the state itself was one of the parties, and to contracts already executed (that is, fully performed). Both these were probably alien to the Framers' intent. Overriding state legislative power by a dubious analogy from the private law of contracts, Marshall held that a grant implies a promise (that is, a contractual obligation) not to reclaim rights conveyed by the grant. He concluded by voiding the Georgia rescission "either by general principles which are common to our free institutions, or by the particular provisions of the Constitution of the United States" (that is, the contracts clause).

Fletcher v. *Peck* provided the basis on which the Supreme Court voided much state legislation throughout the remainder of the nineteenth century. In its heyday, the contracts clause enabled the Court to intrude into the state policymaking process, and thereby to play an expanded role in the regulation of the American economy. It was also pivotal in another way. Marshall cited two bases for voiding the Georgia rescission: the contracts clause, as well as the "general principles which are common to our free institutions" or, as he described them earlier in the opinion, "certain great principles of justice, whose authority is universally acknowledged." These phrases seemed to suggest that the Marshall Court would continue to be hospitable to the broad and vague natural law approach of *Calder* v. *Bull.* (Justice William Johnson, concurring in *Fletcher,* took an even more extreme view, insisting that higher-law principles "will impose laws even on the deity.") That openness to natural law quickly disappeared, however, as the Court jettisoned the natural law doctrine nine years later. Only Justice Story clung to the old higher-law faith in his treatise on the Constitution and in occasional cases (*Terrett* v. *Taylor,* 1815; *Wilkinson* v. *Leland,* 1822; *Commentaries on the Constitution,* 1833). Though echoes of the antique doctrine would occasionally resound after the Civil War, the Court subsumed higher-law principles into other textual bases after *Fletcher* v. *Peck,* and Marshall's "general principles" language turned out to be a dead end.

The Court abandoned higher-law principles in its next major decision striking down the substance of state legislation, *Dartmouth College* v. *Woodward* (1819). To invalidate a New Hampshire statute that tried to convert Dartmouth College, a private institution, into a state university, Marshall relied solely on the contracts clause. He held that a state grant of a corporate charter constituted a contract, disabling the state from later revoking it or modifying it in a way that would frustrate the intentions of the incorporators. After 1819, enthusiasm for traditional higher-law doctrines persisted in state appellate courts, but the United States Supreme Court struck down state legislation only on the basis of some specific provision in the text of the Constitution.

Dartmouth College marked an epochal moment in the history of American corporations. Through the eighteenth century, corporations had been predominantly public entities. They performed public functions such as exploration, governance, education, or transportation; examples include the trading corporations like the Muscovy Company or the Royal African Company, and the universities of Oxford and Cambridge. As public bodies, they were subject to extensive regulation by government. Governments owned some of their stock, nominated some of their directors, and participated in their profits. But beginning in the late eighteenth century, a new type of corporation began to evolve: the private, profit-oriented corporation. It appeared in response to a pressing requirement of English and American capitalism at the threshold of industrialization: the need to amass large amounts of capital for investment. Extant legal vehicles for such investment were proving ever less satisfactory just when demands placed on them became greater. The leading device for amassing venture capital was the partnership, but it suffered from two drawbacks: it terminated on the death or withdrawal of a partner, and each partner was individually liable for the debts of the entire partnership. These impeded the growth of national market economy that required larger and larger investments in the technological offspring of the external combustion engine: steam vessels and railroads. American lawyers experimented with various combinations and mutations of partnerships, but the corporation appeared to be the most promising institutional breakthrough, if its several problems could be eliminated.

The year 1819 witnessed a solution for both these difficulties. The Supreme Judicial Court of Massachusetts, in the case of *Spear* v. *Grant,* upheld the principle of limited liability: A stockholder of a corporation would not be liable for all its debts, but only for the amount of his stock or his subscription. The second resolution came in the *Dartmouth College* case, holding that there were constitutionally based limits, enforceable in the courts, on the extent to which state legislatures could regulate corporations. Without this assurance, investors might have been reluctant to commit their capital to the fledgling private corporation.

Dartmouth College did not settle all questions of government control of corporations; it merely indicated that limits of some sort did exist. The exact scope and contours of those limits were left to be worked out by later courts. Investors and the lawyers who represented them, such as Daniel Webster, sought almost complete exemption from public control, whereas Old Republican ideologues and their Jacksonian descendants demanded that the state retain extensive regulatory powers. This struggle might be visualized as an effort to determine a point on a continuum, ranging from one extreme of total state regulatory control at one end to the opposite extreme of corporate exemption from any sort of public governance. Webster and like-minded lawyers maintained that only the latter condition, a laissez-faire economic order, could encourage and sustain investor confidence and stave off perilous economic experiments such as socialism.

The proponents of state control won out to some extent, securing the opportunity for state legislatures to regulate corporations, at least prospectively. Their triumph was implicit in the *Dartmouth College* opinions themselves, particularly in a concurrence by Justice Story, who conceded that the contracts clause did not prohibit state legislatures from reserving a right in the charters to regulate corporations. This view, in its turn, permitted a variant form of reservation of state authority. New York pioneered with an 1827 statute reserving regulatory power generally over subsequently chartered corporations, and other states followed suit, either by statute or by revision of the state constitution. In that same year, 1827, the Marshall Court held that states could regulate the substance of contracts to be made in the future; it deemed regulatory legislation implicit in all contracts negotiated after the enactment of the statute (*Ogden* v. *Saunders*). Since a charter is a contract under *Dartmouth College,* this decision cleared the way for state regulatory statutes such as that of New York.

The Marshall Court soon employed its newly established powers under the contracts clause to restrain the states' legislative judgement in sensitive areas of public policy. In the 1812 case of *New Jersey* v. *Wilson,* the Court held that an exemption from taxation on land was a contract that a subsequent legislature could not impair by revoking the exemption. This holding was a substantial limitation on the states' vital power of taxation. The states responded by amending their constitutions to prohibit legislative grants of tax immunity. Then in 1819, at the onset of a severe depression that lasted the better part of a decade, the Court used the contracts clause in *Sturges* v. *Crowninshield* to hold a New York insolvency law void because it modified the terms of existing contracts.

The Court's involvement in the snakes' nest of Kentucky land title litigation in the 1823 case of *Green* v. *Biddle* proved even more controversial. At the time Kentucky separated from Virginia to become a new state, the two entered into a compact by which the daughter state recognized land titles granted by its parent state. Subsequently, however, to provide some passage through the morass of title litigation caused by overlapping and repetitive land grants, Kentucky enacted its "occupying-claimant laws," which provided that a squatter had to be compensated for improvements he made on lands if he were ousted by someone with a superior title (usually an out-of-state or absentee speculator, a group disfavored by the squatter-sympathetic state legislature). If he did not receive such compensation, the squatter could take title to the land upon payment of its value less his improvements. The Marshall Court struck down this statute as an impairment of contracts, the contract here being the original bi-state compact. This was a strained holding, even in the eyes of the Court's supporters, and it had mischievous consequences.

In Congress, Kentucky representatives and their sympathizers began an indirect attack on the Court's power of judicial review by proposing legislation, never enacted, that would require some super-majority of the Court (two-thirds, six, or all of the justices, the Court then being composed of seven members) to concur before a statute could be held unconstitutional. The failure of these bills fueled efforts to trim or repeal the Court's section 25 jurisdiction. In Kentucky itself, resistance was more explosive because it was drawn into the vortex of what is known in Kentucky history as the "old court" struggle, so-called because the legislature, disgusted with a holding of the state Court of Appeals that the occupying-claimant laws were unconstitutional, created an entirely new Court of Appeals. For a time, both courts sat, each claiming to be the sole legitimate supreme court of the state. The state legislature, in no mood to tolerate judicial interference with the occupying-claimant laws from any quarter, recommended using state militia to resist enforcement of the judgment in *Green* v. *Biddle.* The new state Court of Appeals announced that it would not be bound by any Supreme Court judgment that did not have the concurrence of a majority of the whole Court (*Bodley* v. *Gaither,* Ky., 1825). Eventually the whole land title controversy dissipated, but the Supreme Court's involvement did nothing to improve its reputation in the minds of southern and western frontier critics.

By common consent, Marshall's greatest opinion is *McCulloch* v. *Maryland* (1819), the bank-tax case. If *Marbury* was the foundation of judicial power in the Marshall era, *McCulloch* was the most important part of the superstructure. Its grand principles and ringing phrases are as vibrantly alive in our own day as they were during President James Monroe's administration. In this case, more than in any other single source, Marshall instructed us on the nature of the American Union and provided the interpretive key to the Constitution.

In the early years of the American Republic, the central constitutional question, if any one issue may be singled out as more important than the others, was whether the federal government possessed "implied powers," that is, powers other than those specifically granted to it in the text of the Constitution. The "expressly clause" of the Articles of Confederation, which confined the powers of the national government to those "expressly delegated," was widely acknowledged, even by

Antifederalists, to be one of the major defects of the Articles. Accordingly, in the First Congress, the framers of what became the Tenth Amendment took care to avoid inserting any comparable limitation on federal authority. Because the question was so important, however, it cropped up almost immediately thereafter in the debate between Alexander Hamilton and Thomas Jefferson over the constitutionality of the congressional charter of the first Bank of the United States. Hamilton defined the word *necessary* in the "necessary and proper" clause of Article I as meaning "no more than needful, requisite, incidental, useful or conducive to," an interpretation adopted almost verbatim by Marshall in *McCulloch.* Jefferson, by contrast, defined the word in its strictest sense: "those means without which the grant of power would be nugatory."

Though bested in the bank argument (because Congress chartered the bank despite his constitutional objections), Jefferson soon returned to the issue, this time joined by James Madison, in the Virginia and Kentucky Resolutions of 1798–99. In these they denied that Congress possessed power to enact legislation limiting individual liberties and urged the states to restrict the national government to its explicitly delegated powers. Observing such claims with growing unease, John Marshall took the opportunity presented by an 1805 case, *United States* v. *Fisher,* to correct the the strict constructionists: "Congress must possess the choice of means, and must be empowered to use any means which are in fact conducive to the exercise of a power granted by the constitution." James Madison remained unimpressed, and as president in 1816 he vetoed a bill authorizing federal expenditures for internal improvements on strict construction grounds reminiscent of his 1798 position. The debates over the admission of Missouri as a slave state, occurring contemporaneously with the decision in *McCulloch,* raised the question of implied powers in their most ominous form.

Against this backdrop of constitutional controversy, Marshall delivered his magisterial opinion in *McCulloch,* adopting Hamilton's 1791 bank arguments and upholding the power of Congress to charter the bank. As in his other great opinions, Marshall first laid out certain "general principles" or axioms of government, from which his conclusions followed irresistibly. He began with the nature of the Constitution itself, reminding his hearers that "we must never forget that it is a *constitution* we are expounding." That Constitution could not, from its very nature, be a detailed enumeration of congressional powers. Rather, it was "intended to endure for ages to come, and consequently, to be adapted to the various *crises* of human affairs."

Granted these axiomatic points, the necessity and existence of implied powers inevitably followed. But before reaching that conclusion, Marshall turned to a discourse on the correlatives of federal and state sovereignty. The federal "government proceeds directly from the people" themselves; consequently, it "is, emphatically and truly, a government of the people," fully sovereign within the sphere of its authority. It followed that the states were not wholly sovereign or autonomous. Federal power thus need not "be exercised in subordination to the States." But conflicts between federal and state authority would inevitably arise in the compound federal system of the United States, and those conflicts must be "decided peacefully," and by the Supreme Court, lest they lead to civil conflict. Thus, after biding his time for twenty years, Marshall repudiated the constitutional theory of the Virginia and Kentucky Resolutions.

After this parade of fundamental principles, the specific holdings of *McCulloch* were almost anticlimactic. Marshall turned to a means-ends test, insisting that if the broad and important missions of the federal government were to be effectively accomplished, that government "must also be entrusted with ample means for their execution." He then adopted a Hamiltonian reading of the word *necessary:* "convenient, or useful, or essential." "Let the end be legitimate, let it be within the scope of the constitution," he intoned in one of the most frequently quoted passages from the opinion, "and all means which are appropriate, which are plainly adapted to that end, which are not prohibited, but consist with the letter and spirit of the constitution, are constitutional." Given such a reading of federal power, it followed that a state could not interfere with the legitimate functions of a federal instrumentality such as the bank, and Maryland's attempt to tax it was invalid. "The question is, in truth, a question of supremacy," he wrote. "The power to tax involves the power to destroy," Marshall added in an often misquoted epigram near the end of his opinion.

McCulloch had a considerable short-term impact. Marshall's "general principles" spoke directly to the hottest and most controversial political issues of the 1820s: the tariff, the bank, federal financial aid for internal improvements, the entire program that Henry Clay in 1824 called "the American System." Troubled southern ideologues and legal thinkers saw in *McCulloch*'s underpinnings for this program the unmistakable signs of "consolidation." This was not merely a theoretical or abstract question for them. The *McCulloch* opinion came down in the midst of the Missouri debates, and its constitutional premises were complicated by questions touching on slavery.

Virginians lost no time in trying to rebut Marshall's constitutional doctrines. With *Martin* v. *Hunter's Lessee* still a sore memory, Judge Spencer Roane and Judge William Brockenbrough published anonymous essays in Thomas Ritchie's Richmond *Enquirer* condemning the principles of *McCulloch.* Vexed by the states' power premises of these essays, Marshall took the unusual step of publishing anonymous essays he himself had composed defending his opinion and refuting his critics, insisting principally that, though the federal government was supreme within the responsibilities assigned to it, significant limitations on its power continued to assure the viability of the federal system and the spheres of the states within it.

Such reassurances did not satisfy proslavery ideologues, foremost among them John Taylor of Caroline, as well as Thomas Cooper and Robert Turnbull of South Carolina, who all denounced the consolidationist tendencies of the federal government under Marshall's nationalizing lead. What most worried these southern critics was the implicit threat to slavery contained in any extension of national power. Denmark Vesey's abortive slave rebellion in Charleston, South Carolina (1822) had alerted them to the precarious condition of internal security in all slave societies. As if that were not bad enough, they sensed a growing indifference, possibly a hostility, toward slavery among people of the northern states, who now returned a majority of the House of Representatives.

Hence ardent southern nationalism, which had characterized the first two decades of the nineteenth century, rapidly waned. At the same time, northern political leaders took up the nationalist outlook the southerners were casting off. Whereas sectionalism had been identified with New England through the War of 1812, it now came to be the hallmark of southern politics. The Webster-Hayne debates of 1830 announced this fact to the world: Daniel Webster defended a nationalist political vision based on Marshallian constitutional principles against the sectionalism based on anticonsolidationist political thinking expressed by Robert Hayne of South Carolina.

The short-term impact of *McCulloch* became absorbed in the intensifying sectional controversy. But after the Civil War settled at the cannon's mouth what Marshall had not been able to secure at the judge's bench, the principles of the opinion resonated more vibrantly than ever, particularly at times of challenge to national authority. The spirit of *McCulloch* permeated the decisions of the 1937–42 period accepting national regulatory power to cope with the emergency of the Great Depression. *McCulloch* figured, too, in the Court's acceptance of the exercise of national power by the public accommodations title of the Civil Rights Act of 1964 and the Voting Rights Act of 1965.

Marshall's last great opinion, *Gibbons* v. *Ogden* (1824), has been as influential as *McCulloch;* but unlike the latter, *Gibbons* proved to be ambiguous at a critical point, passing on an issue that had to be resolved by later generations. To paraphrase an estimate of John Marshall himself, *Gibbons* v. *Ogden* is important simply because it was *there:* it occurred at a vital juncture in American economic development. Like *Dartmouth College,* it nudged the law in a distinctive direction that has been with us ever since.

Lawyers and judges in the early nineteenth century promoted one of two contrasting models of economic development: the traditional one based on government-sanctioned monopolistic economic power and the more modern one based on competition. This distinction was an old one, traceable centuries back into common law doctrines that supported monopolies in the case of unique natural resources (such as sites topographically suited for dams or ferries) and permitted competition in other endeavors (shops, schools, mills). This dualism in the attitudes of law was dramatically captured in the state court decisions of the case that was the predecessor of *Gibbons, Livingston* v. *Van Ingen* (New York, 1812). Chancellor John Lansing condemned the state monopoly grant of steam navigation across the Hudson River as contrary to the public interest. On appeal to New York's highest court, Chief Justice James Kent supported the monopoly on the grounds of "justice and policy." Even as Kent wrote his opinion, however, classical liberal economic thought was undercutting his position. Adam Smith and other eighteenth-century political economists exalted competition as the most efficient and just motive force in modern economies. Legal thought in America did not remain deaf to that powerful idea.

Unlike the *Livingston* case, *Gibbons* v. *Ogden* is remembered for something other than its choice between these models of economic development. Today the commerce clause of the Constitution's Article I, section 8, has become the single most important source of federal regulatory power. Yet before 1824 the Supreme Court had never discussed or interpreted it, chiefly because Congress had enacted no regulatory legislation. Thus Marshall had the opportunity to create basic legal doctrines, and he made the most of it. He defined the federal commerce power as sweepingly as words permitted, stating that it was "complete in itself, may be exercised to its utmost extent, and acknowledges no limitations, other than are prescribed in the constitution." Under such a reading, "the sovereignty of Congress, though limited to specified objects, is plenary . . . vested in Congress as absolutely as it would be in a single government." If discretion in its exercise was to be limited, it must be by the people themselves, at the voting place, rather than by the courts. This broad conception of the commerce power became the foundation for all later commerce clause doctrine. Though contracted at times to narrower limits, the Marshallian conception of commerce has always sprung back to its original capacious scope.

Even with the commerce clause spaciously interpreted, there remained the problem of superiority in the federal system. Here Marshall waffled, uncharacteristically. Given a clash of federal and state legislation on the same subject, a continuum of possibilities for resolving such a clash emerged in the antebellum period. At one extreme, the Court might have held that federal regulatory power was absolutely supreme over any inconsistent state regulation, even if the federal authority were not exercised, simply by virtue of its inherent superiority. This was the position taken by Justice William Johnson, concurring in *Gibbons.* At the other extreme, the Court might simply have reversed these values, holding state power supreme over any inconsistent federal statute. Chief Justice Roger B. Taney later adopted this position in the stress of the slavery controversy. A middle position in the spectrum, which the Court did not evolve until midcentury, would allocate certain subjects to federal supremacy and certain subjects to state authority, depending on their national-versus-local characteristics. Marshall did not adopt any of these positions. He toyed with the idea of federal exclusivity, elaborating the arguments in its favor, but then lamely concluded that "there is great force in this argument, and the Court is not satisfied that it has been refuted." This less-than-resounding conclusion left the door open to a harmful struggle over federal authority until the Civil War.

Marshall may have been mealy-mouthed on the issue, so unlike his approach to other constitutional questions, because a hidden controversy in *Gibbons,* though never brought to the surface explicitly in the opinions, operated as a powerful, invisible determinant of judicial attitudes. That was the question of slavery. The issue of federal-versus-state regulatory power had surfaced the prevous year in *Elkison* v. *Deliesseline,* a United States circuit court case decided by Justice Johnson. In *Elkison,* slavery made its contaminating, disruptive presence felt in the commerce clause area. South Carolinians were originally perturbed by antislavery ideas broached during the Missouri debates, then alarmed by the Vesey Rebellion, which they regarded as a confirmation of their fears. Distraught by the threat to the internal security of their slave society, the Carolinians enacted the first of the Negro Seamen's acts, requiring any black seaman serving on a vessel in Carolina waters to remain aboard his ship. If he came ashore on liberty, the act required that he be seized and held until his vessel departed. If the master of the vessel refused to pay the costs of detention, the sailor was to be sold into slavery.

Johnson, though a native Carolinian, was a fervent nationalist. When the constitutionality of the Negro Seamen's Act came before him on circuit in *Elkison,* he held it void, both as an interference with the federal commerce power and with the treaty power. When his opinion was vociferously condemned in South Carolina newspapers, Johnson wrote newspaper essays himself, anonymously, defending and extending his position. Thus when a commerce clause case came to the Court the next year in *Gibbons,* Johnson could not bring himself to acquiesce in Marshall's ambiguous and incomplete position. Instead he wrote an ultranationalist concurrence that argued for full federal exclusivity. This hidden problem of slavery continued to bedevil commerce clause cases in the Supreme Court until its source, slavery itself, was extirpated.

Gibbons was a popular opinion because many Americans saw it as a bar to hated monopolies. Part of its popularity derived from its being in step with technological advance. Marshall synchronized legal and technological developments, bringing the law abreast of engineering and scientific improvements. But Marshall seemed to sense that *Gibbons* would be his valedictory to the Republic. He therefore left the American people with a melancholy warning that surveyed the constitutional controversies of his lifetime:

> Powerful and ingenious minds, taking, as postulates, that the powers expressly granted to the government of the Union, are to be contracted by construction, into the narrowest possible compass, . . . may, by a course of well digested, but refined and metaphysical reasoning, founded on these premises, explain away the constitution of our country, and leave it, a magnificent structure, indeed, to look at, but totally unfit for use.

He condemned states' power abstractions, warning that only "safe and fundamental principles"—the precepts he had laid before the people since *Marbury*—would sustain the Constitution and the Union.

The last decade of Marshall's tenure was a time of frustration, accommodation, and reluctant concession. With one exception, the constitutional decisions of the Marshall Court after 1824 either fell short of the nationalist scope of the earlier opinions, or met with severe political resistance. And even that one exception—*Craig* v. *Missouri* (1830), in which Marshall struck down a state note issue under the Bills of Credit clause of Article I, section 10—was soon evaded by the Taney Court. Otherwise, from a constitutional nationalist point of view, it was a time of what seventeenth-century New England ministers called declension.

In the same year as *Ogden,* Marshall handed down a foreign commerce decision, *Brown* v. *Maryland,* which prohibited states from taxing the subjects of international trade while they remained in their "original packages"; the correlative was permitting the states' tax power to reach those goods when they had become "commingled" with other property in the state after the original package had been breached. Marshall also eroded his *Gibbons* holding in *Willson* v. *Blackbird Creek Marsh Co.* (1829) by permitting a state to authorize damming of a navigable creek that had been plied by vessels sailing under the same federal coastal licensing act that Marshall had used to strike down the New York monopoly. The state of Georgia and President Andrew Jackson handed Marshall a series of three rebuffs in the various Cherokee cases (*Corn Tassel*'s case, *Cherokee Nation* v. *Georgia* [1831], and *Worcester v. Georgia* [1832]) by ignoring or flouting his decrees that attempted to preserve Indian rights in the face of whites' land greed. Finally, in *Barron* v. *Baltimore* (1833), Marshall held that the restrictions of the federal Bill of Rights did not apply to the states, an extraordinary concession to state autonomy not compelled by the language of any of the original ten amendments except the First.

What caused this melancholy retreat? Several explanations suggest themselves, and in combination they proved decisive. First and most important, the constitutional doctrines of some of these declension-decade opinions were inherently sound, even if they marked a retrogression from the high nationalism of Marshall's earlier years. Among these are the original package doctrine of *Brown* and the recognition of valid state regulatory interests in *Willson.*

The Court was coming under severe political pressures, too, from all around the compass. Its decisions since 1809 had antagonized a powerful and vocal group of states: Virginia, Pennsylvania, New York, Ohio, Kentucky, Maryland, Missouri, South Carolina, Georgia, New Jersey, New Hamsphire, and Massachusetts, nearly all of them seats of Jeffersonian Republican power. The economic depression that began in 1819 only intensified sectional stresses that had been revived by the Missouri debates. The demise of the first party system left the national political structure disorganized and chronically febrile, a situation in which local animosities would not be dampened by the tendencies toward compromise and accommodation that a stable political mechanism imposes. With Andrew Jackson's election in 1828, the Court found itself confronting a powerful antagonist backed by the resources of a dynamic new political party. Jackson did not hesitate to ignore judicial doctrine in such matters as the Cherokee cases, the Bank veto, and the Maysville Road veto (1830). And at the state level, judicial power was being successfully challenged by the movement to elect all judges and by the effort to codify the states' laws.

In this inhospitable climate, the exuberant nationalism of *McCulloch* and the judicial assertiveness of *Cohens* were anomalous. Momentum had shifted to the Court's enemies, and the period between *McCulloch* and

Marshall's death witnessed a host of proposals to strip the High Court of its powers. The New York legislature recommended a scheme, which has resurfaced in our own times, to create a kind of super–Supreme Court composed of the twenty-four chief judges of the state supreme courts, a body that would have ultimate review authority over the real Court's decisions. A variant, proposed (not surprisingly) by a Kentuckian, Richard Johnson, would have made the Senate itself a review panel over Court decisions. Other senators suggested that the Constitution be amended to permit the justices to be removed by processes less strict than impeachment, such as the legislative technique known as removal by address, in which a mere majority of a legislature is competent to fire a judge. Then there was the spate of proposals to repeal or modify section 25.

Despite their widespread support, and the animosity toward the Court in so many states, all these court-curbing proposals failed. Several explanations might be offered for this failure, but the most persuasive is the inherent force and wisdom of the Marshall Court achievements. The legal historian G. Edward White sums up these achievements in the phrase "the American judicial tradition," which Marshall established (White, *The American Judicial Tradition: Profiles of Leading American Judges* [New York, 1976]). This tradition includes three major elements. The judiciary is autonomous from both the executive and judicial branches, immune to any kind of direct political pressure and hence free to hand down decisions on considerations other than expediency, compromise, and policy that are the grist of the political mills. Second, the scope of judicial authority extends to political and policy questions as well as routine legal questions. This authority has been secured without judicial involvement in ordinary politics. Finally, the American judicial tradition has imposed "a set of internalized constraints upon the office of the judge" that restrict the scope of judicial discretion, requiring that all decisions conform to the rule of law.

This tradition depends on an assumption that "the law" has an objective existence outside the political and policy preferences of the judges. That persistent philosophical assumption has often been challenged by the Court's critics in the century and a half since Marshall's death, and the remainder of this volume will survey the resultant controversies. But it is a measure of Marshall's achievement that he set the agenda of this debate. He created the judicial tradition out of the scant and unpromising prospects he found when he took office in 1801. Never has a judge been able to accomplish so much with so little.

Chapter 3

"A constitution intended to endure for ages to come"

DEMOCRACY, SLAVERY, AND CAPITALISM BEFORE THE TANEY COURT

BOTH THE beginning and the end of Roger B. Taney's tenure as chief justice of the United States were marked by extravagant condemnation of the man and his principles. These attacks have distorted our perception of the antebellum Court, and recent scholarship has had to slog its way out of the swamp of misunderstanding and bias to achieve a fair picture of Taney and his Court. When he was nominated by President Andrew Jackson, Taney was blasted by Whigs as "that political hack"; "inferior in talents and learning, and especially in legal reputation, to most, at least, of his associates on the Court." They predicted, "he cannot but experience a sense of inferiority" (quoted in Charles Warren, *The Supreme Court in United States History,* rev. ed. [Boston, 1932], 2:17).

Taney's first opinion in the *Charles River Bridge* (1837) case was especially distressing to legal conservatives. Charles Sumner, who had been Joseph Story's student at the Harvard Law School and continued to be his protégé, said that reading Taney's majority opinion in the *Bridge* case after Story's dissent was like "taking hog-wash after champagne" (Quoted in Warren, *Supreme Court in United States History,* 2:28). An anonymous Whig critic wrote that "old things are passing away. The authority of former decisions, which had long been set as landmarks in the law, is assailed and overthrown . . . the whole fair system of the constitution [is] beginning to dissolve like the baseless fabric of a vision" (quoted in Warren, *Supreme Court in United States History,* 2:30–31). New York's Chancellor James Kent, one of the nation's most respected constitutional authorities, condemned the *Bridge* opinion in private correspondence to Story and in an anonymous law review article: "It abandons, or overthrows, a great principle of constitutional morality" (quoted in Warren, *Supreme Court in United States History,* 2:29). "I have lost my confidence and hopes in the constitutional guardianship and protection of the Supreme Court," he wailed. "What a deep injury has [the *Bridge*] decision inflicted on the Constitution, jurisprudence, and character of the United States! We are fast sinking even below the standard of Pagan antiquity" (quoted in Carl B. Swisher, *The Taney Period,* 1836–1864 [New York, 1974], 95).

Such comments give the impression that Marshall's moderate regime had been overthrown in a legal revolution, replaced by radical and ignorant legal vandals. The Whiggish comparison between Marshall and Taney was not only wrong; even purged of its errors, it remains misleading. Yet the excesses of the conservative reaction have something to tell us about the state of public law in the Jacksonian period. It was a time of profound legal and political change. Conservatives were bemoaning not just the transition from a Federalist to a Democratic legal regime. They perceived correctly that the law itself was undergoing profound shifts.

To begin with, the republican vision that had informed Marshall's jurisprudence was disintegrating. Marshall and his contemporaries had been soldiers and statesmen of the Revolution. Their perspective was that of the eighteenth century. Their image of the constitutional order was classical, symmetrical, balanced, and static. Fundamental constitutional principles were, for them, unalterable and permanent. Their approach to law was teleological, seeing in the growth of law the realization of an immanent, divinely appointed destiny for the American republican experiment.

Changes in American society during the Jacksonian era were rudely dislocating this ideal. Geographic growth alone changed America almost beyond recognition. The Louisiana Purchase (1803) almost doubled the size of the nation; the acquisition of West and East Florida (1810–19) made it a Gulf Coast nation whose territory rimmed the Caribbean; the territorial acquisitions of the 1840s (Texas, 1845; Oregon, 1846; California and the Southwest, 1848) once again doubled America's acreage, and now made the United States a Pacific nation as well.

The dynamic but unstable American economy posed new challenges for the law. To mention just two examples, the recurrent, almost cyclical depressions (1819, 1837, 1857) strained the states' and nation's capacity to structure debtor-creditor relationships; and the voracious demand for capital at the onset of industrialization assured legal conflicts over the allocation of scarce investment resources. Rapid population growth further destabilized an already burgeoning society. The immigration component of this growth was particularly important, for it included many Irish and German Roman Catholics, whose presence provoked nativists while it swelled the Democratic party, traditionally hospitable to new and hyphenated citizens.

The political parties of the era, Whig and Democratic, both held ambivalent attitudes toward contemporary reform movements, but the intense political competition of the period nevertheless served to encourage reform efforts. Temperance and prohibition flourished, generating legal and constitutional struggles. Democratizing political movements in the states produced challenges to the law itself, as well as efforts to improve the administration of justice, such as the abolition of capital punishment and imprisonment for debt. The relationship between the states and the federal government on the one hand and the states and their people on the other seemed open to continuous reconsideration and change. As the republican ideological impetus of the Marshall era lost its force, a movement that exalted democracy and state sovereignty took its place, much to the dismay of the conservatives. Chancellor Kent, acclaimed author of the *Commentaries on American Law* (1826–30), warned that "the Judges of the Supreme Court have no business to be looking with timidity and awe upon the State sovereignties, as if they were the safer and the purer sovereigns" (quoted in Swisher, *Taney Period,* 95). This tendency to exalt state power, soon distorted by the slavery controversy, however, produced inconsistent leanings toward state autonomy and national supremacy.

Legal issues at the state level further contributed to the conservatives' sense of impending catastrophe. Judges of the Revolutionary Era faced a straightforward responsibility: to convert republican ideology into legal doctrine. By the time Taney became chief justice, a new generation of judges, men who had been infants during and after the Revolution, faced a different and more complex task. The law of property provides an apt illustration. For Marshall's generation, the task had been to secure property against expropriation and redistribution by debtor-sympathetic state legislatures. The task facing Taney's generation was quite different. For one thing, new forms of incorporeal (that is, nontangible) property had appeared: franchises, for example. Equally valid and legitimate yet conflicting policy considerations sometimes pulled judges in inconsistent directions. For example, corporate franchises (that is, charters of incorporation) had to be secured against state interference and spoliation, but at the same time the state legislatures had to be free to regulate those franchises in the interests of the welfare of the entire people. Jurists of an earlier era saw this issue in simplistic or passé terms, and it was left to the rising generation, Taney's, to resolve the conflicts by more sophisticated criteria.

Another source of conservative distress was the realization, poignantly felt by both Story and Kent, that they had failed to unify the body of American law. As law reports proliferated, the gush of common law adjudication became a flood threatening to drown the synthesizing efforts of Kent, hailed as "America's Blackstone." Even Story's prodigious output of treatises could not encompass all common law developments. To make matters worse, at the state level, reformers seemed to be attacking the common law itself. Critics assailed it as antidemocratic, demanding that all judge-made law be reduced to legislatively compiled codes. Other reformers horrified Whig jurists by insisting that all judges be elected for limited terms, so as to be democratically accountable to the people.

Higher law came under indirect attack, and "vested rights"—that slogan of an older, static conception of the economic order—seemed threatened. Status-based legal relationships also were besieged, as wives sought a legal capacity distinct from that of their husbands, and abolitionists attacked that ultimate status relationship, slavery. Well might a conservative New York judge, Seward Barcolo, lament: "The ancient muniments [documentary evidences of title to property] . . . are crumbling and falling before the batteries of modern reformers. The old landmarks are being removed. The principles of former times are fast receding from view" (*Holmes* v. *Holmes,* 4 Barb. S.C. 295 [N.Y. Sup. Ct. 1848]). The barbarian hordes not only seemed to be at the gates; in the person of Roger B. Taney, they had actually taken command of the citadel. "A constitution intended to endure for ages to come," as Marshall had called it in *McCulloch,* seemed to conservatives about to succumb after only a generation.

The conservatives' invidious comparison of Taney with Marshall is understandable, even if misplaced. Taney had served as United States attorney general and secretary of the treasury in the Jackson administrations. In the former post, he prepared an official opinion on the constitutional validity of certain state statutes, the Negro Seamen's Acts, in which he expressed doubt that a Supreme Court decision against their constitutionality would bind the states. He confirmed his adherence to this heresy as treasury secretary. He urged President Jackson to veto the Bank recharter bill, and drafted that part of the veto message in which Jackson claimed that a Supreme Court opinion "ought not to control the coordinate authorities of the Government. The Congress, the Executive, and the Court must each for itself be guided by its own opinion of the Constitution." In conservatives' eyes, this made Taney "the ready and most obsequious agent of the severest and most dangerous blow which has been given to our Constitution and law" (quoted in Warren, *Supreme Court in United States History,* 2:14).

Despite these radical ideas (which, in any event, the remainder of his career repudiated), the new chief justice shared Marshall's fundamental values. Both men were determined to maintain a capitalist economic order. Each was dedicated to preserving the claims derived from ownership of property; the differences between them stemmed from Marshall's older, static view of property, and Taney's preference for dynamic property. The vested rights/higher-law orientation of republican jurisprudence was obsolete even before Taney ascended to the bench. Taney's generation subsumed it into newer forms of constitutional protection for private power. Similarly with the elements of republicanism, especially popular sovereignty. Marshall and Story saw their task as having to secure those values. Taney's generation could take that accomplishment for granted, and get on with the next job, to accommodate democratizing trends to the earlier republican structure. Both Taney and Marshall supported constitutional limitations on the legislative power of the states and the federal government. And finally, both were committed to the expansion of federal judicial power. Such similarities make Whig fears seem groundless and hysterical.

But there were two major differences between Taney and Marshall, and the conservatives' anxieties were not altogether misconceived. Unlike Kent and Marshall, Taney and his brethren had a deep attachment to state sovereignty and autonomy. Closely related was their dedication to the security of slavery, a value they cherished all the more strongly as the issue itself became more urgent and disruptive.

Apprehensive conservatives thought they saw their worst fears confirmed as three major decisions came down in Taney's first term (1837) as chief justice (*Briscoe* v. *Bank of Kentucky, Charles River Bridge* v. *Warren Bridge,* and *Mayor of New York* v. *Miln*). Each expanded state power, though not at the expense of national authority. *Briscoe* did indeed seem to overturn a recent Marshall precedent, *Craig* v. *Missouri* (1830). Article I, section 10, prohibits the states from issuing "Bills of Credit" as paper money. In *Craig,* Marshall had struck down a Missouri scheme by which a state loan office issued certificates that served as a surrogate for currency. This decision was intensely unpopular in the specie-poor southern and western states, in which economic development, according to both contemporary belief and modern monetarist economic theory, required an expansive and flexible money supply. In *Briscoe,* Taney gladdened these frontier interests by upholding a Kentucky variant on the Missouri scheme (a state bank issued its notes, which were not backed by the credit of the state, but which did serve to augment the circulating medium).

The impact of *Briscoe* was mild compared to the impression made by *Charles River Bridge,* largely because the *Bridge* case was a compendium of so many major legal and constitutional issues of the Jacksonian era. These included the effect of technological change on the law, the status of corporations, the extent of state regulatory control over economic development, the reach of the contracts clause, the extent to which state regulatory power was to be constrained by the United States Constitution, and a reprise of the monopoly-versus-competition models' contest for supremacy. Any one of these would have made the *Bridge* case a potential landmark decision. Moreover, the case was Taney's maiden opinion (*Briscoe* had been written by Justice John McLean) and thus was something of a bellwether in the new era of public law.

The problem posed in *Charles River Bridge* was whether the Court would construe a corporate charter in such a way as to read into it an implied guarantee that the company would be free from competition by a rival. Taney determined that it would not. In corporate charters, he held, "no rights are taken from the public, or given to the corporation, beyond those which the words of the charter, by their natural and proper construction, purport to convey." Taney used a Marshall decision, *Providence Bank* v. *Billings* (1830), as authority for his dictum that a "state ought never to be presumed to surrender this power" to adopt any policy it chooses to encourage economic development.

In *Charles River Bridge,* Taney also demonstrated his alert sensitivity to the relationship between law and technological development. The *Bridge* case represented not only rival theories of capitalist growth but also a clash between older ways of life and an emergent technology (in this case, railroads, just then beginning to chug over the horizon and change the American landscape). In an eloquent peroration, he wrote:

> If this court should establish the principles now contended for, what is to become of the numerous railroads established on the same line of travel with turnpike companies; and which have rendered the franchises of the turnpike corporations of no value? Let it once be understood that such charters carry with them these implied contracts, and give this unknown and undefined property in a line of travelling, and you will soon find the old turnpike corporations awakening from their sleep, and calling upon this court to put down the improvements which have taken their place. The millions of property which have been invested in railroads and canals, upon lines of travel which had been before occupied by turnpike corporations, will be put in jeopardy. We shall be thrown back to the improvements of the last century, and obliged to stand still, until the claims of the old turnpike corporations shall be satisfied, and they shall consent to permit these States to avail themselves of the lights of modern science, and to partake of the benefit of those improvements which are now adding to the wealth and prosperity, and the convenience and comfort of every other part of the civilized world.

Rarely has a Court so acutely grasped the interrelations of law, economic growth, and technological change. Though Marshall dimly sensed such matters in *Gibbons,* Taney's clearheaded and confident embrace of the technological future distinguished his tenure.

A modern constitutional historian, Stanley I. Kutler, provides the key to an understanding of Taney's decision in his concept of "privilege and creative destruction" (Stanley I. Kutler, *Privilege and Creative Destruction: The Charles River Bridge Case* [Philadelphia, 1971]). Judges recognize that legally accorded privilege sometimes becomes a drag on further economic and technological improvement, hampering change that will benefit society. They then fashion doctrines that achieve a creative destruction of these clogs on progress, promoting improvements and innovation at the expense of vested interests, expectations, and hopes for a continuation of the privilege.

This process of creative destruction is related to two other engines of legal development in the antebellum years. The eminent legal historians Willard Hurst and Morton Horwitz both scout the simplistic notion that courts of the period blindly and reflexively protected vested rights. Rather, Hurst maintains, judges such as Taney extended a judicial preference to dynamic, rather than static, capital, "capital in motion," as he calls it (J. Willard Hurst, *Law and the Conditions of Freedom in the Nineteenth-Century United States* [Madison, 1956]). Though the differences between the two vanish in close cases, static capital produces only sluggish returns that coupon-clipping investors consume or divert to established, conservative, safe investments. Dynamic capital on the other hand seeks riskier, less assured investment opportunities, and in return produces multiplier benefits for the community in addition to the innovative enterprises that it supports directly. In the *Bridge* case, the competitor (new) bridge opened up the northern Massachusetts hinterland to the market and port of Boston, whereas a continuation of the de facto monopoly enjoyed by the old bridge might have stymied that metropolis-hinterland relationship.

Horwitz suggests that American law underwent a transformation in this period, destroying older forms of property rights in favor of newer ones demanded by entrepreneurial elites (Morton J. Horwitz, *The Transformation of American Law,* 1780–1860 [Cambridge, Mass., 1977]). Access to capital and to natural resources such as railroad rights of way and dam sites could not be blocked by invoking talismanic phrases such as "vested rights," "natural law," or "private property." Very much the child of its era, the Taney Court recognized and legitimated the demands of the newer forms of property by clearing away the claims to favor and protection of the older.

Taney's *Bridge* opinion established his claim to greatness because it created a dynamic, adaptable, protean model for subsequent adjudication. Taney achieved a balance between investment opportunity and popular control of economic development. He sensibly spurned the claims of Daniel Webster on behalf of the old bridge to virtual immunity of corporations from public control and for limitless extension of corporate monopoly privilege. He thereby affirmed legislative authority in policy-making. At the same time, he recognized the obsolescence of Old Republican hostility to banking, insurance, and manufacturing corporations, acknowledging the validity of investors' demands for some measure of security for their investments and for assurances that the state legislatures could not arbitrarily frustrate the plans of entrepreneurs.

Story dissented, fearing that Taney's approach was too instrumental, that its concern with policy ends was too direct and overt. Both men sought to promote economic growth, but Story clung to a vision of what Kent Newmyer calls "capitalism made moral and responsible through principled law" (Kent Newmyer, *Supreme Court Justice Joseph Story: Statesman of the Old Republic* [Chapel Hill, N.C., 1985]). Story saw in Taney's ready embrace of policy considerations a fatal disjunction between law and morality, a violation of what Chancellor Kent called the "great Principle of constitutional Morality." But Story stood alone on the Court against the onrushing democratic forces given their head by Taney's *Bridge* opinion. He lamented: "I am the last of the old race of judges. I stand their solitary representative, with a pained heart, and a subdued confidence."

The adaptable quality of the *Charles River Bridge* paradigm was demonstrated almost immediately when a case came to the Supreme Court in 1839 that involved the states' powers to regulate out-of-state corporations. Justice John McKinley on circuit had held that a corporation lacked capacity to enter into contracts outside the state that chartered it. Had the Supreme Court affirmed this extraordinary holding, it would have fragmented the national economy in the name of a state sovereignty abstraction. Yet it was clear that states had to retain some measure of control over out-of-state corporations. To resolve such competing policy considerations, Taney resorted to a *Charles River Bridge*–like solution that balanced these interests. In *Bank of Augusta* v. *Earle,* he held that a corporation was "for certain purposes" a person in the eyes of the law, and like a natural person could make contracts outside the state of its "domicile." A state retained sovereign power to regulate an out-of-state corporation to any extent that it wished, even to the point of excluding it altogether, but it had to do so explicitly. Absent such an express legislative regulation, courts could not invent or hypothesize a public policy for the state by reading such an exclusion into state legislative determinations.

Thus the *Bridge* case, read together with *Providence Bank* and the Marshall and Story opinions in *Dartmouth College,* provided a broad rule of general applicability that struck a dynamic balance between private capital and state regulatory power, between some degree of legal protection and exemption for the private sector and the kind of legislative regulatory control demanded by Jacksonian Democratic ideology.

Taney's only significant substantive departure from Marshall precedents in contracts clause cases came in the Court's elaboration of a balancing model that accorded greater respect to state regulatory power. In *Bronson* v. *Kinzie* (1843), Taney displayed the same dedication to the constraints of the contracts clause as his predecessor had. After the 1837 depression, some states enacted "stay" laws providing relief from mortgage foreclosure by specifying a time within which a delinquent debtor could repurchase foreclosed property, or specifying some minimum percentage of the market value of the property below which property could not be sold at a foreclosure sale. In *Bronson,* Taney voided such a statute as a violation of the contracts clause. Had this case been decided in 1837, it might have provided some reassurance to conservatives alarmed at the accession of a Jacksonian Democrat to the seat vacated by Marshall. The Taney Court also found federal constitutional limitations on state sovereign power in *Dobbins* v. *Erie County* (1842), in which it held that a state income tax statute could not constitutionally reach the income of a federal official, a decision that reaffirmed *McCulloch*'s solicitude for protecting federal power against state encroachment.

In one narrow area of public law, the Taney Court displayed a peculiar ambivalence or reticence about the bases of state sovereign power. Though eminent domain and the police power were closely related, the Court readily accepted the former, while retaining reservations about the latter, an odd approach that requires some explanation.

Eminent domain did not become a source of constitutional controversy until the Jacksonian period, when states began expanding it beyond such traditional, long-acknowledged functions as appropriating road rights of way and authorizing the flooding of milldam impoundments to newer and more controversial uses, such as authorizing railroads to seize land for roadbeds. This novel application of the eminent domain power, in which the state in effect "lent" its sovereign authority to private entrepreneurs, was first sanctioned by New York's Chancellor Reuben Walworth in an 1831 case, *Beekman* v. *Saratoga and Schenectady Railroad Co.,* and eminent domain quickly became acclimated in American law.

But however appealing this new authority might appear to railroad investors, conservative lawyers saw a conflict between it and constitutional safeguards for property and contracts. Thus it was only a matter of time before the issue would come before the Taney Court, and it finally did so in a case, *West River Bridge* v. *Dix* (1848), that resembled *Charles River Bridge.* The state of Vermont destroyed a bridge franchise by incorporating it in a toll-free highway, with payment of compensation for the taking. Webster, again representing the losing side in a bridge case, darkly warned that this kind of expropriation, even if it did comply with the various federal and state constitutional requirements of public purpose, just compensation, and established procedures, was nevertheless a step down the road toward such radical programs as socialism and the abolition of slavery.

But the power of taking property was obviously an inherent sovereign attribute, and in *West River Bridge* the Court's state sovereignty extremist, Justice Peter V. Daniel, upheld the state's power to take private property. Daniel's opinion reflects its author's lifelong hostility to corporations, which he was quite happy to sacrifice to state power. The decision provoked only one dissent, suggesting that nearly all the Court saw *West River Bridge* as fitting nicely into the *Charles River Bridge* paradigm. A Boston editor wrote that "any State has the power to check the assumptions of these corporations, while, at the same time, all necessary privileges of corporations are as well secured as ever, and their real value and utility enhanced by thus harmonizing them with popular sentiment."

From thence to a sweeping doctrine of the police power should have been just a short step. "Police power" is a concept almost coextensive with sovereignty: the power of a state to promote the health, safety, welfare, or morals of its people. Prominent American jurists soon took that step, led by Lemuel Shaw, chief justice of the Massachusetts Supreme Judicial Court and one of the greatest of nineteenth-century judges. In an 1851 case, *Commonwealth* v. *Alger,* the police power doctrine made its formal debut when Shaw defined it as "the power vested in the legislature to make . . . all manner of wholesome and reasonable laws . . . not repugnant to the constitution, as they shall judge to be for the good and welfare of the commonwealth." Shaw went on to say that everyone who owns property

> holds it under the implied liability that his use of it may be so regulated, that it shall not be injurious to the equal enjoyment of others having an equal right to the enjoyment of their property, nor injurious to the rights of the community. . . . Rights of property, like all other social and

> conventional rights, are subject to such reasonable limitations in their enjoyment, as shall prevent them from being injurious, and to such reasonable restraints and regulations established by law, as the legislature [may impose].

Such a doctrine would seem to fit comfortably into the outlook of the Taney Court, emphasizing as it did the states' regulatory power. And in fact, in one of the Court's first major decisions, *Mayor of New York* v. *Miln* (1837), Justice Philip P. Barbour warmly supported "all those powers which relate to merely municipal legislation, or what may, perhaps, more properly be called internal police." Yet neither Chief Justice Taney nor most of his brethren ever explicitly endorsed the police power doctrine; Justice Daniel's *West River Bridge* opinion was as close as the Court ever came to enunciating it. Perhaps the justices did not believe that an appropriate case ever presented itself, though this is unlikely, because several important constitutional controversies of the late 1840s and the 1850s (including the *License Cases,* to be mentioned later) would have served nicely.

Instead the explanation lies in the anxieties of Taney and a majority of his colleagues about the constitutional complications of slavery. Two features of the police power doctrine irritated this sensitivity. First, though the police power was virtually identical with state sovereignty, it might be subject to *federal* constitutional limitations (such as the power to tax, make war, or regulate interstate commerce), and thus be vulnerable if a majority of the American people and states became hostile to some aspect of the states' control of slavery. The Nullification Crisis of 1832 stood as a reminder to southern jurists that the slave states did not always command universal support.

Second, if property rights were always subject to what Shaw called "reasonable limitations, . . . restraints and regulations imposed by law," what was to stop a state from regulating the property in slaves? For example, Shaw's doctrine would readily support a free state's prohibition of bringing slaves into its jurisdiction for a temporary stay. (Shaw, in the celebrated 1836 case of *Commonwealth* v. *Aves,* did precisely that.) Taney was not about to concede any sort of regulatory handle over slavery to the will of legislative majorities anywhere. Thus the police power remained a doctrine ignored rather than elaborated by the Supreme Court before the Civil War. Of course, Taney took care to lay a doctrinal foundation for state power to *protect* slavery, but in doing so he relied on concepts of state sovereignty rather than the police power.

The Taney Court's most enduring positive contribution to American constitutional development lay in its elaboration of judicial power. The

Court produced no single dramatic decision like *Marbury* or *Martin.* Rather, through a series of somewhat technical opinions, it broadened the jurisdictional reach of the federal courts well beyond the bounds established by the Marshall Court.

The Court's aggrandizement of judicial power began with the enigmatic case of *Swift* v. *Tyson* (1842), which exerted a profound influence on the course of American legal development for a century. Section 34 of the 1789 Judiciary Act provided that "the laws of the several states . . . shall be regarded as rules of decision in trials at common law in the courts of the United States, in cases where they apply." This phrasing left unclear whether the "laws of the . . . states" included common law as well as statutes. Much turned on this unresolved question of lawyers' law. If section 34 were to be limited to statutes, then the door would be left open for federal judges to develop what amounted to a federal common law.

Swift presented the problem whether a federal trial court in a commercial law case was bound to accept a common law rule of the state in which it sat. This was an important question as the nation began a recovery from the 1837 depression, because variations in the states' commercial law, especially concerning the negotiability of commercial paper, impeded economic recovery. No one was more aware of the need for uniformity here than Joseph Story, who wrote the opinion for a unanimous Court in *Swift,* holding that federal courts in commercial law cases were not bound by state court decisional law, but rather were free to seek their rules of decision in "the general principles and doctrines of commercial jurisprudence."

Swift's rule came under attack in the twentieth century because it failed to create the uniformity that Story sought. It did produce a uniform *federal* commercial law, but the states continued to go their own ways in common law development, leading to the undesirable situation in which two bodies of law, federal and state, coexisted side by side in the same jurisdiction. This situation led plaintiffs' attorneys to "forum shop," that is, to choose between bringing suit in state or federal courts, depending on which afforded a more favorable substantive law. Hence scholars and judges alike began to condemn the rule. Justice Oliver Wendell Holmes, Jr., dismissed it as "pure usurpation grounded on a subtle fallacy." He sneered at Story's Platonic conception of the law as "a brooding omnipresence in the sky." Eventually Justice Louis D. Brandeis held *Swift* to be unconstitutional in *Erie Railroad* v. *Tompkins* (1938).

Yet in its own day, *Swift* scarcely deserved such unkind treatment. Though we have lost faith in the conception, Story's generation believed in the objective existence of "general principles" of commercial law, to which decisional law could conform and thereby approach unification.

(And we are in no position to deride this goal, for we pursue it ourselves, both in the modern *Restatements* of various bodies of law, and in the uniform laws promulgated by the commissioners of Uniform State Laws, most notably the Uniform Commercial Code.) Moreover, commercial law in Story's day was susceptible to this kind of forced unification into a single body of law. A decade earlier, Story had recommended it as a subject for codification in Massachusetts precisely because it had attained a degree of uniformity. Finally, as a practical matter, a contrary result on the substance of the rule would have undermined the universally acclaimed goal of promoting the negotiability of this form of commercial paper. It would have devalued overnight many outstanding bills of exchange and struck a blow at the nation's credit structure.

Twice it was necessary for the Taney Court to expand the jurisdictional reach and powers of the federal courts by discarding premature and shortsighted decisions of the Marshall Court. The first instance was the decision in *Louisville, Cincinnati, and Charleston Railroad* v. *Letson* (1844), which opened the doors of federal courts to corporations. They had previously been largely excluded as parties in diversity suits (that is, litigation in which federal courts have jurisdiction because the parties are citizens of different states) because of two Marshall precedents. *Strawbridge* v. *Curtiss* (1806) and *Bank of the United States* v. *Deveaux* (1809) required that in order for a corporation to be a party in diversity litigation all its shareholders had to have citizenship diverse from the citizenship of all parties on the other side. Such a jurisdictional rule was a nuisance in the Jacksonian era when stock in corporations was commonly held by residents of different states. Consequently an ever-larger portion of commercial litigation was being excluded from the federal courts. Recognizing the undesirability of the situation, Justice James M. Wayne lowered the old jurisdictional bars in the *Letson* case, holding that, for diversity purposes, corporations were to be deemed citizens only of the states in which they were incorporated. Federal courts thereby entertained an ever-increasing volume of corporate litigation.

Just as *Letson* expanded the business of the federal courts when corporations were parties, the case of *Genesee Chief* v. *Fitzhugh* (1851) opened up federal admiralty jurisdiction. In an 1825 decision, *The Thomas Jefferson,* Justice Story had unaccountably narrowed the constitutional scope of the federal courts' admiralty jurisdiction. In that case he adopted the tidewater jurisdictional limit of the English admiralty courts, which limited maritime jurisdiction to waters whose tidal ebb and flow was perceptible. This limitation was suitable in the British Isles, where no part of England is more than seventy miles from the sea, and tidewater is virtually coextensive with navigability. But it made no sense in the United States, because it excluded federal authority from the extensive freshwater channels of commerce in the American interior, particularly the Great Lakes and extensive river systems such as the Ohio, the Tennessee, the Missouri, and, above all, the Mississippi. The maritime law governing commerce on rivers, canals, and lakes was state law, which was not always consistent.

After Story's death, it was obvious that the tidewater rule would have to be discarded, and Chief Justice Taney did just that in *Genesee Chief,* holding that the test for federal admiralty jurisdiction was navigability, an eminently workable rule that opened the federal courts to admiralty suits arising from the inland waters. *The Genesee Chief* in this respect is akin to *Gibbons* v. *Ogden* and *Charles River Bridge* in that it reflected the impact of technological innovation on the law. The advent of steam navigation on the Great Lakes and the inland rivers and canal systems meant that commerce and the national market extended the commercial life of America's coastal regions throughout the interior. American law had to follow the commerce borne into the interior by steam-powered vessels.

Among the most significant of the Taney Court's contributions to the development of federal judicial power was the political question doctrine. Marshall had anticipated the substance of the doctrine in his *Marbury* distinction between legal and political issues, and Taney briefly alluded to the distinction in his dissent in *Rhode Island* v. *Massachusetts* (1838), arguing that the Court did not have jurisdiction over a boundary dispute between those two states because the question presented was "political." But before 1849, the distinction remained hazy and amorphous. In the case of *Luther* v. *Borden,* decided that year, Taney and Justice Levi Woodbury developed the nascent doctrine at length.

Luther was the delayed judicial resolution of the Dorr Rebellion, a crisis in Rhode Island constitutional development that culminated in 1842. The state had not adopted a republican constitution at the time of American Independence, contenting itself with cosmetic changes to its colonial constitution, the 1663 royal charter. Because the state was in the vanguard of the industrial revolution in America, by the 1830s it was plagued by the related problems of malapportionment and disfranchisement. Reformers sought to open up the suffrage, but met with obstruction by the conservative Whig ruling elite. So in 1842, they adapted the philosophy of the Declaration of Independence to their situation by calling extralegal popular elections for a constitutional convention, drew up a new state constitution, and had it ratified by all adult white male voters. The established government meanwhile revised the existing constitution and refused to recognize the authority of the self-constituted new government under "Governor" Thomas Wilson Dorr. With almost no violence, the regular government then suppressed the Dorrite government, and subsequently instituted some less far-reaching reforms.

Disgruntled Dorrites brought the *Luther* suit to test the legitimacy of the acts of the regular government, including the imposition of martial law. Chief Justice Taney held that courts lacked power to resolve the question whether the Rhode Island government was republican for purposes of the clause in Article IV, section 4, that requires the United States to guarantee all states a republican form of government. Such a question, he held, "belonged to the political power and not the judicial." Hence it was Congress and the executive branch that had responsibility for enforcing the guarantee clause, and not the courts. Justice Levi Woodbury insisted that courts could resolve only the traditional questions of distributive justice that are involved in ordinary litigation between private parties in matters of contract, property, and so forth. To make judges arbiters of issues of political theory, he claimed, would be to make them, rather than the people, the real sovereigns of America.

The 1856 case of *Murray's Lessee* v. *Hoboken Land and Improvement Co.* provides an example of the Court seeming to acquiesce in a limitation of its jurisdiction yet reserving to itself the substance of power, in this case, an extraordinary power at that. At issue was the constitutionality of a nonjudicial distress proceeding against an embezzling federal customs collector, the notorious Jacksonian political crook Samuel Swartwout. In a unanimous opinion by Justice Benjamin R. Curtis, the Court upheld the process, holding that just because a type of proceeding, such as seizure of property, *could* take the form of a traditional action at law does not mean that it *must* do so. In reaching this conclusion, Curtis observed that the due process clause of the Fifth Amendment limited the discretion of Congress. It was "a restraint on the legislative as well as on the executive and judicial powers of government, and cannot be so construed as to leave Congress free to make any process 'due process of law,' by its mere will." Though Curtis was speaking of procedure and not of substance, his observation carried the Court a long way toward the doctrine of substantive due process, which a half century later was to become the source of the greatest increase in judicial power since the emergence of judicial review.

Taken together with one other case, *Ableman* v. *Booth* (1859) (to be discussed later in this chapter in a different context), the Taney Court decisions on the nature and extent of judicial power comprise its most enduring and far-reaching legacy. Collectively they did almost as much for the federal courts' powers as *Marbury, Martin,* and *Cohens,* but they added something missing from Marshall precedents: a sense of wise restraint, a perception that at times a court aggrandizing its powers thoughtlessly will only defeat its own purposes and diminish judicial authority in the long run. Sad to say, this prudential instinct deserted Taney and most of his brethren just when it was needed most.

Given the high order of judicial statesmanship Taney displayed in state regulatory and federal judicial power cases, we might have expected a similar performance in commerce clause cases. With one exception, however, the Taney Court commerce clause cases were curious failures, providing no usable doctrine or judicial supervision of an area that Congress left by default to the courts until the end of the century. An explanation for this failure lurks just below the surface.

One of the three major cases of Taney's first term, 1837, was a commerce clause case, and it set a pattern for doctrinal frustration that persisted through 1851. *Mayor of New York* v. *Miln* gave the Taney Court an opportunity to resolve the ambiguity left by *Gibbons:* was federal power under the commerce clause exclusive of state power? New York required masters of incoming vessels to furnish city officials a passenger manifest; its purpose was control of diseased and impoverished immigrants. Justice Barbour for the majority upheld the New York requirement by relying on a vaguely described general state regulatory authority. (The police power doctrine had not yet been articulated.) Such state powers "are not thus surrendered or restrained; and that, consequently, in relation to these, the authority of a state is complete, unqualified, and exclusive." Barbour simply evaded the commerce clause issue by holding that the New York statute was not a regulation of commerce. The contrast with the spirit of *Gibbons* v. *Ogden* could not have been more stark, especially in the overstated hint of state exclusivity. Story expectably dissented, arguing that the regulation was void as inconsistent with Congress's latent but exclusive power to regulate interstate and foreign commerce. Justice Smith Thompson concurred, attempting to stake out a middle position by upholding the state requirement on the grounds that it remained valid only in the absence of a conflicting federal regulation.

These divisions in the new Court portended continuing controversy over commerce clause issues. The *License Cases* (1847) dredged it up again in a challenge to the states' prohibition of intoxicating liquors. Now the tenuous *Miln* majority splintered. The Court had by this time been increased to nine members. In three companion cases, six of the eight justices present for argument wrote opinions, and two of them wrote more than one. The majority upheld the state regulations, but no doctrine emerged from the cases, given the division among the justices. What did emerge clearly, though, were complications posed by slavery questions. Southern jurists had never forgotten the controversy kindled by the Negro Seamen's Acts, which remained a burning constitutional issue more than two decades after their enactment because Massachusetts and Great Britain continued to demand their repeal. Daniel Webster in his argument fished in troubled waters by explicitly comparing the southern coastal states' interest in controlling the ingress of free blacks to Massachusetts's interest in controlling the importation of liquor.

The questions unresolved in 1847 immediately resurfaced in the *Passenger Cases* of 1849, a replay of *Miln,* but this time with the slavery question even closer to the surface because the states were now attempting to control the entry of persons (diseased and insane immigrants) rather than things, as had been true in the *License Cases.* The New York and Massachusetts immigrant-control measures now stood as surrogates for the Negro Seamen's Acts. Because a bare majority of five voted to strike down the regulations, Taney, Daniel, Woodbury, and Samuel Nelson dissented vehemently. The chief justice warned that if federal treaty and commerce powers could override state powers to control the ingress of people, "then the emancipated slaves of the West Indies have at this hour the absolute right to reside, hire houses, and traffic and trade throughout the southern States . . . leading to the most painful consequences." The majority advanced nine distinct reasons for their positions; all opinions totaled almost two hundred pages in the *United States Reports.* David Currie, a legal scholar who has intensively analyzed the Court's doctrine in these years, aptly described the result as "almost total incoherence, . . . buried . . . in a torrent of verbiage" (David P. Currie, *The Constitution in the Supreme Court: The First Hundred Years, 1789–1888* [Chicago, 1985], 230).

The slavery complications had produced a doctrinal impasse, to say the least, on commerce clause issues. But in an atypical moment of lucidity, the Court managed to extricate itself briefly from its fear-induced confusions in the 1851 case of *Cooley* v. *Board of Wardens.* A majority of the justices managed to suppress their inclination to squabble over slavery matters long enough to produce another statesmanlike and paradigmatic rule of even greater reach than *Charles River Bridge. Cooley* involved a fee for pilotage services imposed by a local harbor authority on vessels moving in interstate and foreign commerce. The majority, in an opinion by Justice Benjamin R. Curtis, upheld the fee by drawing a distinction between matters "in their nature national," "imperatively demanding a single uniform rule, operating equally on the commerce of the United States in every port," and local matters "as imperatively demanding that diversity, which alone can meet the local necessities of navigation." Nationalist dissents by James M. Wayne and John McLean argued for federal exclusivity, and this argument provoked Justice Daniel into a polar-opposite concurrence insisting on *state* exclusivity, but Curtis's lucid opinion enabled the rest to check their inclination to box with shadows and instead to support a doctrine that retains its vitality into our own time.

This respite of reason and moderation was all too brief. Like some Nemesis of Greek myth implacably pursuing lawyers and statesmen since the founding of the Republic, slavery intruded itself insistently into the deliberations of jurists until it destroyed the Union. John Marshall and his colleagues enjoyed the good fortune of having few significant slavery cases come before them, and had the good sense to deflect harmlessly those that did. Marshall realized that, if there was to be a resolution of slavery's constitutional problems, it would have to come from Congress rather than the Court. He also appreciated the futility of challenging sectional interests as determined as the slave power. "I am not fond of butting against a wall in sport," he wrote Story in explaining why he evaded a Negro Seamen's Act case while on circuit.

The Taney Court differed from its predecessor in an important technical way that aggravated slavery issues. As chief justice, Taney was indifferent to the salutary Marshall practice of discouraging dissents and concurrences in the interests of unanimity. He tolerated a proliferation of opinions (six, for example, in the *License Cases,* eight in the *Passenger Cases*). In slavery cases, this tendency had the extremely mischievous effect of permitting one member of the Court to adopt an extreme position, which encouraged others on the Court to write their own extreme concurrences or dissents, and, in turn, contributed to a widening spiral of polarization. Taney participated in this sprawl of opinions as much as any other member of the Court.

Differences between the Taney and Marshall Courts became manifest in the first major slavery case to come before the Court, *Groves* v. *Slaughter* (1841). The case involved the validity of a contract for the importation and sale of slaves in Mississippi, whose state constitution prohibited such importation. It presented two difficult questions for the Court. It called up the problem injected into American constitutional discourse by the Negro Seamen's Acts, namely, the power of the states to control the entry of persons and ideas into their jurisdictions. The imported slaves raised constitutional issues generically similar as those in other contexts posed by free blacks, abolitionists, and abolitionist literature. Second, abolitionists had for a decade been demanding that Congress use its commerce powers to abolish the interstate slave trade. This agitation had left the southerners on the Court touchy about questions of the commerce power as it might pertain to slavery. These two questions, apparent under the murky surface of the opinions in *Miln,* now floated into prominence.

Justice Smith Thompson's plurality opinion avoided both major issues: he simply held that the constitutional provision was not self-executing, so that the contract was valid in the absence of a statute implementing the prohibition. But Justice McLean chose to write a separate concurrence in which he espoused ideas compatible with abolitionist constitutional thought: slaves were persons, not property, for purposes of the United States Constitution; federal power over the interstate slave trade was exclusive under the commerce clause; and slave status derived exclusively from local law. Such provocative ideas prodded Taney into a counter-concurrence of his own, in which he insisted that the states' regulatory power over persons coming within their borders was exclusive of federal commerce power. Justice Henry Baldwin, who was probably insane by this time, went even further than the chief, claiming that federal power could be used only to protect the interstate slave trade, not to inhibit it; owners' rights in their slaves were protected by the due process clause of the Fifth Amendment (a bizarre anticipation of the later doctrine of substantive due process); and slaves were property, not persons, in the eyes of the law. *Groves* was an ominous warning that the Court would not only fracture on slavery cases, but that its members would espouse dangerously dogmatic positions on any questions they took up.

The next year, 1842, a more troublesome issue came to the Court in *Prigg* v. *Pennsylvania:* the sibling problems of fugitive slaves and the personal liberty laws of the free states. Some of the northern states sought to protect their black citizens from kidnapping by slave catchers operating under the legal cover afforded by the Fugitive Slave Act of 1793 by enacting laws that provided protections for personal liberty, such as a guarantee of the right to jury trial. In *Prigg,* which was a test case challenging the power of the states to enact such measures, the Court fragmented again, this time in seven opinions. This proliferation makes it difficult to determine just what *Prigg* held, but a majority did form around at least these points: The 1793 Fugitive Slave Act was constitutional; the fugitive slave clause of the Constitution's Article IV was essential to the southern states' ratification of the Constitution and thus was beyond challenge; and the Pennsylvania Personal Liberty Law in question was unconstitutional because it interfered with the master's rights under the federal act.

These points were relatively uncontroversial (except to abolitionists). Two other issues on which there was no majority concurrence proved more inflammatory. The justices split three ways on the question whether states might enact legislation supporting fugitive recaptures under the federal act. Story, McLean, and Wayne held they could not;

Daniel and Thompson insisted they could; and Taney thought that they must. (A decade later, in *Moore* v. *Illinois* [1852], the Court adopted the Daniel-Thompson view.) Story, speaking only for himself, expressed the second point, which, though it was unique to him, has ever since been taken to be the holding of *Prigg*. He stated that the Constitution's fugitive slave clause did not oblige the states to permit their officials or facilities (such as jails) to be used in fugitive recaptures under the 1793 Act. The reaction to *Prigg* ought to have cautioned the Court that it was dealing with inflammable matters. Though abolitionists at first missed Story's hint and denounced the opinion, they soon came to realize the value of his concession. Several states shortly enacted a second series of personal liberty laws conforming to Story's suggestion, prohibiting the use of sheriffs, jails, and so forth for fugitive recaptures.

Some abolitionist attorneys, including the future chief justice of the United States, Salmon P. Chase, at that time a practicing lawyer who had earned a nickname in Ohio and Kentucky as "the Attorney-General for runaway Negroes," sought to use the law and legal processes to promote antislavery causes from within the system. One fruit of these efforts was *Jones* v. *Van Zandt* (1847), an appeal by a conductor of the Underground Railroad from his conviction for violation of the 1793 Fugitive Slave Act. Chase used the appeal as an occasion for attacking the constitutionality of the act on a variety of constitutional grounds, such as violation of the due process clause of the Fifth Amendment or the civil jury trial provisions of the Seventh Amendment, forcing the Court to reexamine *Prigg* and to confront the challenge to the judicial conscience that Chase presented.

Justice Woodbury took up the task. Before his elevation to the Court, he had been a New Hampshire Democratic politician, and, as such, a faithful adherent to the Democratic party's support for slavery. His *Jones* opinion reflected those political antecedents. He began by dismissing arguments that slavery itself was unconstitutional by stating that the issue was "a political question, [to be] settled by each state for itself," thereby anticipating the political question doctrine of *Luther* v. *Borden*, then still two years in the future. He reiterated Story's *Prigg* dictum that the fugitive slave clause was a "sacred compromise," which made it possible for him to dispose of the moral challenge: "Whatever may be the theoretical opinions . . . as to the expediency of some of those compromises or of the right of property in persons which they recognize, this court has no alternative, while they exist, but to stand by the constitution and the laws with fidelity to their duties and their oaths." Here Woodbury reaffirmed the traditional judicial commitment to obedience to law despite contrary promptings of conscience.

Woodbury's judicial amorality reflects a view unanimously held among American judges that a jurist betrays his responsibility and his oath when he decides according to the commands of conscience rather than law. Put another way, the American judicial tradition requires that the judge must always decide according to law, and not permit his conscientious scruples to override the law. Judge Learned Hand once recounted an incident that occurred when he accompanied Justice Oliver Wendell Holmes, Jr., to work one morning. Hoping to provoke Holmes, Hand said, "Do justice." With apparent agitation, Holmes responded, "That is not my job. My job is to play the game according to the rules." Chief Justice Warren Burger later wrote in the spirit of Woodbury and Holmes: "Our duty . . . is not to do justice, but to apply the law and hope that justice is done" (*Bifulco* v. *United States,* 1980, concurrence).

The Court's next confrontation with slavery issues in *Strader* v. *Graham* (1851) is usually read, correctly, as setting a precedent for avoiding the questions of *Dred Scott* six years later on quasi-procedural grounds. But *Strader* also contained some hints of a dangerous judicial recklessness in handling volatile slavery issues. In *Strader,* Taney repeated the truism that under the Constitution control of slavery was entirely a matter for the states rather than the federal government, "except in so far as the powers of the states in this respect are restrained, or duties and obligations imposed on them by the Constitution of the United States." Read one way, this statement seemed to be a broad hint that the Constitution somehow restrained the states from abolishing slavery or taking any steps inimical to it, as by prohibiting the temporary residence of slaves in free states. He then went on to assert, again in dictum, that the Northwest Ordinance, despite its designated status as "perpetual," was now void, having been superseded by the constitutions of the states carved out of its territory. One implication of this gratuitous assertion was that the states of the former Northwest Territory could introduce slavery within their jurisdictions if they chose. Taney thus seemed willing to upset what free-state residents regarded as fundamental, permanent, and inviolable constitutional settlements.

As one crisis of the Union succeeded another in the antebellum years, two issues precipitated out and came to dominate all other questions in constitutional discourse: the future of slavery in the territories and the constitutional complications surrounding fugitive slaves. *Prigg* had supposedly dealt with the latter conclusively, but Congress's enactment of the new and drastic Fugitive Slave Act of 1850 restored this issue to the Court's agenda, because it inflamed northern opinion and created incident after incident of fugitive recapture or rescue. But it was the territories' problem that came to loom above all others, as northern opinion galvanized around the Free Soil position embodied in the Wilmot Proviso of 1846, which would have excluded slavery from any territories acquired as the result of the Mexican War.

The political process, as filtered through Congress, produced four potential resolutions to the problem of slavery's expansion into the territories. These were:

1. Free Soil: the exclusion of slavery from the territories. This position was widely popular in the free states and became the centerpiece of the Republican party platform after 1854.

2. An extrapolation of the original Missouri Compromise line all the way to the Pacific, with slavery excluded above it and permitted below. As a political matter, this solution was moribund before 1850 and presumably dead after the Missouri Compromise itself was repealed in 1854.

3. Territorial Sovereignty, better known as "Popular Sovereignty." This view called for letting the residents decide slavery's future in the territory. It was the principal plank of the northern Democratic party, led by Illinois Senator Stephen A. Douglas.

4. The expansive proslavery position, first articulated by Senator John C. Calhoun and extended after his death in 1850 by various disciples, ended up in 1860 by demanding that Congress force slavery into all the territories and then protect it.

In addition to these four substantive positions, Congress ever since 1848 had been inviting the United States Supreme Court to take a hand in resolving what was coming to appear more and more to be a problem insoluble by ordinary political means. So when the Court did intrude disastrously into the question in 1857, however ill advised it was on the merits, its involvement was by invitation. In the *Dred Scott* case, Taney and his brethren blundered disastrously, but they were not interlopers.

Dred Scott involved the freedom of slaves who had resided in a free territory and a free state. Taney's opinion for the Court dealt with two major issues: the status of black people, slave and free, under the Constitution; and the power of Congress to exclude slavery from the territories. As to the first, he held that black people, whether enslaved or free, could not be "Citizens" within the ambiguous meanings of that term as it appeared in Articles III and IV of the Constitution. He conceded that states might make blacks citizens if they chose, but that this action could have no effect outside the state's borders, or even any effect within for purposes of the black person's claiming rights under the federal Constitution.

In establishing this idea, Taney committed several major substantive errors that make *Dred Scott* the odious blunder that it was. He asserted in dictum that in 1787 black people were thought to be

> a subordinate and inferior class of beings, who had been subjugated by the dominant race, and, whether emancipated or not, yet remained subject to their authority, and had no rights or privileges but such as those who held the power and the Government might choose to grant them. . . . [In 1776] they had for more than a century before been regarded as beings of an inferior order, and altogether unfit to associate with the white race, either in social or political relations; and so far inferior, that they had no rights which the white man was bound to respect.

Whatever the accuracy of this statement as a historical assertion, it provided Taney with a plausible basis for asserting that his opinion relied on the intention of the Framers.

Taney compounded this racist reconstruction of the past with an impossible canon of constitutional interpretation that has been resurrected and is enjoying some vogue in our own time:

> [No] change in public opinion . . . should induce the court to give to the words of the constitution a more liberal construction . . . than they were intended to bear when the instrument was framed and adopted. . . . If any of its provisions are deemed unjust, there is a mode prescribed in the instrument itself by which it may be amended; but while it remains unaltered, it must be construed now as it was understood at the time of its adoption. It is not only the same in words, but the same in meaning. . . . Any other rule of construction would abrogate the judicial character of this court, and make it the mere reflex of the popular opinion or passion of the day.

Were this prescription taken seriously, the Constitution would shrivel to a parchment museum piece, nothing more than a relic of something no longer alive and vital. Taken together with his dubious history, Taney's interpretive canon suppressed black people in America to some extraconstitutional limbo where they were to remain perpetually, as something less than citizens and legitimately the objects of discrimination and oppression.

Taney then turned to the Missouri Compromise, and the four proposed solutions to the problem of slavery in the territories. By holding the Missouri Compromise unconstitutional, he eliminated both the Free Soil–Republican and the Missouri Compromise–extension proposals. Then, in dictum, he voided the Douglas–northern Democratic proposal of popular sovereignty by holding that what Congress was constitutionally disabled from doing, it could not authorize a territorial legislature to do. That decision left only the southern Calhounite position viable, and Taney ringingly endorsed it in three separate passages in his opinion as constitutional dogma, holding that the only action that the federal government could take with respect to slavery was protection; that Congress was the agent or trustee for the states in the territories; and that Congress must protect the slave owner's claim to ownership of the slave.

Today *Dred Scott* is universally considered a monstrous failure, but scholars disagree on what exactly makes the opinion so vicious. It is pointless to criticize its racism; Taney and his brethren were children of their times. We reject Taney's assumption of the innate racial inferiority of blacks, but that was a failing not unique to him. *Dred Scott* is an egregiously bad piece of judicial workmanship, its logic distorted, its history fabricated, its evidence tortured. But bad as it is, it is not unique. Other equally disastrous opinions come readily to mind, such as *Debs* (1895), the labor injunction case, or the *Income Tax Cases* (1895), in which the majority twisted history and ignored precedent in the service of an ideology. Somehow *Dred Scott* is uniquely, incomparably bad, a monument to the failure of judges. Why?

The principal vice of the opinion lay in its hostility to democracy. Taney attempted to foreclose majoritarian political action for all time on the most pressing problem facing the American people. He withdrew from the majority all power to resolve that problem, except along the lines demanded by a sectional minority. As Arthur Bestor so lucidly observed, in Taney's jurisprudential world, "the court was under no obligation to reflect the views of popular majorities. Policy would be made *for* the nation, but not *by* the nation. Power would be neatly divorced from accountability, action from deliberation" (Arthur Bestor, "State Sovereignty and Slavery: A Reinterpretation of Proslavery Constitutional Doctrine, 1846–1860," *Journal of the Illinois State Historical Society* 54 [1961]: 117–80, quote on 167).

Dred Scott remains an enduring lesson in the limits of judicial power. The great error of the case was not so much that it was decided wrongly, as that it was decided at all. If ever there was need of the political question doctrine, of a recognition that the Court had before it a problem that could not be resolved by judges, it was in the matter of slavery. On the eve of the Nullification Crisis, John Quincy Adams had written: "It is the odious nature of [this] question that it can be settled only at the cannon's mouth." Perhaps that view of the slavery controversy was valid all along, or at least of that part of it involving slavery's expansion into the western empire. But judges could not resolve the issue, certainly not by the imposition of a minority sectional dogma that thwarted democracy and representative government.

Taney was unmoved by the flood of criticism that washed over him. He betrayed no second thoughts about the damage he had done to the reputation of the Supreme Court, or any sense that it was wrong to try to force an extremist minority position on the rest of the nation. He shortly had an opportunity to speak to the other major slavery issue vexing the nation when the case of *Ableman* v. *Booth* (1859) came before the Court. Read in one way, *Ableman* ought properly to be considered a judicial power case that merely happened to be related to slavery, and thus belongs to the line of statesmanlike decisions that included *Swift, Letson,* and *Genessee Chief.* But *Ableman* is also a slavery case that merely happened to involve an expansion of judicial power, and it remains permanently ambiguous, both a failure marked by the faults of *Dred Scott* and a vindication of national judicial power that continues admirable and vital today.

Ableman came to the United States Supreme Court when the Wisconsin Supreme Court issued a writ of habeas corpus to free from the custody of a United States marshal the respondent, a Milwaukee abolitionist, after conviction in a United States district court for violation of the 1850 Fugitive Slave Act for his role in helping a runaway escape. The Wisconsin Supreme Court held the Fugitive Slave Act of 1850 unconstitutional. When the United States attorney general sought a writ of error to bring the case from the Wisconsin Supreme Court to the United States Supreme Court, the chief judge of the Wisconsin court instructed the court's clerk to ignore it.

Taney dealt with this unprecedented stance of judicial nullification magisterially, in the spirit of *Martin* v. *Hunter's Lessee* and *Cohens* v. *Virginia.* He insisted that the national government must possess power to enforce its own laws free from the harassment of state judiciaries, its court, or its marshals: "It was essential, therefore, to its very existence as a government, that [the United States] should have the power of establishing courts of justice, altogether independent of State power, to carry into effect its own laws."

Yet in its immediate context, *Ableman* is a proslavery opinion in the spirit of *Dred Scott.* In dictum, after admitting that he had no occasion for doing so, Taney nonetheless insisted that the Fugitive Slave Act was constitutional. This insistence, coupled with his powerful endorsement of federal judicial power, prostituted judicial nationalism to the service of slavery. Again, Arthur Bestor correctly identified this inverted quality of Taney's deceptive nationalism:

> Federal judicial supremacy did not mean the supremacy of national policy over local or sectional policy. It meant precisely the reverse. It meant the denial to the federal government of any discretionary, policy-making function whatever in the matter of slavery. (Bestor, "State Sovereignty and Slavery," 141)

Taney's opportunities for mischief were not yet exhausted. After *Dred Scott,* anxious Republicans and abolitionists warned that if the United States Supreme Court could force slavery into the territories, it could force it into the free states as well. Abraham Lincoln repeated that fear in his 1858 debates with Stephen A. Douglas, and the issue remained alive until the Civil War erupted. A case, *Lemmon* v. *People* (1860), was appealed to the United States Supreme Court from a decision by the New York Court of Appeals that upheld the power of the state to free slaves being transported through the state to a destination elsewhere. Though the outcome of the case on appeal to the Supreme Court must remain conjectural, it is quite possible that the Taney Court would have reversed the New York decision, thereby depriving the free states of the ability to exclude slavery. In 1858, the Buchanan administration floated a trial balloon arguing that the abolition of slavery in the free states was unconstitutional, and southern congressmen madly boasted that they would extend slavery throughout New England. The whole issue ultimately came to nothing, but not because Taney had too much discretion to meddle recklessly. Instead, the question was overtaken by events. During the war years, Taney supported secession in private correspondence, and drew up draft opinions, presumably to be used as soon as an appropriate case presented itself, that held the Emancipation Proclamation, federal draft, and legal tender acts unconstitutional.

These slavery cases will always obscure and distort our appreciation of the Taney Court. Had Roger B. Taney died in 1856, he would have been remembered as a jurist second in stature only to Marshall, a judge of far-reaching vision who had a sense of balance lacking in the nationalist jurisprudence of the Marshall years before 1824, who had a keener appreciation of the impact of technological change than his predecessor, and who extended the scope of federal judicial power nearly as much as Story, Marshall, and Johnson. But alas, Taney must also be judged by his slavery decisions, which cast a long shadow over his achievements.

Chapter 4

"A constitution adapted to the various crises of human affairs"

CIVIL WAR, RECONSTRUCTION, AND THE RIGHTS OF BLACK PEOPLE

THE AMERICAN Civil War was preeminently a crisis of legitimacy: disagreements over the legality of policies escalated to implicate the legitimacy of regimes themselves. Hence constitutional ideas and debate played a "configurative role," as Arthur Bestor aptly calls it, in the coming of the war, its conduct, and its resolution after the southern armies laid down their arms. The Civil War, in short, was a constitutional conflict, as was its resolution in the period known as Reconstruction. Yet despite the prominence of questions of constitutionality and legitimacy, the Supreme Court's role during the war and Reconstruction appears inconsequential, and this fact requires some explanation. An illuminating comparison is the similarly inconspicuous role of the common law courts during the English Civil War and, later, the Glorious Revolution. Sometimes, it seems, especially at times of revolutionary upheaval, courts are simply *dehors* the action, and properly so.

During the middle and late nineteenth century, economic and social shifts were occurring outside the judicial sphere, beyond the power of courts to control or even to influence in a constructive way. Examples in the United States include the centralization of national power, the obsolescence of slavery and plantation agriculture as economic institutions, the rise of industrial capitalism, the emergence of formalism in many spheres of thought, and the rise of the regulatory state. The legislatures and the executive were better equipped to deal with these matters, and consequently the role of the courts sometimes seemed marginal. Courts were relegated to being spectators on the sidelines, in peripheral ways approving or impeding important developments in American life. Always, the judicial role was reactive. When courts intruded to force a resolution in some direction that seemed compelling to judges, the results were often disastrous—witness *Dred Scott.* It is by now a platitude that war is too important to be left to the generals. We should not forget its judicial analogue: constitutional change is too important to be left to the judges.

But the Supreme Court was not ineffectual or insignificant during the war and Reconstruction. On the contrary—because of the war and Reconstruction, judicial influence was pervasive and the courts' role enhanced far beyond the ambitions of Hamilton and Marshall. The argument is rather that the Court did not initiate, dominate, or control the most important constitutional changes of that era; sometimes that passivity is not a bad thing.

The Court's role during the war certainly began inauspiciously enough. By 1861, Chief Justice Taney had lost all sense of restraint in any matter pertaining to slavery and the Union. Intermittently ill, distracted by grief for his recently deceased daughter and wife, Taney nonetheless clung stubbornly to life and to a determination to preserve the constitutional order as he understood it. That understanding was peculiar by modern or Unionist standards. In private correspondence at the time, the chief justice of the United States supported secession and opposed all measures Lincoln took to bring the departed states back into the Union. Yet, unlike his colleague Justice John A. Campbell, who resigned his seat on the Supreme Court to serve the Confederacy, Taney remained in active service, largely out of a determination to thwart the Republican president.

Taney created a confrontation between himself and Lincoln in *Ex parte Merryman* (1861). The president had authorized suspension of the privilege of the writ of habeas corpus in the Philadelphia–Washington corridor. Army officers arrested and detained John Merryman on charges of sabotage and recruiting for the Confederacy. Taney, seeing an opportunity to denounce Lincoln and his policies, issued a writ of habeas corpus in Baltimore, taking pains to indicate that he was acting not as the presiding judge of the United States circuit court but as the chief justice of the United States in chambers. After army officers refused to honor the writ (on Lincoln's orders), Taney had an opinion printed and distributed immediately, so as to embarrass Lincoln, holding the president's suspension of the writ unconstitutional. Lincoln ignored the opinion as well. Taney derived what satisfaction he could from the manufactured confrontation; his associates on the Court prevented him from concocting others. The last word on the whole incident, in 1939, is that of Robert H. Jackson, who at the time was United States attorney general. Referring to what he considered the abasement of judicial power in the *Merryman* incident, Jackson exclaimed, "One such precedent is enough!"

Jackson was right in not wanting to see a repeat of *Merryman,* but for the wrong reasons. He and many others believed that the Supreme Court had suffered a disastrous loss not only of prestige but also of power in the years after 1857–61. In its extreme forms, this interpretation suggested that the Court was powerless, a whipping boy of vengeful congressional Republicans. The justices were supposedly helpless to stem the flood of unconstitutional programs loosed during the war and Reconstruction. This pitiful state, it was believed, was caused by the magnitude of the Court's *Dred Scott* error and the consequent, retributive loss of power.

Such an interpretation mistakes the Court's relatively reduced role with an absolute diminution of power, and attributes that new and temporary condition to a Republican hostility to the Court as an institution, a hostility that simply did not exist. Rather, as Stanley I. Kutler has observed, throughout the war and Reconstruction the Supreme Court "was characterized by forcefulness and not timidity, by judicious and self-imposed restraint rather than retreat, by boldness and defiance instead of cowardice and impotence, and by a creative and determinative role with no abdication of its rightful powers" (Stanley I. Kutler, *Judicial Power and Reconstruction Politics* [Chicago, 1968], 6). The validity of this view is demonstrated by wartime cases in which the Court asserted the judiciary's role in the constitutional order with a verve not seen since the heyday of the Marshall Court.

One of the most striking examples was *Gelpcke* v. *Dubuque* (1864), involving what amounted to a repudiation of publically issued bonds by the city of Dubuque, whose action was upheld by the Iowa Supreme Court. Newly appointed Justice Samuel Miller described the attitude of his colleagues in a letter to his brother-in-law: "Our court, or a majority of it, are, if not monomaniacs, . . . bigots and fanatics on that subject [debt repudiation]. In four cases out of five the case is decided when it is seen by the pleadings that it is a suit to enforce a contract against a city, or town, or a county. If there is a written instrument its validity is a foregone conclusion" (quoted in Harold M. Hyman and William M. Wiecek, *Equal Justice under Law: Constitutional Development, 1835–1875* [New York, 1982], 369). In such a frame of mind, the Court (with Miller, an Iowan, dissenting) sternly lectured Iowans on public morality and upheld the validity of the debt issue. The Court would not "immolate truth, justice, and the law, because a state tribunal has erected the altar and decreed the sacrifice," Justice Noah Swayne sententiously proclaimed.

Despite this display of judicial power, most principal federal and state wartime measures either did not come before the Court for review or were approved by the Court during the war or after. The case of greatest significance in approving federal wartime policy was the *Prize Cases*

(1863), in which a 5–4 majority of the Court upheld the constitutionality of Lincoln's blockade of southern ports. The Court's opinion in effect permitted the administration to treat the war for certain purposes as a mere insurrection and for other purposes as a conventional war between sovereigns, an ambiguity that proved helpful to Union foreign policy. The decision legitimated not only the blockade but inferentially the whole range of war powers that the president and Congress had assumed.

Otherwise, most major war-related decisions went unreviewed by the Court. These included the war's two greatest accomplishments: the destruction of state sovereignty–oriented constitutionalism and the abolition of slavery. The Lincoln/Republican military coercion of the seceding states, the appointment of military governors, military occupation by Union forces, and the accretion of national power in wartime all contributed to the demise of Jeffersonian/Democratic constitutional attitudes. Congress's abolition of slavery in the territories, the states (by the First Confiscation Act, 1861), the District of Columbia, Lincoln's Emancipation Proclamation, and the slave states' abolition of slavery by constitutional amendment were all *faits accomplis,* neither requiring nor receiving Supreme Court approval. Similarly with presidential and congressional policies raising armies (including the imposition of the draft) and spending funds; despite Taney's desire to condemn them, they were approved by default or by the Court's acquiescence.

Lesser war policies did come before the Court, but only after 1865; all were upheld. These included imposition of a federal income tax (*Springer* v. *United States,* 1881), creation of a national circulating medium (money) and destruction of state bank notes (*Veazie Bank* v. *Fenno,* 1869, and the *Legal Tender Cases,* 1872, discussed below); the criminalization of rebellion and confiscation of rebels' property (*Miller* v. *United States,* 1870), and the destruction of the territorial integrity of a seceding state and concomitant creation of a new state (*Virginia* v. *West Virginia,* 1870).

We should not infer, though, from this abeyance of its policy-validating roles that the Supreme Court was thrust aside and of no account during the war, any more than we should make such an assumption about its place in both World Wars, when it similarly did not play a prominent part. It was in the nature of wartime decisions and policies that the Court's role could be nothing more than peripheral. But the old canard of an impotent and abject Court cowering before the Republicans exerted a firm hold on American imaginations during postwar Reconstruction, in part because the Court was headed by a new chief justice, Salmon P. Chase, who was a jurist of lesser stature than his two predecessors.

Our understanding of the Reconstruction Court is further muddied by an assumption that the sectional dispute over slavery permeated and dominated all politics. Statistical work by Joel Silbey and others indicates that antebellum voters behaved according to traditional political concerns, rather than single-mindedly concentrating on questions of slavery and sectionalism. Much the same is true of the Reconstruction years. Though our focus here is necessarily on questions of Reconstruction, with their sectional and racial complications, life went on; ordinary people, lawyers, and judges were mostly concerned with what would have preoccupied them in more placid times. While the Supreme Court dealt with the controversial problems of Reconstruction, it carried on its ordinary adjudicative functions as well.

A brief survey demonstrates that the many significant constitutional issues the Court disposed of had nothing to do with Reconstruction. The justices concerned themselves with monitoring state taxation programs to assure that they did not Balkanize the national market or run afoul of Congress's commerce regulatory authority. In *Crandall* v. *Nevada* (1866), the majority struck down a Nevada tax on persons leaving the state as being inconsistent with the power of the federal government to require that its citizens come to the national capital or to other states for government service, and the correlative right of the individual citizen to travel among the states. A similar broad-gauged approach led the Court to strike down a state "drummer" tax (a drummer was an itinerant salesman, someone who "drummed up" business). In *Ward* v. *Maryland* (1871), the Court held that the tax interfered with Article IV privileges and immunities of individuals to migrate in pursuit of economic opportunity.

During Reconstruction, the Court also returned to an old piece of unfinished business, the problem of federal exclusivity in the regulation of commerce. The problem posed by *Welton* v. *Missouri* (1876) was whether states could levy a tax, in this case a tax on the occupation of being a peddler, on an instrumentality of interstate commerce. The Court held that, even if Congress had not acted to regulate the subject, the tax was void as an encroachment on the federal regulatory power (in modern times, known as the doctrine of the dormant federal commerce power).

The Court's activist impulse was even more vigilant when states taxed things rather than persons. It struck down a state tax on articles carried in interstate commerce (*Case of the State Freight Tax,* 1873), though it upheld a gross receipts tax on companies that did business in interstate commerce (*Case of the State Tax on Gross Receipts,* 1873). The Court was more hospitable to local taxes in *Woodruff* v. *Parham* (1869), upholding a local tax on sales made at auction; the goods had traveled from elsewhere in interstate commerce, even though these goods were still in their original packages.

The sheer quantity of the Reconstruction Court's activist supervision of legislative policymaking is impressive: it held forty-six state statutes unconstitutional, and, what is more surprising, ten federal statutes. Not all of these were cases of major significance, to be sure. But a look at cases in which the Court voided congressional statutes will demonstrate both the continued vitality of its ordinary (that is, non–Reconstruction-related) judicial function and the extent to which its prestige remained undiminished despite *Dred Scott. United States* v. *Dewitt* (1870) struck down a prohibitive federal tax on a flammable lighting oil compound on grounds that in later cases would cause much mischief, namely, that the revenue purpose was merely a facade for a police power regulation that was forbidden to the federal government.

The best-remembered bit of judicial activism directed at federal legislation came in the *Legal Tender Cases,* though the Court's handling of both cases did little to enhance its reputation as a disinterested and apolitical tribunal. In *Hepburn* v. *Griswold* (1870), Chief Justice Chase held the issuance of paper money, "greenbacks," during the war as legal tender to be unconstitutional—an odd position to take, one would have thought, for someone who had been secretary of the treasury at the time of issue. Chase's opinion, a specimen of bad judicial workmanship, voided the federal legislation in part on the ground that it conflicted with the spirit of the contracts clause. Because the contracts clause by its terms constrains only the states, Chase had to invoke its spirit, since he could not very well call on its letter. But the reference was still metaphysical. He also claimed that the effect of making paper legal tender for preexisting debt was to deprive persons of property without due process of law in contravention of the Fifth Amendment, an anticipation of substantive due process that would have been remarkable had its vehicle, the *Hepburn* opinion, had any merit.

Congress rightly regarded the opinion as insupportable because Chase was catering to his well-known presidential ambitions and his latent, recently revived Democratic political inclinations. Two years later, with the addition of two new members, the Court reversed itself in the *Second Legal Tender Cases,* upholding the constitutionality of greenbacks under Congress's monetary powers. Though this abrupt turnaround may not have enhanced the Court's reputation for consistency, the later opinion was more defensible on the merits. But in any event, the Court through Reconstruction demonstrated that it had a continuing role to play on the constitutional stage, both as to the states and as to Congress. It thereby laid the foundations for its later and more controversial activism.

More impressive evidence of the Court's continued vitality came from Congress itself, which from 1863 through 1875 enacted a sweeping array of statutes that expanded the jurisdiction of the federal courts, including the Supreme Court. The statutes of this decade accomplished a revolution in the federal system, giving the federal courts a more expanded role in the supervision of state policies than was imaginable before the war. It is a truism that a principal result of the Civil War was the establishment of national supremacy. What is not so often understood is that it was accomplished in great measure by exalting the power and jurisdiction of the federal courts. Congress permitted the removal of many cases to federal courts for trial that before the war could have been tried only in the state courts. In 1867, it expanded the habeas corpus powers of the federal courts, converting the Great Writ into a means of testing the legality of confinement by judicial authority, and permitting extensive federal review of convictions in the state courts.

Congress also created a new federal court, the United States Court of Claims, which transferred authority to consider claims against the United States government from congressional committees to federal courts. It passed a new but short-lived Bankruptcy Act, giving federal courts bankruptcy jurisdiction. The capstone of the trend of expanding federal judicial authority was the Jurisdiction and Removal Act of 1875, which for the first time in the nation's history conferred on federal courts both original and removal jurisdiction as broad as the limits staked out in Article III of the Constitution. Because of this jurisdictional grant, Felix Frankfurter and James Landis wrote, the federal courts "ceased to be restricted tribunals of fair dealing between citizens of different states and became the primary and powerful reliances for vindicating every right given by the Constitution, the laws, and treaties of the United States" (Felix Frankfurter and James M. Landis, *The Business of the Supreme Court: A Study in the Federal Judicial System* [New York, 1927], 65). The promise of 1787 had at last been redeemed.

The Court was not bashful about accepting its enhanced role and powers. It respected congressional determinations about the scope of judicial power, both to expand and to contract it, so long as these were within constitutional limits. The power Congress properly gave, the Court accepted; in those few instances in which Congress legitimately withdrew power, the Court acquiesced. This attitude is borne out by three cases that are the ancestors of today's struggles over the power of Congress to deprive the federal courts of original and appellate jurisdiction.

The Constitution's Article III, section 2, provides that the Supreme Court's appellate jurisdiction is subject to "such Exceptions, and under such Regulations as the Congress shall make." Though this clause was central to the struggles over section 25 federal question jurisdiction that almost enervated Marshall, it had not been the subject of much debate or even notice in Congress or the courts before the war. Beginning in 1865, Democrats insisted that the Republicans' program of Reconstruction was unconstitutional. Because these Democrats mistakenly thought they had a majority of the Supreme Court with them, they taunted congressional Republicans that the Court would sooner or later condemn either the whole program of Reconstruction or at least some of its essential components.

Thus when the Supreme Court announced that it would hear an appeal in the case of William McCardle, a Mississippi civilian who had been convicted by a military tribunal of the offense of publishing "incendiary articles" critical of Reconstruction, congressional Republicans became skittish. McCardle was taking advantage of the Court's recently enhanced habeas powers, by seeking a writ under the 1867 Habeas Corpus Act to have his conviction by the military commission reviewed by the Supreme Court. Democrats goaded the Republican architects of Reconstruction in Congress, claiming that the Court would hold the use of military commissions unconstitutional, an action that would gut the effective enforcement of Reconstruction policies throughout the South. Uncharacteristically stampeded by this threat, Republicans enacted a repealer statute, withdrawing habeas review authority from the Court in cases such as McCardle's coming up under the 1867 Act.

In *Ex parte McCardle* (1869), the Court held that under the exceptions and regulations clause, Congress clearly had power to withdraw this small bit of appellate review authority, and it declined to go behind the statute to speculate on Congress's motives in doing so. But it dropped a broad hint to counsel at the end of the opinion, pointing out that the entire remainder of the Court's habeas appellate authority under the 1789 Judiciary Act was left unaffected by the McCardle repealer. Astute counsel quickly took the hint and in *Ex parte Yerger* (1869), the Court accepted jurisdiction of a habeas appeal under the 1789 Act.

Three years later, in *United States* v. *Klein,* the Court held a jurisdiction-removal statute unconstitutional. The *Klein* circumstances were as anomalous as those of *McCardle,* and the precedential value of that case may have been just as circumscribed. Congress withdrew jurisdiction from the Court of Claims and the Supreme Court in cases under the Abandoned and Captured Property Act involving claimants who had been amnestied by President Andrew Johnson, after the Court had held that the presidential amnesty gave them standing under the act to seek indemnification for the taking of their property. In *Klein,* the Court held this jurisdiction-withdrawal statute could not constitutionally be applied to a claimant who had already secured a recovery judgment in the Claims Court, because Congress was unconstitutionally attempting to reverse a judicial decree and apply a rule of decision to a case already litigated. To a great extent, *McCardle* and *Klein* tend to cancel each other out in modern scholarly commentary on congressional exceptions and regulations clause powers, but they attest to the resilience of the Court in meeting challenges to its authority during Reconstruction.

Just as the Court was not intimidated by Congress, so it refused to be cowed by the states, as demonstrated by an extension of the *Ableman* doctrine in *Tarble's Case* (1872). By a coincidence, the Wisconsin courts were again challenging federal authority after the war, this time issuing a writ of habeas corpus to secure release of an enlisted soldier in custody of a recruiting officer of the United States Army on the grounds that he was under age. Justice Stephen J. Field, for a majority of the Court, relied on *Ableman* to hold that state courts lacked power to interfere with federal custody of an individual being held under executive, as well as judicial, authority, reversing a string of state cases decided during the Civil War that assumed state courts had such authority.

John Marshall had established the judicial tradition that the Supreme Court performed its duties outside the realms of ordinary politics; in this sense, he had "de-politicized" the Court. But that tradition did not mean that the Court was never again to be implicated in politics. During the period of Reconstruction, it found itself more involved than usual in partisan, sectional, and ideological controversy, in large measure because the other branches of government, Congress and the President, were operating in a condition of institutional abnormality. For much of the Reconstruction period, Congress, having excluded the representatives and senators of some of the southern states from their seats, functioned without them. President Andrew Johnson was so thoroughly alienated from his nominal party that he was impeached. In such institutional turmoil, it was only natural that some men turned to the Court for a suprapolitical resolution of disputes.

The Court's involvement with the political controversies of Reconstruction began in the case of *Ex parte Milligan* (1866), a case that illustrates the constitutional difficulties besetting any effort to suppress seditious activity by legal process. The Habeas Corpus Act of 1863 required that persons held under military authority be released if a grand jury failed to indict them. Lamdin Milligan was tried by a military commission in Indiana, a state where no hostilities occurred during the Civil War, for various paramilitary activities on behalf of the Confederacy, and he was sentenced to be hanged. He sought a writ of habeas corpus from the

United States Supreme Court, alleging that after his detention a federal grand jury met and failed to return an indictment against him. More broadly, he insisted that his trial by a military commission was illegal in a region outside the theater of war and in which the civil courts were functioning.

The Court unanimously agreed, and in an opinion by Justice David Davis, condemned the extension of military government displacing civilian control in areas outside the theater of war. Davis's opinion was a ringing defense of the traditional guarantees of civil liberty, such as jury trial and procedural due process. But he went further in an ambiguous statement; as understood by his contemporaries, it seemed to say that Congress could never authorize military commissions in areas outside "the locality of actual war" where civil courts were open. This quasi-dictum caused four justices, led by Chief Justice Chase, to disagree with Davis's assertion and maintain that Congress could, if it wished, establish military commissions (though it had not done so in Indiana).

This close division on the Court had political overtones because Davis's sweeping statements seemed to imply that Congress lacked power to authorize military commissions throughout the states of the South undergoing Reconstruction. In late 1866, when the *Milligan* decision came down, this possibility was political dynamite, for it might have effectively aborted Reconstruction. *Milligan* thus contributed mightily to the controversies surrounding the Court at the time, fueling Democratic hopes and Republican fears that the Court might in one way or another declare Reconstruction unconstitutional. In private correspondence, Davis insisted that his opinion implied nothing of the sort, but Congress could not know of such a private reservation (quoted in Kutler, *Supreme Court and Reconstruction Politics,* 67).

The Court's next involvement with Reconstruction policies did nothing to allay Republican fears. In early 1867, a sensitive time because Congress was then debating the policies soon embodied in the Military Reconstruction Act, the Court decided two companion cases known collectively as the *Test Oath Cases,* in which it struck down both state and federal oaths required as a condition for restoration of full citizenship rights (*Cummings* v. *Missouri; Ex parte Garland*). The Court held that these violated the bills of attainder and ex post facto clauses of Article I, sections 9 and 10. Like *Milligan,* both decisions were by 5–4 margins, a situation that never helps the persuasive authority of a controversial opinion.

Emboldened by what they thought was the trajectory of the Court's *Milligan* and *Test Oath* opinions, opponents of Reconstruction decided on a frontal assault on Reconstruction after the Republican-dominated Congress enacted the first of the Military Reconstruction Acts. Southern attorneys tried to enjoin President Johnson from enforcing the statute. In *Mississippi* v. *Johnson* (1867), the Court unanimously spurned this challenge. Even the president, who was an intemperate opponent of the policies embodied in the act, opposed the petition for an injunction, considering it an insupportable challenge to executive authority generally (as indeed it was). Going back to Marshall's *Marbury* distinction between ministerial and discretionary acts, Chief Justice Chase held the president's authority under the act to be discretionary and thus not enjoinable.

Not discouraged by this firm and unanimous opinion, southern attorneys immediately tried again, seeking to enjoin the secretary of war and the general of the armies from enforcing military reconstruction. The Court, in *Georgia* v. *Stanton* (1868), again turned them down unanimously (but with Chase concurring only in result). This time the Court relied on another venerable judicial touchstone, the political question doctrine, holding that what Georgia sought would require the Court to adjudicate political questions left by the Constitution to the determination of Congress and the President. The Mississippi and Georgia Cases, together with *McCardle* (decided the next year), suggested that the Court was not about to accept a head-on confrontation with Congress over the substance of Reconstruction policies.

The Court's final involvement with suits directly challenging political Reconstruction occurred in two cases decided in 1869 and 1871, respectively *Texas* v. *White* and *White* v. *Hart.* The decisions resulted in a resounding victory for congressional Republican theories of Reconstruction, putting to rest any lingering doubts that the Court might invalidate some aspect of Reconstruction. Chief Justice Chase, for a six-judge majority in the Texas case, endorsed the moderate and mainstream Republican constitutional theory of Reconstruction that underlay the Military Reconstruction Acts. He held that, though the seceding states had never left the Union or committed political suicide, their rights as states, as well as some of the political rights of their citizens, had been forfeited or at least suspended by secession.

One of the virtues of the forfeited rights theory was that it comported as closely as a figure of speech can to reality. Its textual constitutional basis was the clause of Article IV that requires the United States to guarantee to every state in the Union a republican form of government. Under the precedent of *Luther* v. *Borden* (and with an irony Chase must have relished, since he was relying on a Taney case to uphold Reconstruction), guarantee clause questions were political and therefore nonjusticiable. Chase went further, however, stating that these particular questions were predominantly for Congress, not the President, to resolve, thus dispelling any idea that the Court sided with the obstructive stand of President Johnson rather than with the congressional Republicans.

The term *Reconstruction* comprehends a bundle of related problems, including the status of seceded states, the status of their white citizens, and, of course, the future of black people, most of them the freedmen of the South. Much historical writing has been based on an assumption that all Reconstruction questions involved the future of black people. Consequently, it is easy to overemphasize that one question to the exclusion of others. Most political issues facing Americans in that era had nothing to do with Reconstruction at all. Yet black people were a presence in all debates on Reconstruction, and any consideration of the subject must explore their fate in the last third of the nineteenth century.

Matters began promisingly enough. As soon as former abolitionist Salmon P. Chase had been sworn in as chief justice, his abolitionist colleague and friend, Senator Charles Sumner, moved the admission of John Rock, a black attorney, to the bar of the United States Supreme Court. Abolitionists thrilled at the symbolic significance of the occasion. Eight years after the chief justice had said that blacks had no rights whites need respect, his successor administered the oath of admission to a black lawyer. But it would take much more than symbolism to sustain the rights of blacks after 1865.

Within a decade, blacks found themselves trapped in a no man's land between implacable racism on one hand and Republican legislation backed by constitutional amendments supporting their rights on the other. This contradiction occurred in part because of differing fundamental assumptions in the North and in the South on the meaning and consequences of emancipation. Northerners assumed that once slavery was abolished the ex-slaves immediately and automatically ascended to all the rights, privileges, and responsibilities of full citizenship, impeded by some racially based disabilities, to be sure, but nevertheless in possession of all civil rights whites enjoyed. Such a view of civil rights as being inherent in the transition from slavery to freedom informed Chief Justice Chase's circuit court opinion in *In re Turner* (1867), in which he nullified a Maryland freedmen's apprenticeship law on the grounds that the Thirteenth Amendment "establishes freedom as the constitutional right of all persons in the United States." Southerners knew better. In the legal regimes of slave societies, emancipation did nothing except exempt an ex-slave from the authority of his master. It conferred no rights except mobility (the right to go where one pleased) and no distinct civil status.

Given these fundamentally different assumptions, the struggle to define and enforce the legal status of the freedmen was bound to be long, difficult, and bloody. For the remainder of the nineteenth century, this struggle conformed to an action-reaction pattern, as Congress assumed the initiative in expanding the rights of blacks, and white southerners together with the Supreme Court maneuvered to negate those rights.

The first and most basic category of freedmen's rights consisted of "civil rights" in the nineteenth-century sense of that term. These comprised mobility, the right to enjoy governmental protection from private violence, the ability to make and enforce contracts, the power to own and convey property, the ability to marry and have a legally protected parent-child relationship, and juridical status (the right to appear in court as party and witness). In southern eyes, each of these could be limited by racial qualifications; for example, it was entirely consistent with southern understandings of the content of civil rights to impose curfews on blacks or prohibit their testimony against whites. As northerners began to comprehend these southern conceptions of civil rights, they moved to compress and summarize their own thinking about rights into a single category: the right of equality before the law, meaning the right of a black person to be treated by the law in every respect, both as to privileges and as to disabilities, as a white person would be treated. Civil rights were variously conveyed by the Black Codes of the southern states, the Civil Rights Act of 1866, and section 1 of the Fourteenth Amendment.

The next category of rights, called "political rights" in the nineteenth century, included the right to vote, the right to hold office, and the right to serve on juries. Rights of political capacity were conferred and secured by section 2 of the Fourteenth Amendment, the Military Reconstruction Acts, the Fifteenth Amendment, and the Force Acts (1870–71) at the federal level, as well as various state constitutional provisions and laws. The final and highest category of rights consisted of social rights, of which the principal ones were equal access to public accommodations and education. Equal access to public accommodations was guaranteeed by the Civil Rights Act of 1875 and equivalent state legislation.

Black people acquired at least the form, and often the substance, of the civil, political, and social rights whites enjoyed. Blacks made contracts, acquired and conveyed property, got access to courts, voted, and claimed entree to theaters and railroad cars. But the bright promise of Reconstruction legislation was soon blighted. Southern Democrats ferociously resented the social revolution that the victorious northern states forced on them. Simultaneously, the Supreme Court hesitated, then stumbled, on the threshold of the revolution in government implicit in the Reconstruction amendments. The remainder of this chapter is the melancholy account of how the Supreme Court and southern Democrats dismantled or enervated these rights so laboriously identified by congressional Republicans.

A major source of judicial conservatism lay in what Harold M. Hyman has identified as state-based federalism, which posits complementary roles for the federal and state governments (Harold M. Hyman, *A More Perfect Union: The Impact of the Civil War and Reconstruction on the Constitution* [New York, 1973], 438–39). The major idea of state-based federalism, distinguishing it from the constitutional order of today, is that responsibility for defining the substantive content of rights, and of enforcing those rights, continued to reside with the states. This outlook, in turn, was based on two related antebellum constitutional ideas, "states' rights" and "dual federalism." The concept of states' rights implied that states continued to possess elements of sovereignty that had not been conveyed to the federal government by the Constitution, and that the federal government had to respect these state sovereign powers. Dual federalism, a phrase coined by the twentieth-century constitutional scholar Edward S. Corwin, summed up a congeries of ideas. Michael Les Benedict enumerates them thus:

> [The states were] the equals of the national government in the federal system; that each of these [state and federal] governments had a complete, independent structure within which to exercise its power and could not require the other to administer its laws; that the powers of each government were completely distinct and independent with each supreme in its own sphere; that the Tenth Amendment confirmed this structure and guaranteed that the national power would not be interpreted in such a way as to subvert the reserved sovereign jurisdiction of the States. (Michael Les Benedict, "Preserving Federalism: Reconstruction and the Waite Court," *Supreme Court Review* [1978]: 39–79, quote on 42)

Most Americans after the war retained some allegiance to this older, prewar conception of federalism. Therefore the freedom of black people had to be achieved within the system of state-based federalism, as much as was possible within the prewar federal structure. The federal government mandated equality of rights for all people in the sense that it expected that blacks would be treated as whites in the matter of all civil rights but not necessarily in the category of political or social rights. The states would continue to have exclusive authority to determine the content of those rights and to enforce them among all their people.

The northern effort to pour some new wine into an old constitutional bottle might have worked had southern whites shared the North's conception of equality under the law, and cooperated in implementing it in good faith. But such an expectation quickly proved to be fanciful. The jurisprudence of slave societies was based on an older concept of equality, summed up in the formula "like should be treated as like," and derived from one of Emperor Justinian's fundamental maxims of law, *suum cuique tribuere:* render to each his own. Justinian's maxim did not require that each get what everyone else got, but merely what he deserved. In a social order based on that idea, blacks did not have any right to claim to be treated as whites in all respects (say, in being free of curfew restrictions or in enjoying the opportunity to enter any occupation they chose). Rather, they could claim only to be treated as other blacks. The chasm between northern and southern conceptions of equality was never adequately understood in the North, with the result that when northern determination to protect the rights and status of the freedmen began to flag, southerners could impose their own vision of a proper legal order within their jurisdictions. To this process, the Supreme Court proved to be an accomplice, because it was constrained by the almost universally shared assumptions of state-based federalism.

The disintegration of legal protection for black rights began amid the multiple ironies of the *Slaughterhouse Cases* (1873), which provided the Court with its first major opportunity to construe the impact of the Fourteenth Amendment. The Louisiana legislature enacted what appeared on its face to be a valid police power regulation that restricted butchering in New Orleans to a single large abattoir. Any butcher could pursue his trade in the Crescent City Company's Grand Slaughterhouse upon payment of a fee.

A group of butchers, all of whom were white men, resented the monopoly thus conferred, with its power to exact a fee from them as a condition of pursuing their trade, and they retained former United States Supreme Court Justice John A. Campbell to challenge the monopoly. Campbell relied comprehensively on the Thirteenth Amendment, the Civil Rights Act of 1866, and three of the four elements of the Fourteenth Amendment's section 1: privileges and immunities, due process, and equal protection. Hence the first of the ironies: the first major case construing the foundations of black rights was brought by white men.

The Court split five to four in response to this challenge; Justice Miller spoke for the majority, rejecting Campbell's innovative and revolutionary argument. (The views of two of the dissenting justices, Joseph Bradley and Stephen J. Field, which inaugurated the substantive due process era, will be explored in the next chapter.) After making an orthodox police power argument sustaining the action of the legislature, Miller turned to each of Campbell's arguments derived from the amendments. He began by rejecting the idea that the statute's restriction on where butchers could follow their trade constituted "involuntary servitude" within the terms of the Thirteenth Amendment. "The one pervading purpose found in [the Reconstruction amendments], lying at the foundation of each,'' Miller claimed, was freedom for black people, not the creation of new or expanded rights for whites. This view would seem to have been encouraging for blacks, suggesting as it did an expansive attitude toward the amendments, at least as they affected blacks. But the direction of Miller's thinking lay elsewhere.

He next took up the privileges and immunities argument, and shattered blacks' hopes that the Fourteenth Amendment would substantially alter the balance of federalism in ways that would protect their newly won liberties. Miller declared that there were two sorts of privileges and immunities, federal and state. Only the former could be secured by federal action. State privileges and immunities, if they may be called that, ''must rest for their security and protection where they had heretofore rested,'' namely, the states. Here lay the decision's second terrible irony, for in this statement, Miller directed black people, for purposes of defining and protecting their rights, to just those bodies, the state governments of the South, which were most hostile to black rights. This reasoning was entirely in keeping with the tenets of state-based federalism, but it meant that the foxes now effectively ruled over the chicken coops. Blacks depended for their rights on the hostile and vindictive ''Redeemer'' regimes just then coming to power throughout the South. This situation would not have been so intolerable if federal privileges and immunities had some significant content. But Miller's conservatism led him to give the narrowest scope possible to federal rights, including things useless to blacks such as the right of access to coastal ports. The only federally protected rights enumerated by Miller that might prove valuable to freedmen were the First Amendment right of assembly and the privilege of habeas corpus. Otherwise, the ''state privileges and immunities'' included nearly all the substantive and procedural rights that would mean anything in the day-to-day lives of blacks in the South.

Miller candidly explained the conservative attitudes that lay behind his doctrine: ''We do not see in those [Reconstruction] amendments any purpose to destroy the main features of the general system'' created by the Constitution. To rule otherwise would produce consequences ''so serious, so far-reaching and pervading, so great a departure from the structure and spirit of our institutions'' as to be unthinkable. They would ''fetter and degrade the State governments by subjecting them to the control of Congress'' and ''constitute this court a perpetual censor upon all legislation of the States.'' It was unimaginable to Miller that the amendments could have been meant to accomplish what some of their sponsors insisted was their true aim: a revolution in federalism, whereby the federal government would take over responsibility for protecting the rights of all citizens in the states that had defaulted.

Though much else in Miller's opinion has been eroded in the past century, the Court has repeatedly reaffirmed the substance of his privileges and immunities reasoning. Only once did the Court rely on the Fourteenth Amendment's privileges and immunities clause to void a state law, and even then the Court reversed itself within five years (*Colgate* v. *Harvey* [1935]; *Madden* v. *Kentucky* [1940].) Consequently today we are still directly affected by Justice Miller's reticence to accept fundamental change in the constitutional order.

Having thus dealt with what he regarded as the most significant of the butchers' arguments, Miller then summarily disposed of the due process and equal protection points. He rejected a substantive due process interpretation out of hand, saying that "no construction of that provision that we have ever seen, or any that we deem admissible" would permit the Court to use the due process clause to monitor the content of legislative policy. To make such a statement, Miller had to ignore both Taney's *Dred Scott* dictum and Chase's more elaborate statement to the same effect in *Hepburn* v. *Griswold,* as well as an extensive body of state law anticipating the substantive due process tradition.

Miller brushed aside equal protection arguments just as abruptly, arguing that only state action "directed by way of discrimination against the negroes as a class, or on account of their race" would ever likely fall afoul of the Fourteenth Amendment. This dictum, too, seemingly supportive of black rights on its face, concealed a hidden betrayal of the aspirations of blacks, for it meant that only explicit and overt state policies could be controlled by the Fourteenth Amendment. Private actions and state action by subterfuge were beyond the reach of the amendment.

Slaughterhouse of itself had no immediate impact on the rights of blacks. But it betokened an attitude toward the construction of the Reconstruction amendments that augured ill for the rights so precariously safeguarded by federal legislation. Just how vulnerable those legislatively secured rights were was demonstrated within a decade by the appearance of the state action doctrine. To understand how damaging this doctrine has been for black rights, it is necessary to begin by comparing the Fourteenth Amendment with the Thirteenth. The second sentence of section 1 of the Fourteenth Amendment begins: "No State shall make or enforce any law . . ." (what follows are the privileges and immunities, due process, and equal protection clauses). It is both clear and reasonable that this sentence inhibits actions taken by states; it is not by its terms a prohibition on the federal government or on private individuals. It is not clear, however, whether the "No State" formulation covers the failure of a state to act; say, its refusal or inability to prohibit private persons from depriving others of civil rights. By contrast, the Thirteenth Amendment and the first sentence of the Fourteenth (which deals with federal and state citizenship) do not contain any "No State" limitation. Consequently they are universal in their application, and do not require the action of a state to actuate them.

These syntactical and logical questions, plus the intentions of those who framed and ratified the Thirteenth and Fourteenth Amendments, would require some definitive interpretation by the courts, especially since they involved questions of the rights of individuals rather than the kinds of abstractions about state status raised in *Mississippi* v. *Johnson* and *Georgia* v. *Stanton.* Courts therefore had an opportunity to construe federal powers broadly or narrowly. A narrow construction, such as was suggested by Miller in *Slaughterhouse,* would constrict the ability of the national government to protect blacks' rights, leaving the freedmen's future in the control of the Democratic, racist, ex-secessionist, ex-Confederate Redeemers who were then taking control of the southern states. A broad construction, on the other hand, would make federal force available to support the freedmen, especially through the instrumentality of the federal courts.

The federal judiciary's first significant encounter with these issues adopted a broad approach hospitable to blacks' rights. In a circuit court case, *United States* v. *Hall* (1871), Judge William B. Woods (who was later to serve as a Supreme Court justice) held that the Fourteenth Amendment empowered Congress "to protect the fundamental rights of citizens of the United States against unfriendly or insufficient state legislation." Denial of equal protection included "inaction" and "omission to protect, as well as the omission to pass laws for protection." Therefore federal laws could operate directly on individuals.

But this encouraging view of federal power under the Fourteenth Amendment was spurned by the Supreme Court, particularly by Justice Joseph P. Bradley, who originally supported the *Hall* position and dissented in *Slaughterhouse,* but who soon changed his mind about the scope of the Fourteenth Amendment. Gradually, almost on a case-by-case basis that stretched over a decade, the Court moved away from *Hall*'s permissive reading of federal powers under the Fourteenth Amendment to the narrowest possible construction of federal authority.

Justice Bradley's circuit court opinion, *United States* v. *Cruikshank* (1876), began the process; it drew a critical distinction that has persisted into our own day. He maintained that congressional power could reach private action under the Thirteenth Amendment, but only if that action was racially motivated. The requirement of racial motive was not necessary under the Fourteenth Amendment, but state action was. On certification to the Supreme Court, Chief Justice Morrison R. Waite affirmed the distinction, stating that the due process clause of the Fourteenth Amendment "adds nothing to the rights of one citizen as against another." Thus an indictment for participating in a lynching that averred that the defendant deprived the victim of life without due process of law was defective; the United States could not punish ordinary homicides, even if it was obvious to all that the killing was racially motivated, as in a lynching or a race riot. Because the southern states were increasingly disinclined to prosecute whites for lynchings and other acts of violence against blacks, the promise of the Reconstruction amendments was becoming ever more hollow. *United States* v. *Harris* (1883) went further, holding unconstitutional the criminal enforcement section of the so-called Ku Klux Klan Act of 1871 (one of the Force Acts of 1870–71) on the grounds that it was overbroad, reaching private violence. (*Cruikshank* merely voided the application of a statute; *Harris* condemned the statute itself.)

This restrictive tendency in the Court's thinking came to fruition in the *Civil Rights Cases* of 1883, in which the state action doctrine was made explicit and ensconced into constitutional interpretation so firmly that it has not yet been dislodged. In this case, Justice Bradley held the public accommodations provisions of the Civil Rights Act of 1875 unconstitutional. The statute provided that "all persons . . . regardless of any previous condition of servitude" were to be provided access to all public accommodations, including inns, railroads, theaters, "and other places of public amusement." Denial was made a federal misdemeanor, with the defendant being civilly liable as well. Bradley first rejected the Fourteenth Amendment as a basis for this legislation, because it prohibits only "State action of a particular character." Civil rights secured by the Fourteenth Amendment could not be deprived by private action, and Congress lacks power to reach such acts under the amendment. (In dictum, Bradley hinted that such congressional power might be found under the commerce clause, a recommendation that bore fruit some eighty years later when the Court sustained the public accommodations section of the 1964 Civil Rights Act on commerce clause grounds: *Heart of Atlanta Motel* v. *United States*, 1964).

More distressing to the friends of black rights was Bradley's reasoning on the Thirteenth Amendment basis for the 1875 Civil Rights Act. Bradley admitted that there was no state action impediment to federal legislation in the Thirteenth Amendment, but he denied that private discrimination constituted either involuntary servitude or a "badge of slavery" prohibited by the Thirteenth Amendment. Bradley expressed the impatience that he and a majority of his brethren felt with such notions: "It would be running the slavery argument into the ground to make it apply to every act of [private] discrimination." "When a man has emerged from slavery," he concluded, "there must be some stage in the progress of his elevation when he takes the rank of a mere citizen, and ceases to be the special favorite of the laws." Consequently the Thirteenth Amendment could not be used to enforce social equality. Its utility was shrunken to cases of involuntary servitude, and it could not reach other forms of racial oppression.

Justice John M. Harlan was the sole dissenter in the *Civil Rights Cases,* as he was to be in *Plessy* v. *Ferguson* (1896), the separate-but-equal case, and his views have been vindicated in our time. Harlan's position on the Court requires particular notice. At the time, he was the only member of the Court who had been a slaveholder (he was from Kentucky). Despite that fact, he was also one of only three members of the Court to have served in the Union forces during the war (the others were Stanley Matthews and William B. Woods). This unusual perspective helped him pierce through the rationalizations, fictions, and formalism that marked the opinions of his brethren in race-related cases. Harlan argued that racial discrimination when practiced by private individuals was a badge of slavery within the reach of the Thirteenth Amendment. This view triumphed in *Jones* v. *Alfred Mayer Co.* (1968), in which petitioners harked back to the 1866 Civil Rights Act as a source of their right to purchase realty free of racial discrimination. Justice Potter Stewart held race discrimination to be a "relic of slavery" and as such the badge of servitude identified by the first Justice Harlan. (With a touch of historical irony, his grandson, also named John Marshall Harlan, dissented in *Jones,* arguing that the statute as thus construed was of dubious constitutionality.)

Despite Harlan's forceful dissent in the *Civil Rights Cases,* the state action doctrine was written into American constitutional law by 1883, and it remains there, though it has been both crumbled along its periphery and attenuated by recent civil rights cases. Second only to Miller's conservative view of the Reconstruction amendments in *Slaughterhouse,* the state action doctrine was the Supreme Court's major contribution to dismantling the structure of the freedmen's rights.

In the late nineteenth century, the Court devised several doctrines and attitudes that resulted in a further erosion of the constitutional status of black people. This erosion occurred especially in three areas: voting, jury service, and public accommodations. In each area, as if it were guided by some malignant impulse that sought to add the judiciary's weight to the burden of oppression, the Court reached results that closed off avenues of relief, reinforced Jim Crow, and abetted both nonviolent and violent segregationist policies.

In the voting rights area, the Court began with the same narrowly focused attitudes that produced the *Slaughterhouse* approach and the state action doctrine. In *United States* v. *Reese* (1876), Chief Justice Morrison R. Waite, Chase's successor, held the voting rights provisions of the 1870 Force Act unconstitutional because they were overbroad, prohibiting any interference at all with voting rather than only those based on racial discrimination. "The Fifteenth Amendment does not confer the right of suffrage upon anyone," Waite observed. This sort of exquisitely constricted approach to the guarantees of the Reconstruction amendments validates Derrick Bell's judgment that "blacks became victims of judicial interpretations of the Fourteenth Amendment and legislation based on it so narrow as to render the promised protection meaningless in virtually all situations" (Derrick A. Bell, Jr., *Race, Racism and American Law,* 2d ed. [Boston, 1980], 33).

By the end of Reconstruction, the white South determined to accomplish legally what it had come a long way toward doing by fraud, intimidation, and violence: the complete exclusion of black voters from the polls. The Mississippi Constitution of 1890 included provisions that came to be known as the "Mississippi Plan." This program included labyrinthine procedures for voter registration, requirements of literacy and understanding of the state constitution, proof of good character, residency, a poll tax, property ownership, disfranchisement of persons convicted of certain crimes, and even the secret ballot (which could be made complex enough to confuse semiliterate voters). Though these provisions were admittedly designed to disfranchise blacks, the Supreme Court in *Williams* v. *Mississippi* (1898) accepted the Mississippi Plan. The Court deliberately shut its eyes to the impact of its ruling in *Williams,* while southerners seized the opportunities presented by that case. Carter Glass, delegate to the 1901–2 Virginia disfranchising constitutional convention that adopted elements of the Mississippi Plan, stated exuberantly: "We have come here . . . for the purpose of finding some constitutional method of ridding ourselves of [black suffrage] forever; and we have the approval of the Supreme Court of the United States in making that effort" (quoted in part in Alexander M. Bickel and Benno C. Schmidt, Jr., *The Judiciary and Responsible Government, 1910–1921* [New York, 1984], 921).

The same attitude pervaded the Court's approach to the problem of excluding blacks from juries. In three 1880 cases, the justices drew lines that invited subterfuge and evasion by white southern officials and resulted in all white juries. Two of the decisions struck down overt exclusion of blacks, whether by statute (*Strauder* v. *West Virginia*) or by explicit actions of the judge in disqualifying prospective jurors on racial grounds alone (*Ex parte Virginia*). But in *Virginia* v. *Rives,* the Court undercut these protections against overt exclusion by ruling that the mere absence of blacks on a jury panel, no matter how systematic, was not evidence of racial exclusion. It took little imagination for southern whites to devise techniques of black exclusion that were implicit and based on a universal understanding of how things work in a segregated society.

A different judicial approach legitimized Jim Crow in public transportation. Chief Justice Waite used the dormant federal commerce power to hold unconstitutional a Louisiana statute that prohibited segregation and discrimination in transportation in *Hall* v. *DeCuir* (1878). Because he stressed the interrelationships of transportation among the states, the effect of the *DeCuir* ruling was to permit any segregating state, by the mere existence of its segregation laws, to void the antisegregation laws of all the others. That this differential result was no accident was demonstrated in *Louisiana, New Orleans, & Texas Railway* v. *Mississippi* (1890), which upheld the constitutionality of a Mississippi segregation statute on the grounds that it affected only intrastate commerce. Clearly, the Louisiana and Mississippi cases were indistinguishable; the differentiating factor was the Court's determination to support state-mandated racial segregation.

Sometimes history's ironies mock malice as well as benevolence. After the intellectual and moral miasma that nourished segregation began to lift, the Court in effect reversed the racial polarities of the Mississippi and Louisiana cases in *Morgan* v. *Virginia* (1946), which used *DeCuir*'s reasoning about the dormant commerce power to strike down a Virginia segregation statute, and in *Bob-Lo Excursion Co.* v. *Michigan* (1948), which upheld a state antidiscrimination measure as it applied to foreign commerce.

Sooner or later, the results-oriented prosegregation bias of the Court would require some sort of justification or rationalization. The Court cannot go on for long promoting a social policy without coming up with some plausible reasons for doing so. These reasons must provide the appearance of impartiality and dedication to some consistent principles. Without such a rationalization, the Court stands naked to the winds of criticism. So it was with segregation. Even though the Court's decisions were in harmony with the mood of those who controlled the direction of racial affairs at the national and state levels, consistency had to be found in reasons as well as results, lest the Court be accused of making purely arbitrary political decisions.

In the Mississippi Jim Crow transportation case, Justice Brewer emphasized that the state supreme court had interpreted the statute to apply only to intrastate commerce. The rationale, however, was threadbare in that case and was obviously insufficient for the more aggressively segregationist statutes likely to come before the Court in commerce clause cases. Something more was needed, and Justice Henry B. Brown supplied it comprehensively in the leading segregation case of the Court's history, *Plessy* v. *Ferguson* (1896).

In *Plessy,* a black passenger evicted from a segregated railway car attacked a Louisiana Jim Crow transportation statute not as a violation of the commerce clause but rather on the Thirteenth Amendment and equal protection grounds in the Fourteenth Amendment. Justice Brown dismissed the Thirteenth Amendment attack by reasoning ratified previously in the *Civil Rights Cases:* discrimination does not amount to involuntary servitude. The equal protection challenge proved more difficult, but Brown surmounted it. He relied heavily on a police power argument, sustaining the state's interest in preserving peace between the races based on "the established usages, customs, and traditions of the people." Besides, he suggested to the black petitioner, a Jim Crow law does "not necessarily imply the inferiority of either race to the other." If blacks thought it did, "it is not by reason of anything found in the act, but solely because the colored race chooses to put that construction on it." In any event, mere laws are "powerless to eradicate racial instincts or to abolish distinctions based upon physical differences." "Social prejudices" he concluded, cannot "be overcome by legislation."

Plessy v. *Ferguson* seems perverse to a modern reader, but it must be understood in the context of its era. Two dominant components of the national outlook of the 1890s make the case entirely compatible with the temper of its times, at least as far as whites were concerned. The first was a formalist mentality, which enabled judges in cases involving blacks to accept a purely formal or nominal equality, no matter how obvious it was to anyone else that that formal condition bore no relation to reality. In Paris Anatole France satirized this attitude in *The Red Lily* (1894), when he wrote of "the majestic equality of the laws, which forbid rich and poor alike to sleep under bridges, to beg in the streets, and to steal their bread."

The more powerful impetus behind judicially sanctioned segregation was a complex of sentiments that coalesced in the 1890s. Reconciliation between the sections was one; the myth of the "Lost Cause," carefully nurtured by numberless southern patriotic and veterans' societies, was another. Another myth was the glorification of the Redeemer political effort, unforgettably captured in the film *Birth of a Nation,* with its images of depraved subhuman blacks threatening white social order and political dominance.

Above all, however, was the ideology of racism, exalting white supremacy and consigning "the Negro to his place." That place, at the turn of the century, was the cotton field and the Jim Crow railway car. The constitutional basis of federalism in the "New South" era was a legal condition known as "suzerainty," under which the federal government controlled the external relationships of the southern states, their foreign policy, and their reintegration into the national market. The concomitant was the southern states' control of their own domestic affairs, which meant white control of black people (plus the related matter of ruling-class annihilation of the Populist challenge). In the era of Reconstruction, which ended in 1877, the racial crusade went under the slogans of "self-government" and "home rule." By the 1890s, the need for pretense disappeared and the movement could now parade under its true colors, white supremacy.

With the general principle of separate but equal established, and southern legislators taking the Court's unspoken hint that southern whites enjoyed a broad latitude in dealing with blacks, the time had come for the Supreme Court to sanction racial segregation in the schools. The Supreme Court promptly obliged, first in *Cumming* v. *Board of Education* (1899), which took it for granted, without argument, that separate but equal was legitimate in the public schools. The problem in *Cumming* was whether a Georgia county's refusal to provide any high school at all for blacks while it provided a high school for whites was constitutional. Justice Harlan, for the Court, had no difficulty holding that it was, reasoning that the county could not afford to maintain two high schools and that shutting down the white high school would do blacks no good. The only remaining question was whether the states could force segregation on integrated private schools. To no one's surprise, the Court held that they could in *Berea College* v. *Kentucky* (1908), upholding segregation on traditional police power reasoning.

After *Plessy* and *Cumming,* the equal protection clause was a dead letter, or, what amounted to the same thing, sunk into a hundred years' sleep by the poisoned apple of Miller's *Slaughterhouse* reasoning, at least as far as black people and white women were concerned. Blacks had had no success at all when they invoked the equal protection clause in the spirit of its abolitionist fathers. Women fared no better. In *Minor* v. *Happersett* (1875), Chief Justice Waite shrugged off a woman's claim that enactment of the equal protection clause removed the gender disability that prevented her from voting. Nothing in the Fourteenth Amendment, Waite responded, was meant to confer the vote on women or to disturb the status quo between the sexes.

A pioneering female attorney, Myra Bradwell, had no better luck trying to overturn Illinois's refusal to admit her to the practice of the law.

Bradwell v. *Illinois* (1873) remains notable today for the concurrence of Justice Bradley, who wrote:

> Man is, or should be, woman's protector and defender. The natural and proper timidity and delicacy which belongs to the female sex evidently unfits it for many of the occupations of civil life. . . . The paramount destiny and mission of woman are to fulfil the noble and benign offices of wife and mother. This is the law of the Creator.

Charles Fairman laconically comments: "As a demonstration of man's superior fitness for the law, this opinion was not a shining example" (Charles Fairman, *Reconstruction and Reunion, 1864–1888,* part 1 [New York, 1971], 1366). That gender bias, and not a general solicitude for state police powers, was the determinative element in these gender discrimination cases was evidenced when another female attorney, Belva Lockwood, applied for admission to the bar of the United States Supreme Court. Waite turned her down, too, without the benefit of a legislative decision one way or the other, citing the practice of the English courts, before whom only men had traditionally practiced.

In these years, there was one suggestion that the equal protection clause might not be entirely chimerical. *Yick Wo* v. *Hopkins* (1886) involved that most isolated and friendless minority of the time, the California Chinese. A San Francisco ordinance required that all laundries be housed in brick or stone buildings. The Board of Supervisors granted nonconforming use permits to carry on laundering in a wooden building to all white applicants and turned down all Chinese applicants. Justice Matthews, in an opinion inconsistent with the prevalent formalism of the day, found that though the ordinance appeared nondiscriminatory on its face, its administration was biased. "Though the law itself be fair on its face and impartial in appearance, yet, if it is applied and administered by public authority with an evil eye and an unequal hand," he concluded, it would run afoul of the equal protection clause. *Yick Wo* was a lonely exception, however, to the dominant approach of the era.

Shortly before World War I, some rays of dawn's light began to penetrate the long, dark night of the equal protection clause. The most striking was the federal government's concerted and vigorous effort to suppress peonage, the system of debt bondage, which was one of several items the southern white ruling class used to reduce blacks to a state of crypto-servitude. Unlike other techniques, peonage was illegal under federal law. A federal statute enacted in 1867, the Peonage Act, was designed to suppress the remnants of the Mexican system of serfdom that lingered in New Mexico Territory. It went unapplied to black involuntary servitude in the South until the turn of the century, when the Justice

Department displayed an uncharacteristically alert interest in suppressing the various forms of debt bondage and crypto-slavery that seemed to be then spreading in the more remote regions of the South.

In a series of remarkable cases, the Justice Department supported vigorous enforcement of the Peonage Act against southern peon masters, and was rewarded with three successive victories. In *Clyatt* v. *United States* (1905), the Court upheld the constitutionality of the Peonage Act, reasoning that debt bondage is involuntary servitude even if it was originally entered into voluntarily by the laborer. The Court also reasserted the idea, long settled but hitherto of little use, that there is no state action requirement under the Thirteenth Amendment, so that the federal government's enforcement powers extended directly to the actions of private individuals, such as peon masters. Encouraged by this hospitable attitude of the Court, the Justice Department and a few federal judges investigated, publicized, and prosecuted peonage cases. *Bailey* v. *Alabama* (1910) sanctioned use of the Thirteenth Amendment to void an Alabama contract enforcement statute which created a statutory presumption of fraud when an employee took an advance and then quit before he had completed his contractual obligations.

The decision in *United States* v. *Reynolds* (1914) reached more widely into the complex and extensive southern system of legalized involuntary servitude. *Reynolds* struck down an Alabama criminal surety act, under which an indigent convicted of an offense and fined was obliged to work for some "surety" who paid it for him. Under such a statute, a black would be arrested, convicted, and fined for some misdemeanor offense, often vagrancy or some trumped up charge. A white planter would pay the fine, and the judge would, in effect, sentence the black to work for the surety for a specified period to pay off the fine. Lest the black laborer harbor thoughts of skipping out on his employer, two other Alabama institutions stood behind the criminal surety system to keep him at his tasks: the chain gang and the convict-leasing system, with their horrors of sadistic brutality and early death. *Reynolds* held the criminal surety system to be debt bondage, and hence proscribed under the Peonage Act.

This welcome respite from the formalist approach also appeared in other cases involving the separate-but-equal doctrine in the prewar period. Behind the aegis of that doctrine, *Cumming* had accepted a situation of separate and unequal, under which, to maintain segregation, a county was permitted to deny a public service to blacks altogether. Such a judicial connivance at absolute deprivation was renounced by newly appointed Justice Charles Evans Hughes in *McCabe* v. *Atchison, Topeka & Santa Fe Railway* (1914). An Oklahoma Jim Crow railroad statute exempted "luxury" cars (sleeping, dining, and parlor cars) from its requirement of equal service, in effect sanctioning the denial of these services to black railroad passengers. Hughes struck the statute down, insisting that there were two sides to the separate-but-equal equation, and that if the South insisted on the first, it had to provide the second. *McCabe* was later to be of precedential value at the beginning of the successful final assault on Jim Crow, when the Supreme Court after 1938 held the southern states to full equality in their dual school systems, a demand so impossible of fulfillment that it would doom segregation.

A similar attitude informed *Buchanan* v. *Warley* (1917), which struck down a Louisville ordinance that prohibited members of one race from occupying a residence on a block in which the majority of residents were of the other race. Justice William R. Day used the Fourteenth Amendment's due process clause to hold that it prevented the state from interfering arbitrarily on a racial basis with property rights. The spurious equality of forbidding whites to move into black neighborhoods was not even a makeweight in the arguments against the due process principle. Finally, in *Guinn* v. *Oklahoma* (1915), none other than Chief Justice Edward D. White wrote for a unanimous Court striking down an element of the Mississippi Plan's disfranchisement of blacks, the grandfather clause, which exempted from the literacy test anyone whose ancestors had been registered to vote in 1866 (or some other date in midcentury). White's willingness to penetrate the facade of the Mississippi Plan was surprising because, as a Louisianan, he was the first southern chief justice since Taney and had served in the Confederate forces. *Guinn* significantly revived the Fifteenth Amendment, though it did not produce a flood of new black voters.

McCabe, Buchanan, and *Guinn* cheered blacks and attorneys for the National Association for the Advancement of Colored People, who had begun to contest Jim Crow and other forms of discrimination in the courts. They signaled that the long night of Court-sanctioned segregation that had lain over the land for the previous generation might be passing and tentatively suggested a process that, forty years later, began to realize the promise of the Reconstruction amendments.

Justice Potter Stewart in 1972 summed up the accomplishments of the Civil War and postbellum periods, emphasizing

> the basic alteration in our federal system wrought in the Reconstruction era through federal legislation and constitutional amendment. As a result of the new structure of law that emerged in the post–Civil War era—and especially of the Fourteenth Amendment, which was its centerpiece—the role of the Federal Government as a guarantor of basic federal rights against state power was clearly established. (*Mitchum* v. *Foster*)

These changes profoundly altered the federal system, establishing national primacy over the states and making possible the eventual success of black people and others in realizing the egalitarian potential inherent in the Reconstruction amendments. But before that occurred, the Supreme Court diverted the revolutionary changes of the Reconstruction era in an altogether different direction.

Chapter 5

"To pass the line which circumscribes the judicial department"

THE FORMALIST ERA, 1873–1937

AMERICAN constitutional law was transformed in the last quarter of the nineteenth century, a time of legal transition comparable only to the era of the American Revolution. Justice Stephen J. Field did not exaggerate much when he declared on the occasion of the Supreme Court's centennial in 1889 that the controversies coming before the Court in the period of his tenure "exceed, in the magnitude of the property interests involved, and in the importance of the public questions presented, all cases brought within the same period before any court of Christendom" (quoted in Charles W. McCurdy, "Justice Field and the Jurisprudence of Government-Business Relations: Some Parameters of Laissez-Faire Constitutionalism, 1863–1897," *Journal of American History* 61 [1975]: 970–1005). The Court met the challenge posed by these cases by developing a comprehensive ideological approach to judging that has been called "classical legal thought."

Legal ideology takes on meaning only in its social context. It is therefore necessary to survey the social and economic backdrop of law-making in the late nineteenth century. Americans lived through an economic revolution they could scarcely grasp. Industrial and finance capitalism transformed the face of America. The factory system made production more efficient and bountiful, while at the same time it made work itself repetitious, mind-numbing, and brutal. Inventions, advances in metallurgy, and the external-combustion engine brought the industrial revolution to the remotest parts of rural America. The shift in energy use from solar-based sources (wood and falling water) to fossil fuels promised a new America in which coal, not cotton, was king. This new energetic order held out the long-run promise of liberating humankind from its biblical fate of sweated labor, but in the short run it created a labor regime almost as coercive as plantation slavery.

The physical impact of industrial capitalism was readily apparent; its financial and managerial dimensions were not, though their effects were as far-reaching. Whole industries became cartelized. Investors and executives, led by John D. Rockefeller of Standard Oil, devised new forms of vertical and horizontal integration. Technological innovations such as the factory system, coal-generated steam power, and industrial chemistry required massive accumulations of capital if they were to be exploited. The partnership and traditional stock corporation were no longer adequate to this task, so lawyers and financiers experimented with investment pools and trusts, while state governments tried to retain some regulatory control over them. When state courts foiled mergers by applying the old corporate legal doctrine of ultra vires, financiers turned to lobbying the legislatures. They were rewarded when New Jersey in 1889 enacted legislation enabling one corporation to own stock in another. This one statute, so simple in retrospect, weakened all state antitrust efforts. (Lincoln Steffens denounced New Jersey as "the traitor state.") American constitutional law now faced a quandary: how could the states exercise any regulatory control over corporate entities that were becoming larger and more powerful than they?

States were not the only entities overawed by corporate giantism. Organized labor was another. If finance and management could combine, reasoned labor leaders, why should not workers also? Management abhorred countervailing centers of power, though. Since the beginning of the nineteenth century, employers had thwarted labor organization by prosecutions for the common law crime of conspiracy. Chief Justice Lemuel Shaw's path-breaking 1842 decision, *Commonwealth* v. *Hunt,* holding concerted refusal to work not to be a criminal conspiracy per se, robbed this weapon of much of its clout, so employers sought other union-busting devices with the same ingenuity they had used to get around state antitrust regulation. They found it in the labor injunction, a potent means of criminalizing union activity.

Some American institutions were beginning to undergo crises of legitimacy. Capitalism at the time rested on assumptions derived from classical economic thought. One of the received texts of classical economics was Adam Smith's *The Wealth of Nations* (1776), with its powerful metaphor of an invisible hand guiding society to greater general welfare through the pursuit of individual self-interest. This structure of thought, as well as the capitalist order it sustained, came under sustained criticism. The nineteenth century was marked by recurrent economic depressions—in 1819, 1837, 1873, and 1893. These business cycles in which government's only role was to stand aloof belied any notion of uninterrupted economic improvement. Poverty in America was more visible than ever, especially in squalid city slums. It was apparent among the new immigrants who formed such a distinctive part of their populations. Henry George captured the sense of bewilderment felt by many in his best-selling *Progress and Poverty* (1879), demonstrating the paradox of increasing material well-being accompanied by pauperization among the working classes.

A different sort of attack on legitimacy confronted American lawmaking institutions, particularly courts and administrative agencies. Criticism of federal judges had been muted after *Dred Scott,* but it had never disappeared. It was ready to flare again when judges seemed to take on policymaking roles. Courts, however, at least had the advantage of being constitutionally sanctioned; administrative agencies were another matter. Their spread after the Civil War seemed to undermine the principle of the separation of powers. Both courts and bureaucracies thus shared a similar problem: how to legitimate their decision-making powers in a republic, since neither was chosen by the people or directly accountable to them? This problem became increasingly urgent as Americans perceived that the managerial, bureaucratic, regulatory state was essential and becoming daily more powerful.

To cope with this turbulent environment, judges had at hand only outmoded structures of thought. In retrospect, their principal innovations, substantive due process and liberty of contract, appear to be belated efforts to shore up the moribund system of classical liberal economics at a time when that system had become obsolete. To them, however, what they called legal science was timeless, classical in its harmony, balance, and logic. The judges' methodological base was an approach to law that we call formalism, a way of doing law that was more a method than a coherent philosophy. It affected all realms of thought, but in law it provided an all-embracing approach to adjudication. Its roots can be traced to the early nineteenth century, and specifically to John Marshall's separation of law from politics.

Because it was above politics, the law was thought to be neutral and autonomous. It was radically different from the temporary expression of majority will conveyed through political organs. Blackstone's idea lingered on: all law had to be compatible with divine or natural law. Superimposed was the tradition Joseph Story expounded, that law was a science. As such, it consisted of a body of principles that could be discovered inductively by the use of reason. These principles could be identified, collected, and systematized from the common law reports, with misstatements weeded out, misapplications condemned. Abolitionist legal thought contributed the concept of individual jural equality: all persons are equal before the law, and consequently none may be subjected to different treatment merely because some majority wants to do so.

The synthetic achievement of formalism did not in itself constitute a body of law, a school of jurisprudence, or a philosophy. Rather, it remained just an approach, or a set of attitudes. Nevertheless jurists sought to apply it systematically as the most promising means of achieving justice in courts. Judges sought to remove from each case all appeals to emotion (prejudice, bias, sympathy) in order that judging might be based not on extrarational impulse, which was capricious, but rather on reason, which was subject to control and the restraints of criticism. Law had to be indifferent to politics, and specifically to the transient and irrational will of majorities, because judges had to uphold the Constitution as supreme law against political demagogues and opportunists. Were it otherwise, law would be reduced to politics, and judges would be little more than legislators. There is little to object to in this collection of principles stated at this level of generality. They may seem quaint to us today, but the goals at least were laudable.

The legal historian Morton Horwitz emphasizes the distinction between public and private law in this period. Public law—that is to say, constitutional law, administrative law, and criminal law in some respects—derived from political acts, and unlike private law was subject ultimately to the will of the people. Public law could undertake the redistribution of wealth. Thus it was potentially coercive and dangerous, and had to be hedged with constitutional restraints designed to assure the autonomy of the individual against the state.

Private law, on the other hand—the law of contracts, torts, commerce, agency, and so on—was based on the exercise of private will. Thus it did not coerce individuals, nor did it redistribute wealth. All transactions and liabilities resulted from the individual's voluntary acts, and were not imposed from above by the state. Private law was essential to the functioning of a free market, as opposed to a regulated one. Regulation by definition is coercive and potentially redistributive, and hence subject to the constraints imposed by constitutional limitations. This private-public distinction, which is specious to our generation, seemed fundamental and compelling a century ago.

The restrictions on public law, derived from the Bill of Rights, constituted the heritage of Anglo-American liberty. Judges felt it their duty to police the doings of public law with a sharp eye, vigilant to catch the state overstepping the limits of its power. In this function, a formalist mentality proved indispensable. Judges saw themselves as mediators between political majorities and individuals and as required always to strike a balance between according the state the powers necessary to govern and protecting the liberties of the individual in the private law realm, free of the coercive and redistributive hand of state power.

Modern constitutional scholarship, tutored by Progressivism and legal realism, has made much of the laissez-faire economic dogmas of the formalist judges. But Michael Les Benedict, a constitutional historian, has recently restored the ideological and ethical component of the formalist outlook, deriving it not from Adam Smith and Herbert Spencer but rather from an old tradition of suppressing state favoritism to preserve individual liberty (Michael Les Benedict, "Laissez-Faire and Liberty: a Re-evaluation of the Meaning and Origins of Laissez-Faire Constitutionalism," *Law and History Review* 3 [1985]: 293–331). American law inherited a hostility to monopolies and governmentally sponsored special privilege, going back at least to the seventeenth century. In early America, this hostility became linked with the vested rights formula of prohibiting the government from taking the property of A and giving it to B, the tradition affirmed in *Calder* v. *Bull.* Jacksonian Democrats of the antebellum era reinvigorated the antimonopoly attitude, while their Whiggish contemporaries on the bench condemned special legislation as violating emergent conceptions of substantive due process. In the late nineteenth century, this juridical heritage produced the axiom that the power of government should not be used to advance the welfare of one interest group at the expense of another. For example, the same reasons that dictated that government not sanction cartels also required that it not sanction unions.

This perspective took on special meaning in the formalist era. Before the Civil War, the functions of both state and federal government were largely promotional and distributive. But as industrialization after the war imposed new costs on society, governments' functions became regulatory and therefore, in the eyes of conservatives, *re*distributive, something alien to the original Constitution and therefore prohibited by it. Judges and other conservative ideologues particularly condemned what they called "class legislation" or "special legislation," whereby a subsidy for one group, such as workers, was exacted by a redistributive shift of the burden and cost of government onto another, such as employees.

Benedict insists that judges did not cynically manipulate this ideological bent to cover or rationalize their solicitude for the haves in their struggle with the have-nots. Instead, they clung to a theory of government that sought to protect human liberty as its highest goal. Conservatives drew the lesson from centuries of governmental intrusion into economic affairs that liberty was most threatened when one interest group seized the powers of government to fatten itself at the expense of others. Thus laissez-faire judges saw themselves as reformers evenhandedly curbing both the rich and the poor from their propensity to use government to promote selfish and antisocial ends.

But of course we see it differently a century later. Formalism was so obviously allied with conservative social and economic bias that its pretensions to neutrality and justice seem a sham. When the formalist approach to judging produced doctrines of substantive due process and liberty of contract that sanctioned class oppression, as when these doctrines repeatedly empowered employers to suppress organized labor, we justly suspect that the formalist method was a cover for a hidden agenda.

Yet the paradox of the formalist era is that the courts were not consistent in their application of formalist method, and this lack of consistency produced obviously incompatible results. Throughout the period between the *Slaughterhouse Cases* of 1873 and the constitutional revolution of 1937, the Supreme Court developed two conflicting streams of precedent in most areas of public law. Each of these streams was identifiable as either formalist or pragmatic in its approach to judging. The inconsistency of the two streams obviously could not go on indefinitely without the law itself appearing irrational and indeterminate, two failings fatal to the rule of law. That inconsistency was resolved by the constitutional revolution that brought the formalist period to a close in 1937.

The judicial hegemony of the formalist era began with two dissents in the *Slaughterhouse Cases* (1873). As noted in the previous chapter, Justice Miller's majority opinion rejected challenges of the Thirteenth Amendment, and privileges and immunities, due process, and equal protection of the Fourteenth Amendment by white butchers to a Louisiana slaughtering monopoly. Miller's approach portended a demure role for the Court. But Justices Field and Bradley in dissent spurned Miller's timorous approach to the impact of the Reconstruction amendments. Field saw in the new privileges and immunities clause a synthesis of Jacksonian Democratic and abolitionist emphasis on the jural equality of individuals, a strange and ironic reconciliation of ideological opponents. Drawing on Justice Bushrod Washington's circuit court opinion in *Corfield* v. *Coryell* (1823) for a definition of "the fundamental rights, privileges and immunities which belong to . . . a free man and a free citizen," Field anticipated the liberty of contract doctrine when he interpreted the Fourteenth Amendment to guarantee an "equality of right, with exemption from all disparaging and partial enactments, in the lawful pursuits of life." Field's approach was subsequently validated in *Yick Wo* v. *Hopkins* in which Justice Matthews voided a racially discriminatory application of a police power ordinance otherwise valid on its face under the equal protection clause as "unjust and illegal discrimination between persons in similar circumstances," thereby ratifying the abolitionist component of the new equality doctrine.

Bradley's dissent in *Slaughterhouse* was more far-reaching. In a brief passage, he conjured up the doctrine of substantive due process out of the natural rights tradition:

> Fundamental rights . . . can only be taken away by due process of law, and can only be interfered with, or the enjoyment of which can only be modified, by lawful regulations necessary or proper for the mutual good of all. . . . This right to choose one's calling, when chosen, is a man's property and right. Liberty and property are not protected where these rights are arbitrarily assailed.

Bradley's words reflected a scarcely noticed yet fundamentally important trend: the transformation of the concept of property from tangible objects (e.g., land, wagons, horses) to intangible rights and expectations, such as the abstract right to sell one's labor or the expectation of profits. The change in the way judges thought about property was to have far-reaching effects.

More important, Bradley transformed what had previously been considered a procedural right, the right to fair and regular procedures in a criminal action, into a substantive right that permitted courts to void statutes because the judges believed that their policy or substance deprived a person of liberty or property. Procedural due process enabled courts to oversee the rules by which trials were conducted. Substantive due process, on the other hand, protected property rights from legislative impairment. Bradley and Field in their different ways spoke for the future, for a conception of law and the judges' role that would dominate the formalist era.

The gradual invasion of substantive due process concepts into American juristic thought created a tension in the development of American law between the new doctrine and the older concept of the police power. For a time, from Reconstruction through 1892, the senior doctrine held its own. The Court, led by none other than Justices Field and Bradley, often reaffirmed the states' police powers and distinguished their positions in *Slaughterhouse.* Beginning with *Paul* v. *Virginia* (1869), upholding the power of the state to regulate out-of-state insurance companies, the Court stressed the need for a vigorous state regulatory power. In *Railroad Co.* v. *Lockwood* (1873), Justice Bradley denied that a common carrier could exempt itself from ordinary tort liability by requiring a passenger to sign a release before boarding, because "the carrier and his customer do not stand on a footing of equality.'' In a case challenging a state's prohibition statute, Field insisted that the Fourteenth Amendment did not interfere with the police power of a state to regulate the use of property for purposes of protecting the health and morals of the community (*Bartemeyer* v. *Iowa,* 1873). Chief Justice Waite in the same vein sanctioned a state prohibition of lotteries against a challenge that such a ban destroyed the charter rights of a lottery corporation. ''The legislature cannot bargain away the police power of a state,'' he declared (*Stone* v. *Mississippi,* 1879).

The high-water mark of the police power came in the *Granger Cases,* principally *Munn* v. *Illinois* (1877). In *Munn,* Chief Justice Morrison R. Waite identified ''the very essence of government'' as ''the establishment of laws requiring each citizen to so conduct himself, and so use his own property, as not unnecessarily to injure another.'' From that premise, and from some old learning concerning the common callings (that is, ferries, bakers, millers, innkeepers), he concocted the doctrine of a ''business affected with a public interest.'' Such businesses, Waite held, were subject to regulation of the fees they could charge, because their proprietors had dedicated them to public service. The owner, ''in effect, grants to the public an interest in that use, and must submit to be controlled by the public for the common good.'' Waite held that the question of the reasonableness of rates was a legislative, not a judicial, issue.

Despite dissents by Field and William Strong, *Munn* stood for more than a decade as the definitive affirmation of police power doctrines. In an extraordinary 1892 case, *Illinois Central Railroad* v. *Illinois,* which involved the state's successful attempt to reclaim title to submerged lands along the Chicago lakefront, Field extended the scope of the police power by adopting the public trust doctrine. He held that the state cannot give away such lands because it holds them in trust for the people. In the same year, the Court reaffirmed *Munn* in another case involving the state's setting of maximum rates for grain elevators (*Budd* v. *New York,* 1892). But this case proved to be *Munn*'s last gasp. In *Budd,* Justices Field and Henry B. Brown joined David J. Brewer in dissent; Brewer argued that *Munn* should be overturned. ''The paternal theory of government is to me odious,'' Brewer snorted. By 1890, after substantive due process had already secured a beachhead on the Court, the balance was shifting against *Munn*'s approval of the police power.

Even opinions sustaining the police power, such as *Munn,* acknowledged that ''in mere private contracts, relating to matters in which the public has no interest, what is reasonable must be ascertained judicially.'' Eventually Justice Field's repeated condemnations of *Munn* had an effect, and ever-stronger dicta began appearing in cases of the 1870s suggesting judicially imposed limits on state police powers. The justices variously revived old natural law doctrines (*Loan Association* v. *Topeka*, 1875; *Davidson* v. *New Orleans*, 1877), voiced unease about the potential reach of the police power (*Stone* v. *Farmers Loan and Trust*, 1886; *Mugler* v. *Kansas*, 1887), and invested corporations with legal personality within the meaning of the Fourteenth Amendment (*Santa Clara County* v. *Southern Pacific Railroad*, 1886), thus extending to them the protections of due process and equal protection that the Framers had originally intended for real people.

While the new doctrines were slowly insinuating themselves in the thinking of justices of the United States Supreme Court, substantive due process met with remarkable success in the state courts. The Massachusetts Supreme Judicial Court revived vested rights doctrines in *Commonwealth* v. *Perry* (1891), holding unconstitutional a law forbidding employers from fining weavers for imperfections, while the more up-to-date substantive due process concept found enthusiastic acceptance in the highest courts of three of the nation's leading industrial states: *In re Jacobs* (New York Court of Appeals, 1885), voiding a statute prohibiting cigar making in residential tenements; *Godcharles* v. *Wigeman* (Pennsylvania Supreme Court, 1886), striking down legislation regulating tonnage rates in iron mills; and *Millett* v. *People* (Illinois Supreme Court, 1886), invalidating state regulation of weighing procedures at coal mine mouths. Even the courts of states not in the vanguard of industrialization, such as Colorado, West Virginia, and Arkansas, found substantive due process doctrines attractive as a means of squelching reform efforts that trenched on property or management prerogatives.

The United States Supreme Court finally adopted substantive due process explicitly in an 1890 opinion by the otherwise inconspicuous Justice Samuel Blatchford. A rate regulation case provided the occasion, a fitting irony since it was rate regulation in *Munn* that ratified police powers. Minnesota created a railroad commission, gave it power to set rates, and made the commission's decisions conclusive on the courts. Holding this arrangement unconstitutional, Blatchford asserted that "the question of the reasonableness of a rate . . . , is eminently a question for judicial investigation, requiring due process of law for its determination. If the company is deprived of the power of charging reasonable rates . . . , it is deprived of the lawful use of its property, and thus, in substance and effect, of the property itself, without due process of law" (*Chicago, Milwaukee & St. Paul Railway* v. *Minnesota*, 1890, known variously as the Milwaukee Road Case or the Minnesota Rate Case). Justice Bradley dissented, correctly observing that the majority "practically overrules *Munn*."

Through the sleight of hand of judicial language, the Court segued from a procedural conception of due process, which would have required only that a person be deprived of liberty or property through established procedures impartially applied, to the radically different substantive interpretation, which consisted of two major new elements not contained in the traditional procedural notion. First, a person had liberty or property rights that were themselves secured by the due process clauses, apart from the processes by which he could be deprived of them. And second, the role of the judiciary was enhanced because its participation was mandatory; it claimed for itself the power to pass on "reasonableness," which in effect meant that it could second-guess legislative policy determinations and their implementation by administrative agencies.

The Court suggested the legislature itself might set rates in the *Budd* case of 1892, but that concession was short lived. The 1898 case of *Smyth* v. *Ames* completed the triumph of substantive due process by voiding legislative rate making that did not permit courts to pass on the reasonableness of the legislative determination. Justice Harlan found himself swept forward by the inertia of his own logic from requiring "just compensation" for the railroad into being forced to elaborate the criteria for determining "the fair value of the property" in the rate-making process. This reasoning in turn launched the Court on a half-century career of making ever-more technical judgments on such things as original costs, earnings capacity, and other such accountants' esoterica. Quasi-administrative judgments drew the Court into such perplexities that finally it gave up the endeavor altogether in 1944, sensibly relinquishing such functions to the expertise of administrative agencies (*Federal Power Commission* v. *Hope Natural Gas Co.*).

Eighteen ninety-five was an extraordinary year in the history of the Supreme Court, for it was then that no fewer than three of the major decisions of the formalist era were handed down, half of all the reactionary benchmarks of the nineties. (These 1890s opinions involved altogether six subjects of major constitutional significance. They were substantive due process, the labor injunction, federal police power, federal income tax, racial segregation, and liberty of contract.) The first, *United States* v. *E. C. Knight,* presented a cluster of related issues: the scope (if any) of the federal police power, the construction of the Sherman Antitrust Act of 1890, and the extent of Congress's power to regulate interstate commerce. Caught between an inchoate but vociferous popular demand for control of trusts and a recognition of the value or the inevitability of economic integration, Congress evaded the issue by obscure statutory language. The Sherman Act prohibited "every contract, combination in the form of trust or otherwise, or conspiracy, in restraint of trade or commerce among the several States, or with foreign nations."

This provision was much less clear than it seemed to be on a first reading. For one thing, Congress probably did not intend to outlaw absolutely every monopolistic combination, but rather only those traditionally disfavored by the common law, namely, those that resorted to unfair trade practices to control a market. Congress may also have intended the act to be limited to interstate marketing practices, though here too the statute was hardly clear.

These various obscurities came to the Court in the *Knight* case, which sought dissolution of a sugar trust that controlled over 90 percent of sugar refining in the United States. For the Court, Chief Justice Melville W. Fuller, a lifelong Democrat, reasserted his party's constitutional tradition of hostility to national regulatory power. He insisted that the police power was an "essentially exclusive" prerogative of the states, and drew on a notion known today as "dual federalism" to suggest a mutual antipathy between the states' police powers and Congress's power to regulate interstate commerce. Then he drew a distinction, wholly artificial to the modern mind but persuasive to the desiccated logic of formalism, between manufacturing and commerce. Only the latter may be regulated by Congress under the doctrine of *Gibbons* v. *Ogden;* the former remains the domain of the states. Another formalist distinction Fuller found persuasive was the distinction between direct and indirect effects on commerce; the latter were beyond Congress's regulatory reach. This distinction proved more tenacious and influential than other elements of Fuller's opinion, and retained its destructive vigor into the 1930s.

The impact of the *Knight* decision was curious. On the one hand, it did not paralyze antitrust enforcement at all, though monopolies themselves continued to multiply. The most that can be said for its short-term influence was that it deflected federal antitrust activities briefly. The Court soon sustained the Justice Department's antitrust efforts in *Addyston Pipe and Steel Co.* v. *United States* (1899) and *Northern Securities Co.* v. *United States* (1904). The decision did not inhibit Theodore Roosevelt's and William Howard Taft's comparatively vigorous trustbusting efforts. The Sherman Act soon became a lethal weapon in suppressing labor organization. Yet the formalistic logic, dual federalism approach, and the direct-indirect distinction were doctrines that beguiled the Court for more than a generation. These ideas eventually eclipsed federal police powers for a time, particularly the commerce power.

The premises of *Knight* are alien to the modern mind, but scholars have attempted to explain them as an effort to preserve to the states their traditional role of regulating corporations or as the Court's effort to try its hand at regulating the national economy in a time when the bureaucratic apparatus had not yet come into being. An overtly political explanation of the majority opinion remains persuasive, however. Chief Justice Fuller and three of his most influential colleagues—Edward D. White, Rufus W. Peckham, and Field (the last then in his dotage)—were orthodox antebellum Democrats whose conceptions of federalism had not enlarged since 1860. Fuller and Peckham, moreover, were men of meager intellectual and professional attainments, mediocrities as justices despite their influence. Allied with the doctrinaire conservative David J. Brewer, they imposed an outmoded constitutional vision on a new era. Trembling before the ghost haunting Europe, the specter of socialism, which Karl Marx had welcomed a half century earlier, troubled by memories of the communism and violence of the Paris Commune, anxious over the doctrines of syndicalism and anarchism that beset Europe, worried by the wave of assassinations on the continent, provoked into repression by labor organization and violence, these men with blindered minds concocted doctrine out of obsolete ideological systems to cope with a reality they misunderstood and feared.

The justices' formalist mentality also enabled them to legitimate racial segregation in the teeth of the equal protection clause. *Plessy* v. *Ferguson* joined the other grotesqueries of the decade in its distance from reality and in the harm caused by the imposition of thought-structures on varied economic and social relations. The Court's incapacity to make its a priori ideas conform to reality also caused harm in the field of labor relations. United States Supreme Court justices, like their brethren on the lower federal courts and the state courts, distrusted labor organization. With Justice Field, they could imagine themselves feeling sympathy for the individual worker in his struggle with powerful corporations, and they tolerated laws extending protection to workers especially subject to victimization, such as women or the male employees of hazardous enterprises. But organized labor conjured up for them only stereotypes derived from the violence that had bedeviled unions since the war. When lower courts began experimenting with labor injunctions as a means of stymieing unionization, the Supreme Court received the innovation warmly.

As *Plessy* anointed Jim Crow, so did *In re Debs* (1895) sanction the labor injunction. Growing out of the struggles of the American Railway Union with the Pullman Palace Car Company in Chicago, the case catapulted Eugene Debs into national fame, and his subsequent imprisonment led him into socialism. A lower federal court used the Sherman Antitrust Act against the union, holding it a conspiracy in restraint of trade. Justice Brewer did not disapprove of that innovative and dubious application of the statute, but he chose to uphold Debs's conviction for contempt on other grounds: the power of Congress to regulate the mails and interstate commerce. In an enthusiastically nationalistic opinion,

Brewer declared that "the strong arm of the national government may be put forth to brush away all obstructions" to commerce and the mails.

The labor injunction was a particularly sinister way to suppress working people because it trampled on their First, Sixth, and Eighth amendment rights. Typically the process would work this way: A United States attorney hostile to unions and seeking to break a strike would find a sympathetic federal judge and persuade him to issue an injunction, often in an ex parte hearing, allowing no opportunity for the union organizers to be present and object. The injunction would restrain not only violence and concerted refusal to work, but also rights of speech, press, and assembly protected by the First Amendment. The organizers would protest outside court and refuse to comply with a judicial order they rightly believed violated the Constitution. The judge who had issued the order would then find them in contempt, in a hearing that did not permit presentation of issues to a grand or petty jury, and fine and jail them. Neither the fines nor the jail sentences were mild. Thus men would be sent to prison, without a jury trial, for attempting to vindicate their constitutional rights. This outcome was precisely the virtue of the injunction to its conservative enthusiasts, since juries often proved either sympathetic to workers or at least willing to evaluate critically the overwrought claims of imminent violence pushed by employers and their legal abettors.

The last of the 1895 triad of cases, *Pollock* v. *Farmers Loan and Trust Co.*, struck down the federal income tax on grounds even more dubious than the justifications of the labor injunction. The Court had previously held that a Civil War income tax was constitutional (*Springer* v. *United States,* 1881), but that decision raised only a flimsy barrier to conservatives who feared that the modest 2 percent flat-rate tax was the camel's nose of socialism, expropriation, and class warfare. "The Act . . . is communistic in its purposes and tendencies," warned the eminent Wall Street lawyer Joseph H. Choate, and he found an echo in Justice Field's concurring opinion, in which the aged and fuddled justice brought his career to an inglorious close with an apocalyptic vision: "Where is the course of usurpation to end? The present assault upon capital is but the beginning. It will be but the steppingstone to others, larger and more sweeping, till our political contests will become a war of the poor against the rich."

The opinion for the majority of the Court by Chief Justice Fuller avoided this sort of hysteria, but it disingenuously explained away contrary precedent and artfully invented legal distinctions to hold that an income tax was a direct tax and thus, under Article I, section 9, had to be apportioned. Because apportionment was a practical impossibility, the effect of Fuller's holding was to doom the tax. He frankly avowed that his purpose was "to prevent an attack upon accumulated property by mere force of numbers." Proponents of an income tax had the last word, however, reversing *Pollock* through ratification of the Sixteenth Amendment (1913), the third time a decision of the Court had to be overturned by the people. (The previous two were the Eleventh Amendment, reversing *Chisholm* v. *Georgia,* and the Fourteenth, reversing *Dred Scott.*)

The Court completed its work of erecting a fortress of conservative judicial dogma in the 1890s when it made explicit the doctrine of liberty of contract that had been suggested in the *Slaughterhouse* dissents. The legal historian Lawrence Friedman has aptly called the nineteenth century "the golden age of the law of contract" (Lawrence M. Friedman, *A History of American Law,* 2d. ed. [New York, 1985], 275). Though he was referring primarily to private law, his remark is equally applicable to public law, beginning with Marshall's landmark opinion in *Fletcher* v. *Peck* (1810), extending through the contracts clause decisions of the antebellum courts that restricted state power, and culminating with Justice Peckham's opinion for the majority in *Allgeyer* v. *Louisiana* (1897). In that case, Peckham recast Field's and Bradley's 1873 suggestions about an individual's right to pursue a calling in the updated terms of substantive due process. Peckham asserted that the term *liberty* in the Fifth and Fourteenth amendments

> means not only the right of the citizen to be free from the mere physical restraint of his person . . ., but the term is deemed to embrace the right of the citizen to be free in the enjoyment of all his faculties; to be free to use them in all lawful ways; to live and work where he will; to earn his livelihood by any lawful calling; to pursue any livelihood or avocation, and for that purpose to enter into all contracts [necessary to do so].

Allgeyer involved insurance contracts, but the broad and abstract generalizations chosen by Peckham soon spread to cover employment contracts. Because formalism assumed jural equality between both parties in a contractual relationship, such as two farmers haggling over the price of a horse, the liberty of contract doctrine assumed that the worker had as great a liberty to sell his labor as a corporation had to buy it. This assumption led judges to gut legislation meant to protect workers from grasping employers.

The Court's ideological and doctrinal innovations of the 1890s were ratified in the case that has given its name to the era: *Lochner* v. *New York* (1905). *Lochner* has become in modern times a sort of negative touchstone. Along with *Dred Scott,* it is our foremost reference case for describing the Court's malfunctioning. Those who want to condemn judicial activism or a particular decision such as *Roe* v. *Wade* claim that the modern Court has relapsed into a *Lochner* mentality. Obviously, *Lochner* has something to say to our times.

In *Lochner,* a five-man majority, speaking through Justice Peckham, struck down a New York law limiting the hours of adult male workers to sixty. Expanding on the liberty of contract doctrine that Field and he had articulated, Peckham insisted that the police power of the state was restrained by a judicially supervised reasonableness test: All legislation and the policy behind it had to appear to a judge to be "a fair, reasonable and appropriate exercise of the police power of the State." Peckham condemned laws that tried to protect workers as "mere meddlesome interferences with the rights of the individual." "The real object and purpose" of the sixty-hour law, he concluded, "were simply to regulate the hours of labor between the master and his employees."

Such a frank substitution of the justice's political, social, and economic views for those of the people's elected representatives appalled the four dissenters. Justice Harlan, no friend of labor, objected that Peckham had ignored persuasive medical and social-scientific evidence on the dangers of long hours in the baking occupation. Holmes, on the other hand, penned a classic brief essay on the judicial function, denying that policy considerations should play any role in judging, beyond their minimal role of demonstrating that a reasonable person could make the policy decision that the legislature did. "The 14th Amendment does not enact Mr. Herbert Spencer's Social Statics," he reminded the majority. He went on:

> A constitution is not intended to embody a particular economic theory, whether of paternalism and the organic relation of the citizen to the State or of laissez faire. It is made for people of fundamentally differing views, and the accident of our finding certain opinions natural and familiar or novel and even shocking ought not to conclude our judgment upon the question whether statutes embodying them conflict with the Constitution. . . . I think that the word liberty in the 14th Amendment is perverted unless it can be said that a rational and fair man necessarily would admit that the statute proposed would infringe fundamental principles as they have been understood by the traditions of our people and our law.

It may be that *Lochner* is more important to us today than it was in its own time. Understanding this momentous decision is difficult for our generation because the case itself has become a byword, an embarrassment of the United States Supreme Court which even modern conservatives condemn. So prevalent is this odium that the case's name has the unique distinction of having been transformed into a verb. We speak of "lochnerizing" when we wish to imply that judges substitute their policy preferences for those of the legislature. In its day, it was merely one of a line of cases involving the rights of labor, and not necessarily the most widely noted or influential. The cases that involved the rights of individual and organized workers, like so many other matters of the time, divided into two inconsistent streams of precedent, with *Lochner* being the foremost of those cases that set back the cause of organized labor and that oppressed the status of working people in their dealings with employers. After *Debs* validated use of the labor injunction, the floodgates of judicial hostility toward organized labor seemed to burst open. *Loewe* v. *Lawlor* (1908; known as the *Danbury Hatters' Case*) extended the provisions of the Sherman Antitrust Act to the activities of organized labor, permitting a civil award of treble damages against striking hatworkers. That ruling was bad enough, but Chief Justice Fuller's opinion suggested that the Court was prepared to go to any lengths to suppress labor organization. Fuller's *Danbury Hatters* opinion was an inversion of his *Knight* opinion, holding that a Danbury, Connecticut, hat manufacturer was engaged in interstate commerce (though the sugar trust was not), despite the similarity of the economic activities of both firms. In place of his artificial *Knight* direct-indirect distinction, Fuller insisted that the defendants' "acts must be considered as a whole."

As if to emphasize the antilabor bias of the Court, in *Adair* v. *United States* (1908) Justice Harlan voided federal legislation prohibiting yellow-dog contracts imposed by railroads. (Yellow-dog contracts were hiring agreements specifying that the employee could be fired for joining or organizing a union). Harlan struck at the law from two salients. First, he held that it violated liberty of contract doctrines derived from the due process clause of the Fifth Amendment; liberty of contract had till then been derived only from the Fourteenth Amendment. Second, Harlan held the statute beyond the range of Congress's commerce clause powers because its content lacked "some real or substantial relation to or connection with the commerce regulated," another artificial test worthy of the *Knight* case.

Seven years later, in *Coppage* v. *Kansas* (1915), the Court applied the liberty of contract reasoning of *Adair* to void comparable state yellow-dog legislation, thus creating a no man's land that neither federal nor state government regulatory power could reach. The problem of the regulatory no man's land was bound to recur as long as the Court continued to promulgate inconsistent lines of precedent without attempting a reconciliation or rationalization of them. Justice Mahlon Pitney, speaking for the *Coppage* majority, was not squeamish about avowing the economic outlook that underlay liberty of contract:

> No doubt, wherever the right of private property exists, there must and will be inequalities of fortune; and thus it naturally happens that parties negotiating about a contract are not equally unhampered by circumstances. [But it] is from the nature of things impossible to uphold freedom of contract and the right of private property without at the same time recognizing as legitimate those inequalities of fortune that are the necessary result of the exercise of those rights.

Of course, Pitney was correct. A regime of law organized around a fundamental right of state protection for unequal accumulations of property must concoct a doctrine of liberty of contract. Any sort of alternative approach that lacked full protection for the doctrine would be potentially redistributive. Therefore, as has been said of the comparable and contemporaneous English doctrine, "freedom of contract means the freedom of the rich to impose terms."

Yet in this era, the Court also handed down numerous decisions supporting state and federal efforts to protect workers, as if *Lochner* and *Adair* did not exist. In *Holden* v. *Hardy* (1898), the Court sustained a Utah statute limiting the hours adult males could labor in mines and smelters, on the grounds that their occupations were dangerous and thus within the regulatory capacity of the states. Then the Court went far toward drawing the teeth of the labor injunction in *Gompers* v. *United States* (1914) when it reversed the conviction of Samuel Gompers and other leaders of the American Federation of Labor for contempt of court. Holmes for the majority insisted that contempt convictions were in their nature criminal and thus subject to the usual constraints on the application of penal laws, including the statute of limitations.

Muller v. *Oregon* (1908) upheld a statute limiting the working day of women to ten hours, a result that in itself was not incredible, since *Lochner* by its terms was limited to adult males. The opinion rested firmly on sexist, eugenicist, and social Darwinist assumptions. The surprising feature was that Justice Brewer, the most formalist member of the Court at the time, accepted and thereby legitimated the "Brandeis brief." Louis Brandeis, then in private practice, argued the case as counsel for the state, and submitted a brief that relied principally on medical and social-scientific authorities rather than orthodox legal sources, thus injecting a realistic note into the formalist judging tendencies of the time. *Bunting* v. *Oregon* (1919) went far beyond *Muller* in sustaining state legislation setting maximum hours for both sexes and accepted some regulation of the touchier matter of wages by allowing the legislature to prescribe minimum overtime rates.

Though scholars throughout the twentieth century have treated the turn-of-the-century Court as being single-mindedly committed to laissez-faire values, and thus hostile to most forms of state and federal regulatory activity, the Court actually sustained most legislation coming before it. The early-twentieth-century legal historian Charles Warren, determined to refute the notion of the Court as a citadel of reaction, published several studies after World War I arguing for *The Progressiveness of the United States Supreme Court,* as he titled one of them. He observed that in 422 cases the Court handed down between 1889 and 1918 that involved the states' police powers it sustained the challenged legislation in 369 (87 percent).

The Court's willingness to accept most regulatory initiatives before World War I was demonstrated in its reaction to the emergent federal police power. Though the Democratic tradition, as expounded by Chief Justice Fuller and Justice Peckham, as well as the newer conservative Republican outlook of such justices as Waite and Brewer, condemned the very idea that the federal government had police powers in the area of domestic regulation, the concept found surprisingly ready acceptance after the turn of the century. The triumph of the idea was sudden, almost stunning. In rapid succession, the Court upheld federal power to destroy commerce in lotteries (*Champion* v. *Ames,* 1903), to tax a substance off the market (the *Oleo Case, McCray* v. *United States,* 1904), and to regulate objects moving in interstate commerce (*Swift and Co.* v. *United States,* 1905). *Swift* was notable for Justice Holmes's emphasis on the "stream of commerce." This metaphor was doubly important. It seemed to undercut, if not implicitly overrule, the direct-indirect distinction of *Knight;* and it signaled an apparent triumph of a more realistic vision of commercial reality than that of formalist dogmas. Both impressions were refuted after the war, but for a time federal police power seemed to have triumphed over the obstruction of the Fuller bloc.

Acceptance of a federal regulatory role appeared most dramatically in antitrust cases. The Court acquiesced in enforcement of the Antitrust Act in *Northern Securities Co.* v. *United States* (1904) and in *Standard Oil Co.* v. *United States* (1911). The Court in the latter case adopted a variant of the "rule of reason," consonant with President Theodore Roosevelt's attitudes toward trusts, holding that the Sherman Act was not meant to outlaw literally all combinations, but only those that unreasonably restrained trade. Congress seemingly ratified this approach by enactment of the Clayton Act in 1913, which forbade those trade practices whose effect was "to substantially lessen competition." Congress in the Clayton Act also tried to prohibit application of the Antitrust Act to labor unions, an effort frustrated by the Court in its swing back to reaction after the war.

The Court just as readily accepted major Progressive regulatory innovations: the Pure Food and Drug Act in *Hipolite Egg Co.* v. *United States*

(1911), the Mann Act (the so-called White Slave Trade Act, prohibiting transportation of females across state lines for immoral purposes) in *Hoke* v. *United States* (1913), and the Adamson Act mandating an eight-hour workday on railroads in *Wilson* v. *New* (1917). Thus it seemed by 1917 that federal regulatory power would meet with no serious obstacles in the Court. That expectation was brusquely shattered, however, in cases involving a surprising subject: child labor.

The abolition of child labor was one of the less controversial Progressive reform objectives. Few any longer promoted child labor with the enthusiasm of Alexander Hamilton a century earlier. Apologists for the notion of working children in factories confronted a powerful phalanx of influential reform interests, including organized labor. Thus, the application of federal police power to outlaw child labor ought not to have stirred up powerful opposition; the issue in some ways was akin to abolishing lotteries or prostitution, the sort of thing no one could resist with good grace. But when Congress in 1916 prohibited the interstate traffic in articles manufactured by child labor, the Court struck the statute down in *Hammer* v. *Dagenhart* (1918). Justice Day's opinion was an unexpected throwback to *Knight* and *Lochner.* He drew a *Knight*-like artificial distinction between things harmful in themselves and things inherently harmless; Congress might control the former, but not the latter. He also relied on *Knight*'s manufacturing-commerce distinction, denying Congress power to reach the production of goods before they moved in interstate commerce. He questioned Congress's motives, suggesting that Congress had no real intention to regulate commerce but merely sought to usurp a state function. Finally, Day resurrected the Tenth Amendment and dual federalism to rope off the area of child labor as being exclusively within the domain of the states.

Taken aback by this unexpected hostility to its newly sanctioned commerce regulatory power, Congress returned to the subject via taxation, levying a prohibitive tax on articles produced by child labor. The Court, now in the reactionary mood characteristic of the 1920s, struck that measure down too in *Bailey* v. *Drexel Furniture* (1922) on grounds similar to *Hammer.* Chief Justice William Howard Taft questioned Congress's motives, saying that it sought to levy a penalty, not a tax; insisted that it invaded the prerogatives of the states denied to the federal government by the Tenth Amendment; and extolled the "sovereignty of the states." In frustration, Congress resorted to its ultimate weapon, submitting a constitutional amendment giving it power to prohibit child labor, as it had done with the subject of income taxes in the Sixteenth Amendment. The amendment failed of ratification, though later public opinion polls revealed that a majority of American people mistakenly thought that it had been ratified.

The unpopularity of some of the Court's decisions between the *Income Tax Cases* of 1895 and the second *Child Labor Case* of 1922 provoked a vociferous political and popular movement to curb the Court's pretensions. Populists, socialists, and Progressives (led by the chief Bull Moose himself, Theodore Roosevelt) denounced the Court for usurping the executive prerogative of the veto. Lawyers and judges filled pages of the law reviews with scholarly critiques of judicial activism. Historians and political scientists surveyed the foundations of judicial review. Congressmen proposed bills and constitutional amendments that would have curtailed the Court's jurisdiction, required a supermajority to hold legislation unconstitutional, changed the federal bench to an elective judiciary, or permitted the recall of judges or their decisions. Two constitutional amendments of the era reversed Supreme Court precedent: the Sixteenth (the *Income Tax Cases*) and the Nineteenth (in effect reversing *Minor* v. *Happersett* [1875], which had held that the Fourteenth Amendment did not confer the right to vote on women).

Aside from the amendments, however, the only actual political response to what President William Howard Taft in 1911 called "hidebound and retrograde conservatism on the part of courts" was, paradoxically, to strengthen, rather than to curtail, the powers of the Supreme Court. The Judiciary Act of 1914 expanded the Court's appellate jurisdiction under section 25 of the 1789 Judiciary Act, and the Judiciary Act of 1925, popularly known as the "Judges' Bill," abolished appeal as of right on constitutional issues, conferring in its place broad discretionary jurisdiction under the writ of certiorari. Thus the Court, as it had done a generation earlier in Reconstruction, survived a period of popular and political criticism with its powers enhanced, not weakened.

Caution and hesitancy, rather than incoherence or contradiction, characterized the Supreme Court's reaction to the appearance of the bureaucratic administrative state. Though such decisions as the *Milwaukee Road Case* and *Smyth* v. *Ames* suggest hostility by the justices toward administrative regulation, a juster explanation may be their reserve in the face of innovation. After the Civil War, the American economy required massive amounts of governance that had not been necessary before the war. The maintenance of a transcontinental railway system, for example, required creation of private and public managerial and regulatory bureaucracies. Gasworks, traction companies, electric power companies, telegraph companies, and railroads were natural monopolies that could not be disciplined by traditional market instrumentalities.

For a time, federal courts, including the Supreme Court, served as surrogate regulatory agencies in the absence of the real thing. Mary C. Porter claims that, particularly with respect to public utilities and rate regulation, "the Court, by balancing the interests of investors and consumers, turned itself into something of a federal regulatory agency" (Mary C. Porter, "That Commerce Shall Be Free: A New Look at the Old Laissez-Faire Court," *Supreme Court Review* [1976]: 135–60). But judges were obviously unfit for this new duty, constitutional considerations aside. As experience in railroad reorganization and receivership demonstrated by the 1890s, the sheer volume of administrative minutiae and the flood of highly technical, unfamiliar, quasi-scientific details threatened to overwhelm the courts. Consequently Congress stepped in first by creation of the Interstate Commerce Commission in 1887 and later with the Federal Reserve Board and Federal Reserve banking system (1913) and the Federal Trade Commission (1914). Meanwhile, long-established executive departments, such as Agriculture and Justice, took on quasi-administrative responsibilities with respect to national forests, public lands, and trust regulation, and a wholly new department, Commerce and Labor, was created in 1903 to gather information about industrial relations and the American economy.

To the legal mind, it soon became obvious that these new regulatory bodies, plus those of the states, needed legitimation. They seemed to be a fourth branch of government in a republican structure designed for only three. They blurred the lines required in separation of powers theory by taking on functions previously performed by the legislative, executive, and judicial branches. Federal judges, who had been reminded by their critics since the early nineteenth century that they were unelected and hence suspect, were not disposed to look kindly upon this new breed of unelected and unresponsive officials who wielded governmental power over corporations and individuals.

Judges, lawyers, and administrative theorists suggested three bases for legitimating administrative agencies. First, the function of the agencies was solely allocative rather than redistributive. That is, they sought to promote economic efficiency, rather than to take A's property and give it to B. Second, they exercised their powers because authority to do so had been delegated to them by the legislative branch. They were, in effect, an arm of the legislature, performing functions that were too detailed or tedious for the legislators themselves to do, and they did so under continuous legislative oversight. Third, and most important, they exercised their powers because they were experts, who functioned as an apolitical bureaucracy.

These various legitimating theories all rested on a particular conception of the public interest. Charles Francis Adams, one of the earliest of the professional regulators, believed that the administrator's function was that of harmonizing and compromising the inconsistent desires of different interest groups. He and other turn-of-the-century administrators were hostile to coercive regulation. They thought it possible for an agency to gather enough data to formulate a persuasive conception of the public interest and to induce parties to the regulatory proceeding to conform to that vision.

The various novel ideas produced a period of confusion over administrative agencies. The Supreme Court and Congress in effect entered a dialogue extending over two decades, in which each branch tentatively and ambiguously sketched out its concept of administrative function and was corrected by the other. The subject of this dialogue was the Interstate Commerce Commission (ICC). Congress in creating it was none too clear about what it expected of the agency. Responding to this uncertainty, the Court at first denied finality to administrative fact finding, permitting federal circuit courts to review factual determinations *de novo* (*ICC* v. *Alabama Midlands Railway,* 1897). It also denied the ICC power to set railroad rates (*ICC* v. *Cincinnati, New Orleans & Texas Pacific Railway Co.,* 1897). Justice Brewer, who wrote the latter opinion, favored a laissez-faire vision of how the economy should operate, whereas the ICC and their regulatees, the railroads, preferred a cartel model, seeking legitimacy for their pooling arrangements, rate bureaus, and so on.

In the Hepburn Act of 1906, Congress ambiguously returned to the issue, bucking the question of the rate-setting authority back to the courts. The Supreme Court responded to Congress's vague hint of displeasure by accepting administrative fact finding as final in *Illinois Central Railroad* v. *ICC* (1907). Perhaps emboldened, Congress then expanded the ICC's policy-making and rate-setting functions in the Mann-Elkins Act of 1910, and the Court accepted this broadened administrative role in *ICC* v. *Illinois Central Railroad* (1910). For the moment, the matter rested but the congressional-judicial accord was overturned by the Taft Court in the 1920s, when the Court swung back to a revived laissez-faire outlook.

In a comparably tolerant frame of mind, the Court also proved hospitable to some of the major progressive reforms of the era. Conservatives had stood aghast at the Populist program embodied in the Omaha Platform of 1892, with its demands for nationalization of the railroad, telegraph, and telephone systems, confiscation of corporate landholdings, and a graduated income tax. Progressives and other reformers promoted a wide variety of other reform proposals, including the measures of direct democracy: initiative, referendum, recall of legislation, recall of elected officials and judges, and recall of judicial decisions. This last alarmed conservatives, who cheered President Taft's veto of the Arizona Enabling Bill in 1911 because the incipient state's constitution contained a provision for judicial recall. Such innovations on representative government would be "likely to subject the rights of the individual to the possible tyranny of a popular majority," Taft intoned. In this spirit, conservatives maintained that any reforms that short-circuited the representative process would be unconstitutional, as inroads on the republican nature of American government. This, in turn, suggested to them an avenue of constitutional attack on the initiative and referendum themselves, as well as on the substance of some laws enacted by those innovations in the western states.

The Supreme Court disappointed them, however, in *Pacific States Telephone and Telegraph Co.* v. *Oregon* (1912), turning aside a challenge to the constitutionality of the Oregon initiative process that had imposed a gross-receipts tax on businesses. Chief Justice White held the issue to be nonjusticiable and therefore beyond the competence of judges to resolve, because it implicated the republican guarantee clause of Article IV and was therefore a political question. As a direct result of the *Pacific States* decision, state and lower federal courts upheld nearly all items on the Progressive agenda that came before them.

"Lochnerizing," Aviam Soifer has written (unpublished manuscript study), "did not really arrive until after World War I." The Court passed through one of its most regressive phases in the 1920s, in part because of four men pilloried in the next decade by journalists as the "Four Horsemen": Willis Van Devanter, James McReynolds, Pierce Butler, and George Sutherland. They were abetted by the generally conservative Chief Justice Taft and Edward Sanford, leaving only Holmes, Brandeis, and Harlan F. Stone to speak for progressive trends in the law. But the regression also reflected a Court caught in shifting jurisprudential currents. Traditional ideas of judicial philsophy had become obsolete, and newer ones were only then being elaborated.

Jurists of the old school implicitly believed in what the legal scholar Edward White has called the "oracular theory of judging" (G. Edward White, *The American Judicial Tradition: Profiles of Leading American Judges* [New York, 1976], 149). But the day of the oracular theory had already passed, and judges laboring in its grip seemed at first out of touch, then antiquated, then reactionary, and finally obstructive. The oracular theory presupposed the existence of timeless principles of justice embodied in the United States Constitution. The judges' function was chiefly to restrain the coercive power of government in order to protect the liberty of the individual. Judges discovered and applied these principles in the suprapolitical act of judging, a process marked by reason rather than by will. Though conceding that judges were frail humans with their own political, social, and economic biases, the oracular theory insisted that those prejudices did not influence their judgments. Judges discovered law; they did not make it. Much less did they make it to suit their own class interests. The law thus discovered conformed to the fundamental principles of the Constitution.

Several decades of political and professional criticism had discredited the oracular theory but by war's end nothing had arisen to take its place. Holmes's writings off the bench, plus his opinions on the Massachusetts Supreme Judicial Court and the United States Supreme Court had so far influenced only professional opinion. Benjamin Cardozo's two influential books, written with one eye cocked toward his lay readership (*The Nature of the Judicial Process,* 1921, and *The Growth of the Law,* 1924), were only beginning to have an impact, and even at that some conservatives denounced them as heretical.

Roscoe Pound, then dean of the Harvard Law School and the most influential of the critics of the old order, criticized the oracular theory as "slot-machine jurisprudence." (What he called a slot machine was not the one-armed bandit of Nevada but rather the mechanical forerunner of today's computers.) He endorsed Holmes's dictum that "the life of the law has not been logic: it has been experience." Judges are not automatons who mechanically verify whether the text of a statute conforms to a constitutional limit. Rather, he maintained, judges made law and that law had social and economic impacts. Law was always contingent, a product of its time and place. Thus he agreed with Holmes and Cardozo that law reflected extant customs, traditions, and mores. He endorsed the pragmatist insistence that a human construct such as the law had to be judged by its results rather than by deductive and syllogistic reasoning from a priori principles. In the late 1920s, this structure of thought, which came to be called sociological jurisprudence, was followed by a set of attitudes that its proponents called legal realism, a positivist philosophy of governance that rejected the autonomy of legal principles and the predictability of judicial decision making. Abetting these jurisprudential trends was the decay of the old idea that law was a science and in its place the claim that expertise had a role in governance, to harmonize the conflicts among interest groups by suasion and by accumulating vast amounts of economic data.

Judges, always reluctant to move too far in advance of societal consensus, were caught in a difficult position. Traditional legitimating explanations of what they did as judges had broken down, but had not yet been replaced by comparably powerful and persuasive alternative ideas of the judicial function. Hence the judges' performance, from the distance of more than a half century, may seem either erratic or regressive. Perhaps it was; but we should allow them at least the recognition that the jurisprudential grounds were shifting under their feet, and they labored without validated guides to the future.

In some of its decisions, the Court of the 1920s demonstrated an openness to recent developments in government. It spurned a challenge to the Prohibition Amendment (the Eighteenth) posed by Rhode Island on states'-rights grounds (the *National Prohibition Cases,* 1920). It validated the intrusion of the federal government into postwar railroad planning and management represented by the Transportation Act of 1920, including its recapture clause that in effect forced moneymaking lines to support their poorer relations (*Railroad Commission of Wisconsin* v. *Chicago, Burlington, and Quincy Railroad,* 1922, and *Dayton-Goose Creek Railway* v. *United States,* 1924). The chief justice adopted Holmes's stream of commerce approach to questions of national commerce in sustaining the federal police power over stockyards in *Stafford* v. *Wallace* (1922).

But the general tenor of the Court's decisions was conservative, so much so that contemporaries perceived it, in Edward White's phrase, as a "citadel of reaction." Its labor decisions were the worst of a bad lot. After *Muller* and *Bunting,* a reasonable attorney might have concluded that *Lochner* had either been overruled *sub silentio* or at least was moribund. Such an attorney would have been shocked by *Adkins* v. *Children's Hospital* (1923), in which a majority of the Court struck down a minimum wage law for women. Justice George Sutherland's formalistic opinion read into the Constitution a "moral requirement" of a "just equivalence" between labor performed and wages paid. Conceding an "ethical right" to a "living wage," Sutherland nevertheless held that "the fallacy of the proposed method of attaining it is that it assumes that every employer is bound at all events to furnish it." He rejected Brandeis brief-type statistics as "only mildly persuasive." Even Chief Justice Taft, no radical, was dismayed at such notions. In dissent, he cited the inequality of woman's bargaining position, the "evils of the sweating system," and the impropriety of judges holding statutes "invalid simply because they are passed to carry out economic views which the Court believes to be unwise or unsound." But Taft's strictures could not move his fellow conservatives, and the Court continued to carry on an antilabor crusade.

Congress in the Clayton Act of 1913 had vaguely attempted to exempt organized labor from antitrust prosecutions by providing that labor was "not a commodity or article of commerce," and had flatly prohibited labor injunctions unless necessary "to prevent irreparable injury to property." The Court nullified these provisions in a series of cases that upheld use of the labor injunction to stop secondary boycotts (*Duplex Printing Press* v. *Deering*, 1921) and to halt picketing in a primary boycott (*American Steel Foundries* v. *Tri-City Central Trades Council*, 1921). For good measure, the Court also voided a state statute that prohibited injunctions against peaceful picketing (*Truax* v. *Corrigan*, 1921).

State police power fared little better in cases that did not involve labor questions. The leading case was *Wolff Packing Co.* v. *Court of Industrial Relations* (1923), which voided a Kansas statute requiring compulsory arbitration for labor disputes in certain vital industries. Taft resurrected the *Munn* conception of businesses affected with a public interest, only to restrict it to three narrow categories that rationalized such prior decisions as *Munn, Holden,* and *Muller* but choked off any possibility of future growth. The Court displayed hostility to the states' police power in striking down statutes that regulated coal-mining activities underneath residences (*Pennsylvania Coal Co.* v. *Mahon*, 1922), the weight of bread sold at retail (*Jay Burns Baking Co.* v. *Bryan*, 1924), theater ticket scalping (*Tyson & Brothers* v. *Banton*, 1927), employment agencies (*Ribnik* v. *McBride*, 1928), and ice retailing (*New State Ice Co.* v. *Liebmann*, 1932). The Court also regressed to its 1890s mentality in cases involving a new federal regulatory agency, the Federal Trade Commission, denying it power to define unfair trade practices (*FTC* v. *Gratz*, 1920) and permitting courts to revise Commission fact finding (*FTC* v. *Curtis Publishing Co.*, 1923).

Though Charles Evans Hughes, returning to the Court as chief justice to replace Taft in 1930, and Benjamin Cardozo, replacing Holmes in 1932, leavened the doctrinal inclinations of the Court somewhat, the old formalist mechanical jurisprudence of the Fuller and Taft Courts survived intact as the nation slid into the Depression. The activism and experimentation of Franklin D. Roosevelt's New Deal programs were bound to collide with the oracular approach to judging of four justices (Van Devanter, McReynolds, Butler, and Sutherland).

At first, however, state regulatory responses to the economic stresses of the depression met with a narrow 5–4 acceptance. Two decisions expressed broad themes that seemed to reaffirm the proregulation stream of precedent available to the Court. *Home Building and Loan Association* v. *Blaisdell* (1934) accepted a Minnesota statute imposing moratoria on mortgage payments. Though an emergency cannot create powers not in the Constitution, it may "furnish the occasion for an exercise of power" already there, the new chief justice wrote. He affirmed Holmes's approach to judging:

> It is no answer to say that this public need was not apprehended a century ago, or to insist that what the provision of the Constitution meant to the vision of that day it must mean to the vision of our time. If . . . it is intended to say that the great clauses of the Constitution must be confined to the interpretation which the framers . . . would have placed on them, the statement carries its own refutation.

Justice Owen Roberts, who joined the Court in the same year as Hughes, upheld price controls in *Nebbia* v. *New York* (1934), effectively overruling *Wolff Packing* while freeing *Munn* of Taft's constraints. "Neither property rights nor contract rights are absolute; . . . equally fundamental with the private right is that of the public to regulate it," he maintained.

The Court also sustained federal regulatory authority in two cases. The first, a group of related suits collectively known as the *Gold Clause Cases* (1935), upheld the government's power to void clauses in private contracts stipulating payment in specie by an exercise of the monetary powers. A year later, in *Ashwander* v. *Tennessee Valley Authority,* the Court sustained regional planning and public enterprise on the basis of the federal government's defense and commerce powers.

But beginning in the spring of 1935, the Court invalidated federal and state economic regulation in a string of decisions that brought on the constitutional crisis of 1937. A unanimous Court in *Schechter* v. *United States* (1935) held the regulatory codes authorized by the National Industrial Recovery Act of 1934 to be unconstitutional as an excessively broad delegation of legislative authority to the president and to private groups. *Schechter* was not an unreasonable or extremist opinion, and may have in fact not been regretted by the Roosevelt administration, since the NRA "Blue Eagle" regulatory bodies were not working as FDR had hoped, and the program was floundering. *United States* v. *Butler* (1936) was another matter. Striking down the Agricultural Adjustment Act, a six justice majority speaking through Roberts embraced a broad, Hamiltonian conception of the government's power to appropriate funds for the general welfare, but nevertheless voided the legislation on Tenth Amendment grounds, an ominous sign for federal regulatory power.

Butler was at least plausible, if farfetched. Two other 1936 decisions, however, went to extremes in striking at state and federal powers. *Carter* v. *Carter Coal Co.* (1936) was triply shocking. First, the Court's majority ignored that the suit was brought in violation of a federal statute and was, like the *Income Tax Cases,* also collusive, and thus beyond the Court's jurisdiction. (An 1850 precedent, *Lord* v. *Veazie,* held that federal courts may not entertain collusive or feigned suits.) Second, Justice Sutherland, who wrote the opinion, reverted to *Knight* as authority for the direct-indirect limitation on federal commerce power, a precedent most lawyers considered repudiated by this time. Finally, he ignored the severability provision in the statute (a clause that stated that if one part of the statute were to be held unconstitutional the remainder should not thereby automatically fall but should be judged on its own merits), thereby demonstrating that the justices willfully disregarded an explicit statement of Congress of its own intent. The Court in effect told Congress that it did not mean what it expressly said it meant. *Carter* was all the more revolting because it struck down a federal regulation governing coal production in the name of states' rights, after all the major coal states had appeared as amici urging that the statute be sustained.

Morehead v. *Tipaldo* (1936) was just as disturbing. The Court held unconstitutional a New York statute requiring a minimum wage for women, citing as authority *Adkins,* another precedent most thought defunct. *Carter* and *Morehead,* read together, suggested that the evil of the regulatory no man's land might now not only reappear, but be expanded to exclude all federal and state efforts to cope with the economic difficulties of the Depression.

The Court's obstruction plunged the nation into a judicial constitutional trauma. This condition, however, was not the result of the so-called court-packing crisis of 1937. Roosevelt's ill-conceived court-packing plan, by which he proposed to add a new judge to any federal court for every sitting judge who reached the age of seventy and refused to retire, was only the trigger, not the crisis itself. Rather, the grave impasse into which the nation was forced was a situation of judically imposed stasis, an immobility approaching catatonia. Five men—the Four Horsemen plus the erratic Roberts—clinging blindly to an outworn judicial outlook, denied governmental power, state and federal. Americans sensed, as FDR stated in his Fireside Chat announcing the court-packing plan, that it was not the Constitution that stood in the way of effective government at a time of national distress, but rather a twisted and insupportable interpretation of the Constitution.

Twice in its history, the Court has forced the nation into an impasse amounting to a crisis of constitutionalism, and it is instructive to compare the two situations. At the most obvious level, the *Dred Scott* Court and the Court of the Four Horsemen obstructed majoritarian political processes and prevented legitimate political majorities from having their way in the name of an abstract and obsolete judicial program that sought to shield a minority of wealth from the effects of democratic politics.

At a deeper level of analysis, though, it becomes apparent that the Courts induced the crises by their conceptions of the Constitution. Both saw it as a rigid, inflexible, and unyielding document, changeable only by the amendment process. Both insisted that the words of the document could mean only what they meant to the Framers, and that the intervening generations of experience were irrelevant to constitutional interpretation. Both imposed on the document their own reading of the text—in each instance, a forced and unnatural one—and deluded themselves into believing that their interpretation was the true meaning, identical with the Framers' intent, and embodying some supposed inherent and objective content. Both, in short, were the products of judicial hubris which feared changed and the results of republican self-government.

The 1937 impasse was resolved along lines retold many times. The Senate rejected FDR's proposal; one by one, the Four Horsemen retired; Justice Roberts veered again; and FDR got eight new appointments between 1937 and 1941. Doctrinal realignment followed, and the Court finally resolved the anomaly posed by the inconsistent lines of precedent it had been creating since the 1890s by systematically destroying one of them. Numerous decisions from 1937 through the war years sustained federal or state regulation and demolished the obstructive precedents. *West Coast Hotel Co.* v. *Parrish* (1937) overthrew *Adkins* and *Morehead* to uphold a women's minimum wage law. In an eloquent valedictory dissent, Justice Sutherland insisted that it was not he and his three brethren who had been to blame for the impasse; it was the Constitution itself. "The meaning of the Constitution does not change with the ebb and flow of economic events" was his final *cri du coeur. NLRB* v. *Jones Laughlin Steel Corp.* (1937) overruled *Schechter* and *Carter* in upholding the National Labor Relations Act, and *United States* v. *Darby* (1941) upheld the wages-and-hours provisions of the Fair Labor Standards Act. When Congress severely restricted the injunctive power of federal courts in labor disputes, the Court upheld the measure as being within Congress's power to control the jurisdiction of federal courts in *Lauf* v. *E. G. Shinner* (1938.) Thus were two generations of Court hostility to labor organization buried. *Steward Machine Co.* v. *Davis* (1937) upheld the Social Security Act. *Wickard* v. *Filburn* (1942) demonstrated how far the Court was willing to go in sustaining congressional commerce power. It upheld federal regulations that forbade a farmer to consume grain that he had grown on his own farm in the name of Congress's power to regulate interstate commerce. Such a result was possible once the *Knight* mechanical distinction of direct and indirect effects had been discarded, and a practical effect standard substituted in its place.

After World War II, the Court seemed to go out of its way to repudiate the entire structure of economic substantive due process decisions, articulating a standard of extreme deference to legislative policy decisions in economic matters. In *Lincoln Federal Labor Union* v. *Northwestern Iron & Metal Co.* (1949), Justice Hugo Black emphasized that the

"Allgeyer-Lochner-Adair-Coppage line of cases," as he called it, had been abandoned. Post–1937 decisions "leave debatable issues as respects business, economic, and social affairs to legislative decision," Justice William O. Douglas added in *Day-Brite Lighting Co.* v. *Missouri* (1952). In *Williamson* v. *Lee Optical Co.* (1955), Douglas justified the extreme deference standard, which would uphold economic legislation if the Court could imagine any conceivable reason for the legislative decision, by noting that "the day is gone when this Court uses the Due Process Clause [to] strike down state laws, regulatory of business and industrial conditions, because they may be unwise, improvident, or out of harmony with a particular school of thought." The final word on substantive due process came from Justice Black in *Ferguson* v. *Skrupa* (1963): "We refuse to sit as a 'super legislature to weigh the wisdom of legislation.' [Whether] the legislature takes for its textbook Adam Smith, Herbert Spencer, Lord Keynes or some other is no concern of ours."

Thus the formalist *Lochner* era came to an ignominious end. The Court repudiated all its premises: the Constitution embodies unchanging and unchangeable principles not affected by time and place; judges neutrally and impartially apply those principles to particular fact situations; the Constitution's meaning was fixed at the framing and cannot change over time; adjudication is a logical process uncontaminated with individual bias.

But in discarding these notions, the modern Supreme Court has discovered that it lacks plausible alternative principles that would offer the same comprehensive explanation for the justices' work. Thus the modern Court is sometimes embarrassed by lack of a credible justification for its authority, and, by one of history's ironies, stands condemned by some as being no less arbitrary than the formalist *Lochner* Court.

Chapter 6

"A government entrusted with such ample powers"

FOREIGN AFFAIRS, EXECUTIVE AUTHORITY, AND THE COURT

BEFORE World War I, the Supreme Court rarely had occasion to comment on the powers of the presidency and Congress in the conduct of foreign affairs. A few early cases involving the effect of treaties, the *Canter* case of 1825 on the territories, the *Prize Cases* of 1863, and the *Insular Cases* comprised virtually the whole body of precedent on the subject. The Great War changed all that. The Court did not again remain aloof from questions involving war and foreign policy. Suddenly, urgent problems involving separation of powers, federalism, and civil liberties came before the Court. The Court did not thwart the military or foreign policies of a popular president, and so did not itself become the focus of controversy, as it had in 1937 in the domestic sphere. But it did play an important role in policing the boundaries established by separation of powers and federalism doctrines, and it legitimated the innovations of the strong chief executives of the twentieth century.

America's involvement in World War I brought with it an unprecedented expansion of national authority. The federal government undertook a repressive campaign to stifle opposition to its policies. In response, libertarians coalesced into a sometimes effective resistance, defining the content of civil liberties and urging restraints on the new Leviathan. The growth of federal and executive authority made Lincoln's innovations, the only basis for comparison, seem modest by comparison. Yet the Supreme Court unhesitatingly ratified these radical alterations in the constitutional balance, sometimes at a serious cost to civil liberties.

The first of the wartime issues presented to the Court was the constitutionality of military conscription. In the *Selective Draft Law Cases* (1918), opponents of the draft challenged conscription on the grounds that Congress lacked power to raise armies by a draft, and that such a draft constituted the "involuntary servitude" abolished by the Thirteenth Amendment. In a prolix, nationalist opinion characteristic of his style and attitudes, Chief Justice Edward D. White brushed these objections aside, treating the Thirteenth Amendment arguments as not even worthy of refutation. The Court similarly disposed of challenges to Congress's power to enact wartime prohibition under its war powers (the *War Prohibition Cases,* 1919; *Rupert* v. *Caffey,* 1920). These cases implicitly ratified the remarkable expansions of federal regulatory power embodied in the 1917 Lever Act and related legislation, which by war's end had centralized the direction of American economic life through price and production controls.

The expansion of federal and executive power in wartime had created some problems for the civil liberties of American citizens during the Civil War, but not to the extent experienced in World War I. The era of the first Red Scare witnessed reenactment of federal sedition laws, creation of federal surveillance agencies, zealous federal prosecution of political dissidents, a comprehensive panoply of state antisubversion laws, supplemented informally by local and vigilante action against radicals and ethnic minorities. The prosecution of critics of the war and political deviants produced a spate of cases which came up on appeal to the United States Supreme Court. These cases furnished the occasion for the Court's creation of modern First Amendment law.

In *Patterson* v. *Colorado* (1907), Justice Holmes had stated that the First Amendment and comparable provisions in the state constitutions prohibited only prior restraints on publication, not subsequent criminal prosecution for the content. This ruling raised a problem never satisfactorily resolved at common law: whether a mere "bad tendency" toward social harm was enough to make a defendant criminally liable for speech, or whether a tighter "proximate cause" relationship must be proved, establishing a close linkage between word and antisocial act. Americans accepted, in theory at least, John Stuart Mill's distinction between opinions and acts, as well as his observation that even the expression of opinions might go beyond the bounds of legitimate liberty if the context of their utterance constituted "instigation to some mischievous act." These distinctions provided the basis of First Amendment law for a half century.

The problem of free speech in wartime quickly came before federal judges, first in the court of then District Judge Learned Hand in the *Masses* case (*Masses Publishing Co.* v. *Patten,* 1917). Congress in 1917 enacted the Espionage Act, a statute making it a federal offense to cause insubordination in the military services or to obstruct recruitment. Enjoining the postmaster from refusing to accept an issue of the *Masses* for mailing, Hand drew a careful distinction between legitimate "agitation" and "direct incitement to violent resistance." But he was reversed on appeal, and as he himself admitted, his views attracted little support.

Closer to the mainstream was Justice Holmes's classic formulation in *Schenck* v. *United States* (1919), another Espionage Act prosecution: "The question in every case is whether the words used are used in such circumstances and are of such a nature as to create a clear and present danger that they will bring about the substantive evils that Congress had a right to prevent. It is a question of proximity and degree." In this same opinion, though, Holmes diluted the fact-specific stringency of his newly minted clear-and-present-danger test by making the "tendency" of the act an element of the crime. He reinforced this emphasis by his unforgettable illustration: no one has a right to shout "fire!" in a crowded theater.

The antilibertarian potential of Holmes's ambiguous test was soon realized in a case coming up the same year, *Abrams* v. *United States,* under amendments to the Espionage Act known as the Sedition Act of 1918, a statute that harked back to the Sedition Act of 1798. Objecting to the conviction of Russian immigrant socialist pamphleteers for distributing leaflets protesting the Allied invasion of the Soviet Union in support of the White anti-Bolshevik forces, Holmes found himself moving into a more libertarian position. Insisting that his clear-and-present-danger test required nothing less than "the present danger of immediate evil," Holmes adopted a philosophical position derived from John Milton's *Areopagitica* and the enthusiasms of Thomas Jefferson in his more libertarian moments: "The best test of truth is the power of the thought to get itself accepted in the competition of the market."

Holmes's effort did little to stem the first Red Scare, and his brethren explicitly adopted a bad-tendency test in *Pierce* v. *United States* (1920). Yet despite affirming convictions based on the tendency-distended clear-and-present-danger test, the Court soon moved in more libertarian directions in a case involving a state sedition act, *Gitlow* v. *New York* (1925). Though upholding the conviction of an American Communist, Benjamin Gitlow, under the New York statute, Justice Edward T. Sanford offhandedly announced that the protection of the First Amendment was extended to the activities of the states, thus beginning the process of "incorporation" of the Bill of Rights as a limitation on state power. The majority upheld the constitutionality of the New York act, leading Holmes to dissent. He insisted that the state could not proscribe the substantive communication of ideas unless those ideas posed some immediate threat of a substantive evil the state has power to prevent.

Several years later, when the Court upheld a California criminal syndicalism law in *Whitney* v. *California* (1927), Justice Louis D. Brandeis penned an eloquent dissent (in form, actually a concurrence) that has become a classic of libertarian literature. "The function of speech [is] to free men from the bondage of irrational fears," he reminded his brethren in a call for courage and public virtue in protecting the freedom of political debate. In the long run, the libertarian potential of the Holmes-Brandeis clear-and-present-danger position was to prevail, but a half century and a second Red Scare intervened before the Court was able to free itself from the "bondage of irrational fears" Brandeis had cautioned about.

Another Holmes decision on executive power left a legacy to later times, but this one was mischievous. After the war, the state of Missouri mounted an anachronistic states' rights challenge to the federal treaty power, insisting that a migratory bird treaty with Canada could not supercede the state's control over wildfowl in Missouri flyways. Of course the justices spurned this conceptual throwback to pre–Civil War constitutionalism, but in doing so Holmes, writing for the Court, uttered some careless dicta on the scope of the treaty power (*Missouri* v. *Holland,* 1920). Reading the punctuation and syntax of the supremacy clause of Article VI for all they were worth, Holmes suggested that "Acts of Congress are the supreme law of the land only when made in pursuance of the Constitution, while treaties are declared to be so when made under the authority of the United States." This cryptic observation raised troubling questions: did Holmes mean to imply that the fundamental charter restrained only the statutory exercise of federal power, but not the treaty-making power? Could a treaty accomplish objectives forbidden by the Constitution?

This troubling possibility returned to haunt American policy makers after World War II. In 1954, conservative Republicans annoyed by Presidents Franklin D. Roosevelt's and Harry S Truman's conduct of foreign affairs plus conservative Democrats who feared that the United Nations Charter might invalidate racial segregation in the American South supported the Bricker Amendment, which specified that "a provision of a treaty which conflicts with this Constitution shall not be of any force or effect" and that "a treaty shall become effective as internal law in the United States only through legislation which would be valid in the absence of a treaty." This proposed constitutional amendment failed, largely because of President Dwight D. Eisenhower's opposition, but the lingering possibilities of Holmes's dicta were not dissipated until Justice Hugo Black offered the assurance that "no agreement with a foreign nation can confer power on the Congress, or on any other branch of Government, which is free from the restraints of the Constitution" (*Reid* v. *Covert,* 1957). This late dictum finally laid to rest all unresolved doubts about whether Congress might evade constitutional restraints by treaty.

If the treaty power is bounded by the Constitution, is the power of the president in the conduct of foreign affairs similarly constrained? That question has retained a perennial relevance throughout American history. It was first debated in newspaper essays by James Madison and Alexander Hamilton in connection with President George Washington's unilateral proclamation of neutrality in 1793 during the wars of the French Revolution. Madison, writing under the pen name "Helvidius," insisted that Congress ought to have a role in the decision for neutrality, in part because the powers of the president were enumerated and circumscribed by Article II. Hamilton, writing as "Pacificus," scorned that view, seeing Article II as a plenary grant of all conceivable executive power to the president, especially in the conduct of foreign affairs. "The general doctrine of our Constitution then is," wrote Hamilton, "that the executive power of the nation is vested in the President; subject only to the exceptions and qualifications, which are expressed in the instrument."

The Helvidius-Pacificus polarity reappeared several times before World War I, notably in debates over presidential power sparked by the Mexican War and the Civil War. But the extraordinary expansion of presidential authority between 1917 and 1918 presented the issue acutely. The World War I–era Court had no trouble with the expansion of federal power generally in wartime, but the more focused issue of presidential power did not reach it until 1936.

United States v. *Curtiss-Wright Export Corp.* (1936) involved the problem of the president's statutory authority, conferred by the Neutrality Acts of the 1930s, to embargo arms sales to combatants. Justice George Sutherland, who in domestic matters was eager to restrict the president's and Congress's authority, produced a Hamiltonian treatise on presidential power over foreign affairs. He affirmed "the very delicate, plenary and exclusive power of the President as the sole organ of the federal government in the field of international relations—a power which does not require as a basis for its exercise an act of Congress," but which must nevertheless operate within constitutional restrictions. Sutherland emphasized the need for secrecy in the conduct of foreign relations, requiring for the president "a degree of discretion and freedom from statutory restriction which would not be admissible were domestic affairs alone involved."

Sutherland anticipated, and to some degree legitimated, the expanded role of the presidency after World War II. The vast sweep of powers he accorded the executive office was fraught with constitutional problems, especially in the hands of a vigorous president. World War II produced an expansion of federal and executive authority against which even the experience of World War I paled by comparison. Once again, the Supreme Court did not thwart any major executive or congressional initiatives but, with one major exception, it demonstrated a greater sensitivity to problems of civil liberties the wartime accession of power posed.

After the bombing of Pearl Harbor, Congress promptly reenacted much of the World War I–era economic and security legislation, and then authorized even more extensive control of national economic life, including rationing, price and wage controls, and government regulation of production. Chastened by its recent experiences in compounding the emergency of the depression, the Court readily acquiesced in these regulatory intrusions. Symptomatic of the mood of the justices toward economic restrictions was the observation of Justice Wiley Rutledge, dissenting in a case upholding wartime price fixing. Because "war calls into play the full power of government in extreme emergency," he insisted that "citizens must surrender or forego exercising rights which in other times could not be impaired" (*Yakus* v. *United States,* 1944).

The Court monitored the infringement of civil liberties during World War II more closely than it had in World War I. In 1944, it reversed the conviction of an anti-Semitic, pro-German pamphleteer for violation of the reenacted Espionage Act by applying a stringent clear-and-present-danger test (*Hartzel* v. *United States,* 1944). The Court similarly adopted an extremely narrow conception of the meaning of the Constitution's requirement of "the same overt Act" (Article III, section 3) for a treason conviction, reversing the conviction of a German-American who had befriended German saboteurs in the United States (*Cramer* v. *United States,* 1945).

The Court did not, however, hamper the most destructive government assault on American liberty during the war, the Japanese relocation program. In 1942, the army, acting under the authority of one of FDR's executive orders, began to implement a three-step program that placated the racism, greed, and war hysteria of West Coast whites, who had long resented the economic diligence and clannishness of the Japanese-Americans who lived among them. Making no distinction between alien Japanese and the Nisei (American-born citizens of Japanese ancestry), the army asserted that all Japanese constituted a potential fifth column. It therefore first imposed a curfew on all West Coast Japanese, and then ordered their exclusion from Washington, Oregon, and California. The victims were forced to evacuate their homes and abandon their businesses, farms, and fisheries, and they were displaced to what were euphemistically called "Relocation Centers"—in reality, racial concentration camps.

The Court sanctioned this program of relocation. In *Hirabayashi* v. *United States* (1943), it sustained the constitutionality of the curfew program. (More than forty years later, the convicted petitioner, Gordon Hirabayashi, by that time a retired Canadian college professor, reopened the proceedings, alleging that the FBI had suppressed evidence in his original trial that would have proved not only his loyalty but that of the overwhelming number of Japanese-Americans. In 1986, his conviction was vacated on other grounds.) Yet Chief Justice Harlan Fiske Stone made a concession that was to have an incalculable impact a decade later. Racial discrimination was "odious to a free people whose institutions are founded upon the doctrine of equality." This concession availed the Japanese nothing at the time, but it anticipated the Court's attack on segregation in the 1950s.

Justice Hugo Black subsequently defended the exclusion order in *Korematsu* v. *United States* (1944), a strained piece of logic chopping that he and Justice William Douglas, also a member of the majority, nevertheless defended to the end of their lives. Taking care to distinguish the detention program, which he did not pass on, Black upheld Japanese exclusion as a matter of wartime necessity, justified by the possibility that some of the 40,000 Japanese nationals relocated, as well as a smaller number of the Nisei, might retain loyalties to the emperor.

Black too made a concession that was to undermine other forms of racism later. "All legal restrictions which curtail the civil rights of a single racial group are immediately suspect," and are subject to "the most rigid scrutiny." Here, however, they survived that scrutiny because of "pressing public necessity" and the Court's reluctance to second-guess military commanders in the field in a period of national crisis. Fred Korematsu, too, sought to have his conviction overturned, and in 1984 succeeded. Congress, reflecting the more sober attitudes of modern times, then considered reparations to the survivors of the relocation program, a proposal opposed by the Reagan administration, which objects to hindsight criticism of military and civilian leaders.

The Court was not wholly insensitive to the plight of Asian minorities during the war, though. On the same day it handed down *Korematsu,* it also ordered a writ of habeas corpus for a Japanese-American held at one of the detention camps on the grounds that the government could not detain a person of unquestioned loyalty (*Ex parte Endo,* 1944). After the war, in *Duncan* v. *Kahanamoku* (1946), it struck down the imposition of military government in Hawaii by the territorial governor and the army immediately after Pearl Harbor. The Court found especially offensive the military governor's imposition of military courts throughout the islands for trial of civilians and his suspension of the writ of habeas corpus.

Recent American experience with total war invites comparison with earlier periods. In the Civil War and in World War I, no responsible official suggested the suspension of constitutional guarantees of liberty during wartime. Yet both times the constitutional fabric was strained at the expense of civil liberties. The powers of the presidency expanded, with the later acquiescence of Congress. The Court did not interpose any bar to the growth of executive and federal power over the nation's economic life in World War I. After the Civil War and World War II, however, it objected to some wartime excesses. During wartime, considerations of national security restrained the Court from more active oversight, and its intervention on behalf of minorities harassed by wartime loyalty efforts, was always too late. The Court also accepted wartime imposition of what constitutional historian Herman Belz has called a "quasi-constitutional dictatorship" (Alfred H. Kelly, Winfred A. Harbison, and Herman Belz, *The American Constitution: Its Origin and Development* [New York, 1983], 571), encouraged by Congress's active participation in creating or ratifying the structure of presidential authority.

The configuration of constitutional institutions and powers that emerged after World War II was markedly different from that of the pre-1939 world. The United States found itself, or chose to place itself, in an unending state of national emergency, as one foreign policy crisis succeeded another in the Cold War era. One constitutional concomitant was federal planning and direction of the economy, symbolized by the Employment Act of 1946, with its commitment to use federal authority to achieve maximum employment, production, and purchasing power. Another consequence of the Cold War was the militarization of American foreign policy, ratified by a directive of President Harry S Truman known as "NSC 68," which committed the United States to a spiraling arms race with the Soviet Union in pursuit of containment.

Finally, a third feature of Cold War constitutionalism was the prevalence of the "national security state," a condition in which Cold War foreign and domestic policies continuously interacted. As American fears of the Soviet Union escalated after 1947, the United States created a formidable internal security apparatus of executive agencies and legislative committees in the federal government and the states, charged with finding supposed Communists and subversives. This reaction induced a witch-hunt mentality on the part of many Americans and their political leaders, in which they saw themselves beleaguered from without by a powerful, nuclear-armed foe, the U.S.S.R., and from within by its abettors, a conspiratorial web of ideologues, activists, traitorous spies, and people entertaining radical ideas on political and social problems. In this frightened new world the Supreme Court played a prominent role.

After the outbreak of war in Europe in 1939, the federal government and the states wove an extensive net of antisubversive legislation. The

Alien Registration Act of 1940, popularly known as the Smith Act, created the federal crimes of advocating the overthrow of the federal or state governments by force or violence, of organizing or knowingly belonging to groups advocating such action, or of conspiring to commit such acts. After World War II, the Truman administration put in place an investigative program that was meant to uncover "disloyal" persons in the federal service, while Congress created or continued various standing committees, such as the House Un-American Activities Committee, the Senate Investigating Subcommittee, and the Senate Internal Security Subcommittee.

The Internal Security Act of 1950, otherwise known as the McCarran Act, required registration of so-called Communist-front groups, created a Subversive Activities Control Board, and authorized the maintenance of concentration camps for the detention of potential saboteurs in periods of what the act called an "internal security emergency." (The SACB and the camps were dismantled some twenty years afterward.) The Communist Control Act of 1954 came close to outlawing the Communist party. All these federal measures were backed by a complementary array of state antisubversive statutes, some of them holdovers from World War I, and by legislative or executive investigative activities that paralleled the exploits of Joseph McCarthy and HUAC.

Between 1950 and 1959, a divided United States Supreme Court confronted these measures in a predominantly conservative mood, emphasizing the values of judicial restraint, respect for legislative policy judgment and the exercise of the states' police power, and the need for balancing individual liberties against the supposed requirements of national security. The Court's majority was hostile to any notion of an absolute First Amendment protection for the rights of speech, press, and association, stressing instead the countervailing need of the state to preserve itself in an era of international tension. It displayed these attitudes most clearly in the appeals of the first round of Smith Act convictions, *Dennis* v. *United States* (1951).

The principal leaders of the American Communist party were convicted of violation of the Smith Act's conspiracy provisions in a trial heavy-handedly presided over by United States District Court Judge Harold Medina. They appealed their conviction to the United States Court of Appeals for the Second Circuit. In a 1950 opinion, *Dennis* v. *United States,* Judge Learned Hand affirmed. Hand still preferred his 1917 test as a criterion for persecutions for speech, and considered Holmes's *Schenck* formulation inferior. But in his *Dennis* opinion he undertook to restate the clear-and-present-danger test in terms suitable to his perception of the situation of the United States in the Cold War world.

The result was a basic reformulation of the Holmes formula: "In each case [judges] must ask whether the gravity of the 'evil,' discounted by its improbability, justifies such invasion of free speech as is necessary to avoid the danger." This formula decisively altered the old test, shifting its emphasis from timeliness and tight causal connection to the seriousness of the substantive evil that the government feared. The qualification "discounted by its improbability" proved a feeble counterweight to the sanction Hand's formulation gave to those panicked by bugaboos. Under the Hand gravity-of-the-evil test, if the feared consequences are serious enough—and nothing could be more serious than the destruction of the United States government—the improbability of their occurrence can do little to deter those who would suppress speech.

In the Supreme Court, a 6–2 majority, speaking through Chief Justice Fred Vinson, affirmed the convictions and explicitly endorsed Hand's test. With a mixture of fear and impatience, Vinson reminded libertarians that the United States confronted a real and serious conspiracy linked to a foreign enemy. Thus the First Amendment protection of speech confers "not an unlimited, unqualified right." Rather, the "societal value of speech must, on occasion, be subordinated to other values"—in this case, national survival. In a sense, the Court had now come full circle, back to the practical and antilibertarian application of the clear-and-present-danger test as it was originally formulated by Holmes in *Schenck*. The Court had clearly drifted away from Holmes's sobered second thoughts in the *Abrams* dissent and the passion of Brandeis's call for courage and self-confidence in the *Whitney* dissent. This nervous approach set the tone for the next half-dozen years.

Throughout the McCarthy period, the Court remained hospitable to federal and state attempts to suppress radical ideas and political activities. Even before *Dennis,* it had adopted an expansive view of the federal commerce regulatory power to uphold the anti-Communist oath requirements imposed on union officers by the Taft-Hartley Act of 1948 (*American Communications Association* v. *Douds,* 1950). Thereafter, the Court's conservative majority upheld state loyalty procedures, including loyalty oaths and firings of public sector employees who had refused to testify concerning their political beliefs or associations. In *Adler* v. *Board of Education* (1952), for example, the Court sustained New York's World War I–era Feinberg Law, which made membership in subversive organizations a disqualification for holding a position as a school teacher. So long as the state statute could be construed to prohibit only knowing membership in organizations espousing the doctrine of overthrow of existing government by force and violence, the Court sustained such an exercise of the police power.

Such tolerance for state and federal subversive hunting evaporated suddenly in 1956, and thereafter the Court dismantled its doctrines that supported the security apparatus of the Cold War. Several decisions shocked conservatives. The Court voided a state prosecution of a prominent Communist, Steve Nelson, for sedition against the United States on the grounds that federal law had preempted that field, leaving no room for independent operation of state law (*Pennsylvania* v. *Nelson,* 1956). In the same year, it confirmed a national revulsion at the government's use of perjured witnesses by vacating a registration order made by the Subversive Activities Control Board on the basis of testimony by Harvey Matusow, a confessed perjurer (*Communist Party* v. *SACB,* 1956). In 1957, to the consternation of McCarthyites, Justice Harlan voided the conviction of several Communist party leaders in *Yates* v. *United States* on the grounds that they could be punished only for advocacy of action, not advocacy of doctrine. This opinion was a significant modification of the *Dennis* gravity-of-the-evil test, in the direction of imposing a more stringent burden on the prosecution, and thus made Smith Act prosecutions of Communists more difficult.

Then in 1957 Chief Justice Earl Warren chastised the House Un-American Activities Committee in *Watkins* v. *United States,* damning congressional investigations for exposure's sake. In a related case, *Sweezy* v. *New Hampshire* (1957), the Court similarly condemned an investigation by state Attorney General Louis Wyman into the political beliefs of a leftist economist on a visiting appointment at the University of New Hampshire, on the grounds that the investigation intruded on the appellant's First Amendment rights. Elated liberals saw in these 1957 decisions the imminent demise of the entire investigative apparatus of McCarthyism. Outraged conservatives responded by introducing several bills in Congress that would in effect reverse the *Nelson* and *Watkins* results by curtailing the jurisdiction of the Court. But like earlier jurisdictional-limitation efforts, all but one failed, owing in some measure to a widespread conviction that the Court was too important an institution to be hobbled by political reactions to politically controversial decisions. The one statute that was enacted, the so-called Jencks Bill, actually improved procedures for challenging government witnesses.

In 1959, the Court momentarily retreated from its offensive against Cold War internal security intrusions. Liberals, hoping that the icy tone of the *Watkins* majority opinion portended a finding that HUAC itself was unconstitutional, or less expansively, that the First Amendment might inhibit HUAC's investigations, were disappointed by *Barenblatt* v. *United States* (1959). In that case Justice John M. Harlan upheld a contempt citation by the committee on the grounds that its activities were an exercise of "the ultimate right of self-preservation." But this holding proved to be only a temporary blip in the Court's otherwise consistent hostility to the domestic repercussions of the Cold War. The Court condemned the use of "faceless informers" in legislative investigations (*Greene* v. *McElroy*, 1959); hinted at, and then confirmed, a new constitutionally protected right to travel abroad in voiding the State Department's denial of a passport to leftists (*Kent* v. *Dulles*, 1958; *Aptheker* v. *Secretary of State*, 1964); and overruled the *Adler* decision and struck down the Feinberg Law in *Keyishian* v. *Board of Regents* (1967).

The culmination of this libertarian line of decisions came in *Brandenburg* v. *Ohio* (1969). The Court in a per curiam opinion voided a World War I–era state criminal syndicalism statute, confirmed Justice Harlan's advocacy-of-action test in *Yates*, and, overruling *Whitney* v. *California* (1927), endorsed the eloquently libertarian dissent of Brandeis. Justice Douglas concurred, objecting to any advocacy test at all and insisting that the line be shifted to the distinction "between ideas and overt acts." He wrote, using a phrase later widely quoted, that only "where speech is brigaded with action" can the state step in to inhibit political activity. He flatly condemned the clear-and-present-danger test as an unconstitutional incursion on rights secured by the First Amendment, taking a swipe along the way at "judges so wedded to the status quo that critical analysis made them nervous."

Brandenburg capped a trend that characterized the Warren Court in cases involving political expression. Moving steadily away from the retrogressive *Dennis* content-oriented approach toward First Amendment issues, the Court in the Warren years steadily expanded the scope of an individual's ability to engage in political activity. In 1974 the Court announced a First Amendment–based right of political association in *Communist Party of Indiana* v. *Whitcomb*. Though not going so far as Justice Douglas had demanded in *Brandenburg*, by endorsing his ideas-action distinction, the Court made it impossible for either federal or state governments to punish an individual for political activities or associations that did not involve actions that the government had power to prohibit. In this state of things, the Holmes *Abrams* and Brandeis *Whitney* dissents have the last word—for now.

The second Red Scare faded to a poisoned memory as the Cold War abated. But the constitutional problems arising from America's foreign involvements and from the consequent growth of presidential power have not diminished in recent years. If anything, the Supreme Court is called upon more frequently than in other peacetime periods to mediate constitutional conflicts, but with this difference: whereas the constitutional issues of the Red Scare periods involved principally cases of personal liberty, the recent cases deal chiefly with separation of powers questions, and only secondarily with civil liberties.

The Court's second major confrontation with Cold War constitutional issues came in the steel seizure case, *Youngstown Sheet and Tube Co.* v. *Sawyer* (1952), a suit establishing some limits to war-induced hypertrophy of executive power. In April 1952, while the Korean War was still in a phase of stalemate, President Truman forestalled a steel strike by ordering the secretary of commerce to seize affected steel mills and run them under national authority. He cited no specific authority for his act except that accorded him as commander in chief by the Constitution.

A divided (6–3) Court held that his actions were unconstitutional. Justice Black, in a brief majority opinion, stressed separation of powers and concluded that Truman had intruded on Congress's domain. He rejected the administration's argument of an inherent, Hamiltonian executive prerogative that justified a president's assumption of legislative powers.

Justice Robert H. Jackson's concurrence has proved more influential in the generation since, because he suggested three models of president-Congress interaction the Court might find itself mediating. In the first, in which the president acts pursuant to explicit congressional authorization, his powers are at their maximum. In the second, in which Congress has not spoken, the president's powers are in what Jackson called "a zone of twilight," and executive and legislative powers are concurrent and of uncertain scope. Finally, in the third situation, in which the president acts in defiance of Congress's expressed policy, "his power is at its lowest ebb, for then he can rely only upon his own constitutional powers minus any constitutional powers of Congress." Jackson's formula has proved to be a flexible outline for thought on the problem, not automatically foreclosing or ratifying any particular action but rather injecting a sense of elastic, inherent limits on presidential authority. Jackson did, however, remind Truman and his successors that "men have discovered no technique for long preserving free government except that the Executive be under the law, and that the law be made by parliamentary deliberations."

Tocqueville's insight, that Americans eventually convert their political disputes into judicial ones, retained its validity in the 1960s and 1970s. Many Americans sought a judicial resolution of the constitutional questions raised by America's involvement in Vietnam. They asked the courts to address two issues. First, did the actions of Presidents Eisenhower through Nixon committing American forces to the escalating Southeast Asian war exceed the range of the president's powers under the Constitution? Concomitantly, was America's participation in the Vietnam War unconstitutional because Congress had not declared war? Second, did

American involvement violate some restrictions of international law, or, conversely, was it sanctioned by various treaty obligations?

Lower federal courts generally avoided these questions, finding them to be nonjusticiable because they presented political questions that the Constitution left to be resolved by other branches of government, not the courts. In those few cases in which lower federal courts held the issues justiciable, they found against the petitioners on the merits (e.g., *Orlando* v. *Laird,* U.S. Court of Appeals for the Second Circuit, 1971). The United States Supreme Court steadfastly refused to review these decisions. Because denial of certiorari or refusal of leave to file a petition is wholly discretionary, the Court did not have to assign reasons for its decision not to hear argument, and it never did. Implicitly, however, the Court seemed to endorse the positions of some lower courts that either the presidents' actions were constitutional or that no court could sensibly deal with the question because of the magnitude and delicacy of foreign policy issues involved (*Massachusetts* v. *Laird,* 1970; *Holtzman* v. *Schlesinger,* 1973). Commentators as well as lower federal judges assumed that its unstated reason drew on the doctrine of political questions, a topic of renewed relevance after the 1962 decision in the first reapportionment case, *Baker* v. *Carr.*

Richard M. Nixon was single-handedly responsible for generating more constitutional disputation than any other president, including Jefferson, Lincoln, and the first Johnson. His disdain for cooperation with Congress and for the restraints of the rule of law, together with his confusion of the powers of his office with sovereignty, assured that his administration would be unusually productive of constitutional litigation. Thus one of the useful legacies of his five years in office was a body of law limning the powers of the presidency.

In *United States* v. *United States District Court for the Eastern District of Michigan* (1972), the Court was confronted with a characteristic attempt by the Nixon administration to operate free of the constraints of law. The Justice Department had conducted extensive wiretapping against American political dissidents in the United States. In a criminal prosecution of several of these dissidents, the defendants demanded that the government disgorge evidence produced by such warrantless surveillance. The United States Attorney General, John Mitchell, declined, asserting that such disclosure would be prejudicial to the "national interest." The trial court nevertheless ordered disclosure, and was sustained by the United States Supreme Court. Justice Lewis Powell framed the issue in terms of a need to balance the right of individuals to enjoy the liberties assured by the Fourth Amendment's guarantee against unreasonable searches and seizures as against the government's need and duty to protect "the domestic security." From this perspective, it then rejected all the government's arguments against the requirement of judicial authorization for a wiretap. But the Court emphasized that the considerations involved in such a case were different from warrantless wiretapping of foreign nationals, surveillance conducted outside the United States, and surveillance used in the conduct of foreign affairs. In such cases, Fourth Amendment requirements might not constrain the government, at least not so strictly.

This setback proved trivial, though, compared with the administration's troubles during the impeachment efforts against Nixon. The bundle of crimes and improprieties known as Watergate disclosed innumerable instances of the administration's determination to evade or violate the laws. These culminated in the confrontation of *United States* v. *Nixon* (1974), caused by President Nixon's refusal to turn the Watergate tapes over to Special Prosecutor Leon Jaworski. Nixon resisted on three grounds (1) He claimed the president is not amenable to ordinary judicial process; the extraordinary process of impeachment was the only procedure constitutionally available to subject his conduct to formal scrutiny; (2) he asserted executive privilege for the tapes, and further argued that the scope and validity of that claim were nonjusticiable; and (3) even if the two preceding issues were decided adversely to him, he maintained that the tapes nevertheless were within the zone of executive privilege.

Chief Justice Warren Burger, a Nixon appointee, held against the president on each of these issues and ordered production of the tapes, a move that assured Nixon's downfall and resignation from office. Basing his position on the bedrock of *Marbury* v. *Madison,* the chief justice insisted that it is the province of the Court to determine the law. He therefore rejected the nonjusticiability argument, insisting that the Court must retain its authority to moderate clashes among the branches of government. Though he emphasized the deference to be accorded the president's claim of confidentiality, Burger nevertheless rejected Nixon's demand for absolute immunity and held him amenable to ordinary judicial process, especially in a case, as in the Watergate tapes litigation, in which that process was an incident of a criminal prosecution. Burger relied on "our historic commitment to the rule of law" as overriding the conflicting claims of executive confidentiality. Nixon's pretensions to what his critics called "the imperial presidency" were shattered.

The outcome of the Nixon cases was influenced by his antagonism to Congress and his consequent defiance of legislative restraints. In cases in which later presidents operated within statutory limits, respectful of congressional authority, the Court proved to be much more sympathetic to presidential power. In *Dames & Moore* v. *Regan* (1981), it upheld presidential nullification of the attachment of Iranian assets as part of the resolution of the Iranian hostage crisis because the president's acts conformed to authorizing legislation and Congress had acquiesced in his actions. The Court went further in *Immigration and Naturalization Service* v. *Chadha* (1984), holding the legislative veto unconstitutional as a violation of the separation of powers because Congress intruded on the province of the executive branch.

It is an iron rule of American historical development that foreign policy crises increase the powers of the presidency. The United States will surely never return to the more peaceful era before 1940 when the national agenda was not dominated by endless foreign policy crises, real or manufactured. Thus we can expect to witness an unending tendency for the presidency to push its growth to the outer bounds of constitutional authority. And just as surely, we can expect to see challenges to that growth. Being the legalistic people that Tocqueville identified, Americans will continue to demand that the Supreme Court supervise the presidency's growth.

Recent experience suggests some broad outlines of the Court's likely response to that challenge. We have left behind us forever, like the Garden of Eden, the simpler world of republican virtue the eighteenth-century Framers tried to secure. Thus it sounds naive and futile to demand that the modern presidency function within the budgetary and informational constraints Madison and Jefferson envisioned for it. Yet their goals still remain compelling. They feared an unrestrained executive, aggrandizing power either because Congress proved too supine to resist or because some foreign or domestic crisis seemed to call for the man on horseback. Modern chief executives aggrandize power in ways the Framers could not foresee. But the challenge the Framers confronted remains with us still. The growth and exercise of presidential power threaten individual freedom and the rule of law. Whether the Courts in the third century of our national life under the Constitution will be able to restrain the presidency as effectively as they did in the second century will determine the future of constitutionalism in America.

Chapter 7

"A superior, paramount law"

SUBSTANTIVE EQUAL PROTECTION

SINCE THE constitutional revolution of 1937, American public law has been dominated by a paradigm that first appeared in a 1938 case of no importance, *United States* v. *Carolene Products.* It was tucked away in a footnote that merely qualified a statement in the text of the opinion. Two-thirds of the note was originally drafted not by Justice Harlan Fiske Stone, the author of the opinion, but by his law clerk, Louis Lusky, a young lawyer fresh out of Columbia Law School. *Carolene Products'* footnote 4 contained concepts that have dominated constitutional development for the past half century.

Justice Stone first restated an idea he thought his brethren did not fully appreciate. Judges should be less willing to presume a statute constitutional if it "appears on its face to be within a specific prohibition of the Constitution." To this idea, he added two more categories of constitutionally suspect statutes: laws "which restrict those political processes which can ordinarily be expected to bring about repeal of undesirable legislation"; and "statutes directed at particular religious, . . . national, . . . or racial minorities." The second category was actually just a particularized application of the first. "Prejudice against discrete and insular minorities" was constitutionally proscribed because it tended to "curtail the operation of those political processes ordinarily to be relied upon to protect minorities."

Stone later characterized the formula of footnote 4 in a slogan others have endorsed: the Bill of Rights, especially the First Amendment, identifies certain liberties as occupying a "preferred position" (*Jones* v. *Opelika,* 1942, dissent), often called the "constitutional double standard." The values it elevates are called "preferred freedoms." The Court quickly accepted this new orientation. Four judges—Douglas, Black,

Wiley Rutledge, and Frank Murphy—enthusiastically promoted the idea of preferred freedoms, whereas Felix Frankfurter doggedly and unsuccessfully assailed it.

The preferred position doctrine shifted judicial concern from the value of liberty to that of equality. Liberty, in this context, connotes an individual's exemption from the regulatory authority of government. The equality ideal connotes the equal status and opportunity of all people in a governmental system that has power to enforce public policy made by a majority. After World War II, Justice Robert Jackson began to explore the implications of this incipient shift in his concurrence in *Railway Express Agency* v. *New York* (1949). He argued that the Court should be slow to invalidate legislation on due process grounds, because such a decision has the effect of removing the subject matter from any governmental control at all. By contrast, when the Court voids a law on equal protection grounds, it does not prohibit all regulation, but merely requires that any regulation the government chooses to impose must fall impartially on everyone. In Jackson's interpretation of the liberty-to-equality shift, the relationship between Court and legislature would be modified in a major way. No longer would the Court exercise a judicial veto, or function as a third house of the legislature. Instead, judicial review would now merely send the legislature back to the drawing boards to extend the scope of its handiwork.

The *Carolene Products'* paradigm and its implicit equal protection agenda have guided the work of the Court for the past fifty years. Despite Frankfurter's strenuous objections, the Court has observed the double standard consistently, providing only the most minimal review of laws that infringe or control property interests, while subjecting laws that fall within one of the three *Carolene Products'* categories to a heightened and usually fatal scrutiny. The most prolific of those categories was the Stone/Lusky reference to "discrete and insular minorities," which turned judicial attention to the long-dormant equal protection clause and produced a body of law some scholars have termed substantive equal protection.

Before World War II, the equal protection clause had been almost a dead letter in the Constitution. Justice Holmes suggested its insignificance in his sneering remark that reliance on the clause was "the usual last resort of constitutional arguments" (*Buck* v. *Bell,* 1927). The reasons for the clause's shriveled scope go back to Justice Miller's *Slaughterhouse* dictum stating that the only laws affected by the clause were those "directed by way of discrimination against the negroes as a class, or on account of their race." For a time, the Court struck down explicitly race-discriminatory legislation (*Strauder* v. *West Virginia,* 1880), as well as facially nondiscriminatory laws applied "with an evil eye and an unequal hand" (*Yick Wo* v. *Hopkins,* 1886). But *Plessy* destroyed even this limited concession to the ideals of the Framers by its formalistic approach to racial discrimination, and the equal protection clause thereafter languished.

The modern era of substantive equal protection began with frontal and flanking attacks on the separate-but-equal doctrine by the National Association for the Advancement of Colored People. The head-on assault, which sought to have the Court repudiate separate but equal and overrule *Plessy,* constituted a high-risk gamble for Thurgood Marshall and other NAACP strategists. It was not at all evident in the early 1950s that equal protection was an idea whose time had come, and if the gamble failed, *Plessy* might be reaffirmed, perhaps forever, as an element of American constitutional law. The flanking attack demanded that, if southern states cling to *Plessy,* the separate facilities must be truly equal. But this would be a frustratingly slow and piecemeal process, inviting evasion and procrastination stretching into infinity. So despite the dangers posed by the frontal strategy, the NAACP resolved to attack state-mandated racial segregation directly.

The NAACP was vindicated in *Brown* v. *Board of Education* (1954), one of the most significant decisions in the history of the Court. Only a generation after it was handed down, *Brown* seems like an elemental force in American constitutional law, something so essential that the Constitution was unfinished before 1954. After *Brown,* American constitutional law could never again be the same. *Brown* opened doors that could never be shut, not just for black Americans but for all who saw themselves the victims of inequality and discrimination. It also implied a new role for the Supreme Court and other federal courts, a role that has been called "judicial legislation." Previously, the courts' "legislative" functions were negative: they wielded the equivalent of a veto. After *Brown,* federal courts assumed positive roles in mandating policy alternatives, running school systems and prisons, prescribing administrative details for entitlement programs, and willy-nilly becoming ombudsmen for many who thought that legislative programs might be better run. The momentum of the *Brown* opinion impelled the Court into areas of public policy that previously would have been unthinkable for it to consider.

In *Brown,* Chief Justice Earl Warren wrote for a unanimous Court; that unanimity itself was one of the big surprises of the decision. He dismissed conflicting evidence on the Framers' intent concerning school segregation as "inconclusive." Warren therefore turned to the psychological impact of segregation on the intellectual and social development of black children, which he found devastating. Segregation of itself "generates a feeling of inferiority" among blacks, a point he buttressed by the famous footnote 11, a Brandeisian reference to psychological and other social-science authorities. Footnote 11 acted as a lightning rod in the opinion, attracting the wrath of segregationists who accused the Court of writing social science and not law. Warren entombed *Plessy,* without explicitly overruling it: "Separate educational facilities are inherently unequal." The day of equal protection had dawned.

As the Court was soon to discover, however, condemning segregation was simple, compared with enforcing integration. It turned to that difficult and frustrating problem in the case known as *Brown* II (*Brown* v. *Board of Education,* 1955), in which it demanded "good faith implementation . . . with all deliberate speed." But the lessons of history ought to have taught the justices that the resistance of segregationists, abetted by the ingenuity of southern attorneys, would translate "all deliberate speed" into "never."

The Supreme Court quickly encountered imaginative varieties of "massive resistance," as it was called, by the southern states. The Court steadfastly rejected every segregationist ploy, from outright defiance in the 1957 Little Rock desegregation crisis to resurrected (and immediately reburied) theories of nullification and interposition, to the shutdown of the entire public educational system in Prince Edward County, Virginia, to so-called freedom-of-choice plans, and so on through a seemingly endless catalog of subterfuge, evasion, and chicanery, to say nothing of the violence that dogged the early civil rights movement. As the years wore on, the Court's patience grew ever thinner until it was forced into the advanced position it adopted in *Green* v. *County School Board* (1968). In that case the Court left behind the approach of its earlier cases, which had focused on the intent to discriminate, and now directed its attention to the effects of de facto segregation. Now means now, the Court impatiently declared; "delays are no longer tolerable."

The next major milepost in the desegregation venture was busing, a remedy it endorsed in *Swann* v. *Charlotte-Mecklenburg Board of Education* (1971). The Court forthrightly resolved the dilemmas implicit since 1954, abandoning the earlier and ineffectual search for formal equality, requiring instead the effective achievement of substantial equality. But as it did so, the Court found itself confronting the combined problems of residential segregation, subtle racism, and opposition by the political Right. Having shed a crude, overt racism, conservatives now extolled formal equality as the true meaning of the equal protection clause, trusting that social inertia would block further black progress and preserve the racial status quo. Formal equality denotes simply the absence of overt de jure discrimination; it limits remedies to individuals, not groups, and then only to those who can demonstrate that they personally were the subjects of discrimination; and above all, it demands proof of intent to discriminate as the essential condition of governmental action rather than a showing of the effects of discriminatory practices. It is an updated version of nineteenth-century formalism. Spurred by successive Republican administrations (Nixon, Ford, and Reagan), Congress has expressed its displeasure with busing; some states attempted to prohibit the practice; and conservatives unsuccessfully promoted constitutional amendments that would have banned it. The question moved to the fore of the so-called social issues of the 1980s.

Another major initiative of the Court narrowed the state action doctrine originally announced in the *Civil Rights Cases* of 1883. The state action doctrine exempted most forms of racial oppression from federal authority, leaving blacks in the South to the empty recourse of state power, to which *Slaughterhouse* had originally consigned them. In 1948, however, the Court created a massive, open-ended exception to the state action doctrine in *Shelley* v. *Kraemer.* This case involved state court enforcement of a racially restrictive covenant in the sale of residential real estate. The Court found this enforcement to constitute state action and thus to be within the power of Congress to prohibit. "Equal protection of the laws is not achieved through indiscriminate imposition of inequalities," asserted Chief Justice Fred Vinson in his most memorable aphorism.

This restriction of the state action barrier opened the doors of federal courts to numerous civil rights plaintiffs vindicating rights and pursuing remedies originally granted to them under Reconstruction-era civil rights legislation, especially the Civil Rights Act of 1866. Of these statutory rights and remedies, the most important today is the statute known simply as "1983", meaning section 1983 of Title 42 of the United States Code, originally enacted as a section of the 1871 Force Act, which gives private individuals a civil cause of action for damages or equitable relief against any person who, "under color of" any state statute, custom, or usage, causes them to be deprived of any right under the federal Constitution or laws.

The Court steadily narrowed the state action concept after 1948 to the point at which some observers thought it would vanish, leaving all private conduct subject to the sanctions of federal power. The Court found state action, for example, when a state leased commercial space in a state-owned building to a private lessee who discriminated (*Burton* v. *Wilmington Parking Authority,* 1961), and when the people of California enacted an amendment to the state constitution prohibiting open-housing legislation (*Reitman* v. *Mulkey,* 1967). But this promising trend stumbled in the face of Justice William H. Rehnquist's hostility to the expansion of federal remedial power. In *Moose Lodge* v. *Irvis* (1972), a majority of the Court followed Rehnquist in refusing to find state action in a state's licensing of a private discriminator. Thus state action remains a barrier to federal remedial action against discrimination by private persons, not so daunting as it had been before 1948, but nonetheless an impediment to section 1983 actions.

The state action doctrine inhibits federal power only under the Fourteenth and Fifteenth amendments because of express language in the text of those amendments ("No State shall . . ."; "shall not be denied or abridged . . . by any state"). No such textual limit appears in the Thirteenth Amendment. But except for peonage cases, federal remedial power under the Thirteenth Amendment was a dead letter because of indifference throughout most of the twentieth century. That attitude changed abruptly in 1968, when in *Jones* v. *Alfred H. Mayer Co.* the Court upheld Congress's power to prohibit private discrimination under powers given it by section 2 of the Thirteenth Amendment. Appellants, an interracial couple denied housing by a developer, sued under section 1982, a statute descended from the 1866 Civil Rights Act's provisions recognizing a right to buy and sell property. The *Jones* case partially vindicated Justice John M. Harlan's dissent in the *Civil Rights Cases,* especially his contention that Congress had sweeping powers to reach discrimination as a badge of slavery. (Ironically, his grandson and namesake dissented in *Jones* on the grounds, among others, that Congress's power under the Thirteenth Amendment was dubious.) *Jones* revived the modern descendants of the 1866 Civil Rights Act's substantive provisions, and stiffened Congress's remedial authority.

The early civil rights cases glossed over some dilemmas lurking in the problem of racial discrimination. The most troublesome was the distinction between de jure segregation, that is, separation of the races required by law, and de facto segregation, separation that resulted from historical trends such as neighborhood residential patterns. This, in turn, presented another dilemma, the question of whether *Brown*'s remedies, whatever they might be, applied only to intentional discrimination or extended to the effects of discrimination.

The Court has dealt ambiguously with the problem of purpose-impact distinction. It has consistently held that a racially differential impact alone is not sufficient to condemn a statute. But this barrier is not so formidable as it first seems, for in *Washington* v. *Davis* (1976) the Court held that differential impact may be evidence of discriminatory purpose, and that upon a showing of impact the burden of proof shifts to the state to demonstrate that the inferential linkage to discriminatory intent does not exist in reality. This was a prudential ruling; Justice Byron White for the majority noted that if the Court permitted effect to be an irrebuttable proof of intent, it would cast a cloud of constitutional suspicion over "a whole range of tax, welfare, public service, regulatory, and licensing statutes that may be more burdensome to the poor and to the average black than to the more affluent white."

One of the most hotly disputed issues in modern civil rights struggles has been the use of so-called benign racial classifications to give minority applicants an advantage in securing some governmentally provided benefit. Affirmative action programs have come under attack from whites who contend that any minority preference automatically discriminates against some unoffending member of the majority who is denied the benefit given to a black person or other minority under the preference. On this issue, the Court has spoken with studied ambivalence. The problem here is comparable to the now obsolete issue of freedom of contract. If parties were to be put on a footing of real and effective equality in the bargaining relationship, government would have to intervene on the side of the weaker; otherwise a formal system of bargaining equality would invariably work to the advantage of the wealthy and powerful. Similarly with the posture of formal "color blind" equality: formal equality will generally perpetuate the effects of discrimination, leaving blacks permanently disadvantaged.

In the leading case on this topic, *Regents of the University of California* v. *Bakke* (1978), the Court managed to split 5–4 to strike down a numerical preferential admissions program at the Cal-Davis medical school, while simultaneously splitting 5–4 to *uphold* the school's ability to take race into consideration as one factor in its admissions policy. In a brief and eloquent dissent/concurrence, Justice Thurgood Marshall reminded his brethren that for almost two hundred years the Constitution supported discrimination against blacks. "Now," he continued, "when a State acts to remedy the effects of that legacy of discrimination, I cannot believe that this same Constitution stands as a barrier." But a majority of the Court refused to accept his logic or his reading of history. A hopelessly divided Court did, however, uphold the federal government's racial preference set-aside program in government contracting (*Fullilove* v. *Klutznick,* 1980), without being able to agree on a doctrinal basis for doing so.

When someone challenges a statute under the equal protection clause, the Court resolves the question through an inquiry that embodies *Carolene Products'* double standard. If the statute involves economic regulation, the Court subjects it only to minimum scrutiny. But if it is a civil rights question, the Court invokes strict scrutiny, which is almost always fatal to the law involved. Strict scrutiny comes into play if the court finds that the statute either (1) involved suspect classifications, the prime example being racial ones; or (2) affected fundamental rights. But strict-scrutiny categories expanded steadily throughout the Warren years. The Burger Court did not reverse the Warren precedents, but it did refuse to extend them further.

Strict scrutiny imposes two tests: the end or objectives of the law must be "compelling" (not just desirable or useful or reasonable) and the means has to be the "least restrictive" available. Both the means and the ends tests require the Court to substitute its judgment about policy for that of legislatures. Suspect classifications proved easier to justify. It has always been clear that the equal protection clause barred overtly racially discriminatory laws. In this broad view, *Plessy* was a historical deviation from the Framers' intent. Even the foremost opponent of expanded equal protection scope on the Court today, Chief Justice Rehnquist, concedes a vigorous role for the clause when the Court is confronted with such legislation. He went so far as to extend the category to include "national origin, the first cousin of race," an uncharacteristic departure from his usual textualist approach (*Trimble* v. *Gordon,* 1977, dissenting opinion). The controversial application of the suspect-classification approach comes in its extension to groups characterized other than by race. The effects have been mixed and restricted largely to women.

Gender classifications are not so automatically or so deeply suspect as racial ones, but the Court has looked on them with disfavor in recent years. It was not always so: until the Warren Court, women's claims to equal treatment were dismissed without being taken too seriously. But in the leading sex discrimination case of the modern period, *Craig* v. *Boren* (1976), the Court adopted an "intermediate-level" scrutiny test, requiring "important governmental objectives" and means "substantially related" to those ends. When the Court sustains gender-discriminatory laws, as in the exemption of females from draft registration, it falls back on the old formula of permitting legislatures to discriminate among groups "not similarly situated" (*Rostker* v. *Goldberg,* 1981). But this position does not signal a lapse to partriarchal attitudes. The Court's first female member, Justice Sandra Day O'Connor, made that clear when in 1982 she cautioned against legislative reliance on "archaic and stereotypic notions" and a "mechanical application of traditional, often inaccurate, assumptions about the proper roles of men and women" (*Mississippi University for Women* v. *Hogan,* 1982).

Of the two strict-scrutiny subcategories, fundamental rights has been the more controversial. Legal commentators disagree among themselves whether the equal protection clause implies any distinct substantive values (such as the right to an adequate diet, or the treatment of all human beings with the same basic dignity) or whether it is devoid of such values and only embodies the old equitable idea that like shall be treated as like.

In influential law review articles, Charles Reich (1964) and Frank Michelman (1968) argued that welfare entitlements were a form of "new property," and, as fundamental rights, had as valid and enforceable a claim to constitutional protection as property rights of the more traditional sort (Charles A. Reich, "The New Property," *Yale Law Journal* 73 [1964]: 733–87; Frank I. Michelman, "On Protecting the Poor through the Fourteenth Amendment," *Harvard Law Review* 83 [1969]: 7–59). The Court first took up this idea in a case striking down state requirements that applicants for welfare assistance reside in the jurisdiction for one year, *Shapiro* v. *Thompson* (1969). The basis of Justice William Brennan's holding was not especially controversial. Such durational residence requirements burden the right of interstate travel and migration, a right identified as fundamental as long ago as *Corfield* v. *Coryell* (1823) and repeatedly reaffirmed throughout the nineteenth century. But Brennan also loosely recognized a claim of welfare families "to obtain the very means to subsist—food, shelter, and other necessities of life." This claim suggested that such a right might be guaranteed by the due process or equal protection clauses.

While this radical new concept of entitlements as a constitutional right was being debated in the law reviews, the Warren Court identified fundamental rights as an element of equal protection in cases that struck down property-owning or residential barriers to the ballot (*Harper* v. *Virginia Board of Elections,* 1966) and that established the right to counsel for indigent criminal defendants appealing their convictions (*Douglas* v. *California,* 1963). Thus the basic notion of fundamental rights became solidly established, but one of the major questions on the Burger Court's agenda was whether that new category included equality of education or access to minimum levels of the necessities of life.

In several ways, the Burger Court disappointed those hoping to see the Court discover such new rights in the equal protection clause. It has, by a historical irony, used the liberal double standard to defeat liberal social objectives. That is, the Court has taken the *Carolene Products* deferential review approach for cases involving economic regulation and applied it to the new property cases to defeat claims to entitlement rights. Thus in *Dandridge* v. *Williams* (1970), Justice Potter Stewart categorized an equal protection claim to a certain quantum of welfare benefits under the Aid for Dependent Children program as involving "state regulation in the social and economic field," and thus not liable to the heightened or strict scrutiny called for in cases involving nonmaterial rights.

San Antonio School District v. *Rodriguez* (1973) was even more disappointing to proponents of substantive equal protection. Respondents in that case had challenged the Texas method, common to all the other states, of financing public schools by a combination of local property taxes and contributions from a state fund known as the School Foundation. Different school districts were able to provide more or less funding for schools depending on the levels of taxable wealth in their areas. Under this system, wealthy suburban areas enjoyed better public schools than some inner-city and rural districts. This disparity, respondents claimed, violated their children's right to equality of access to educational benefits. A 5–4 majority rejected this claim. Speaking for them, Justice Powell stated flatly that "at least where wealth is involved, [the equal protection clause] does not require absolute equality or precisely equal advantages." It was "not the province of this Court to create substantive constitutional rights in the name of guaranteeing" equal protection.

Powell's opinion was grounded on prudential considerations. To accede to the respondents' claim "would occasion in Texas and elsewhere an unprecedented upheaval in public education," and the Court had no stomach for rewriting state public finance systems. But in the 1982 case of *Plyler* v. *Doe,* the 5–4 majority shifted to strike down Texas's refusal to provide any schooling at all to the children of illegal aliens. Brennan for the majority held that a complete denial of educational benefits violated one of the basic goals of the equal protection clause: "the abolition of governmental barriers presenting unreasonable obstacles to advancement on the basis of individual merit." *Plyler* thus salvaged some remnant of liberal social objectives from the apparently closed category of fundamental rights.

In retrospect, the result in *Rodriguez* was foreordained. Were the Court to find in substantive equal protection a guarantee of access to goods and services (shelter, education, medical assistance, minimal dietary levels), it would be performing the wealth-redistribution function it has consistently abhorred throughout the twentieth century. This, even many liberals concede, is a function best left to legislative judgment.

Though protection of discrete and insular minorities has proven to be the *Carolene Products'* category that has absorbed most of the Court's attention, the other two have also played important roles in the Court's agenda. Stone's concern about "legislation which restricts those political processes which can ordinarily be expected to bring about repeal of undesirable legislation" has figured importantly in the Court's work since 1960. John Hart Ely, in his influential 1980 essay *Democracy and Distrust,* argues that the functions of "clearing the channels of political change," as he terms the second paragraph of the *Carolene Products'* footnote, constitutes one of the two essential functions of the Court today (the other being the matter of seeing to it that minorities are adequately represented in the political process). Such a "participation-oriented, representation-reinforcing approach to judicial review" offers the advantage that it leaves the controversial core of modern judicial review—the identification, definition, and selection of values—to the political process. Judges become umpires of that process, seeing to it that everyone has a chance to participate in the game on equal terms with everyone else. But they do not define the values of society, leaving that responsibility to their ultimate masters, the people, whose will is expressed through the representative process.

The preeminent problem in the second *Carolene Products'* category is reapportionment. At first malapportionment did not trouble the Court. Justice Frankfurter in *Colegrove* v. *Green* (1946) rejected a challenge to Illinois districting: "From the determination of such issues this Court has traditionally remained aloof." But as Frankfurter wrote, this posture was already being eroded by various cases involving the political rights of black people. In a series of voting rights cases since the 1920s, the Court consistently struck down state laws that by various subterfuges excluded blacks from voting in primary elections (e.g., *Smith* v. *Allwright,* 1944; *Terry* v. *Adams,* 1953). Then, in *Gomillion* v. *Lightfoot* (1960), the Court overturned an Alabama gerrymandering scheme designed to exclude nearly all blacks from voting in Tuskegee, a historic center of black culture in the deep South.

These black voting rights cases prepared the ground for the momentous reapportionment case, *Baker* v. *Carr* (1962). In that case Justice Brennan authorized lower federal courts to take jurisdiction of suits challenging malapportionment, relying on their equity powers to fashion relief under the equal protection clause. Brennan hemmed in the political question doctrine to narrow the range of questions considered nonjusticiable, thereby thrusting the federal courts directly into what Justice Frankfurter in *Colegrove* had warned was a "political thicket." In a harsh dissent, Frankfurter condemned the majority's action as resting on circular reasoning and reflecting the choice of one political philosophy—encapsuled in the slogan "one man, one vote"—over competing ones hallowed by American political tradition. Frankfurter ineffectually insisted that reapportionment was a classic political question, but his demand that it be left to the electoral process for correction only illustrated the self-defeating futility of his position.

Conservatives reacted to *Baker* and subsequent reapportionment cases by promoting a constitutional amendment that would have permitted one house of a state legislature to be apportioned on other than population grounds. But the Court forged ahead to the one person–one vote principle foreshadowed in *Baker,* raising it to the status of constitutional command two years later in *Reynolds* v. *Sims* (1964). "Legislators represent people, not trees or acres. Legislators are elected by voters, not farms or cities or economic interests. . . . Diluting the weight of votes because of place of residence impairs basic constitutional rights under the 14th Amendment just as much as invidious discriminations based upon factors such as race or economic status," wrote Chief Justice Warren. The whole series of reapportionment decisions of the Warren years proved to be popular, and the effort to overturn them by amendment went nowhere.

Some First Amendment cases display the Court's concern with the self-correcting character of the political process. The *Carolene Products'* dictum explicitly included "restraints on the dissemination of information," and this phrase in turn meant that the First Amendment was implicated in the Court's quest for clearing the channels of political participation. All its efforts to do so since World War II have taken place in the context of a dictum in the 1942 case of *Chaplinsky* v. *New Hampshire,* in which Justice Frank Murphy stated:

> There are certain well-defined and narrowly limited classes of speech, the prevention and punishment of which have never been thought to raise any constitutional problem. These include the lewd and obscene, the profane, the libelous, and the insulting or "fighting" words—those which by their very utterance inflict injury or tend to incite an immediate breach of the peace. It has been well observed that such utterances are no essential part of any exposition of ideas, and are of such slight social value as a step to truth that any benefit that may be derived from them is clearly outweighed by the social interest in order and morality.

Thus the Court has always considered First Amendment issues with the unchallenged assumption in mind that certain kinds of speech categorically lie outside the zone protected by the amendment. This categorization approach has been weakened in the last generation as First Amendment protections have expanded, yet the Court seems instinctively to return to the concept, however devoid of substantive content it may now seem to be.

Since the 1960s, a trend has become visible in First Amendment–political freedom cases. In the first phase, dating from 1964 to 1971, the Court expanded opportunities to disseminate political information. From 1973 on, the Court has continued to expand those opportunities for the wealthy segments of American society, while constricting it for those lower on the socioeconomic scale. The first phase began with *New York Times* v. *Sullivan* (1964), the basic press freedom case of American constitutional law. In order to sustain its conclusion that a public figure must show malice, rather than mere falsity, to succeed in a libel suit against a newspaper, the Court identified "a profound national commitment to the principle that debate on public issues should be uninhibited, robust, and wide-open." On the basis of this principle, it not only struck down Alabama's common law of libel as applied to public figures, but retrospectively the Sedition Act of 1798 for good measure.

The Court further promoted an open political process in the *Red Lion* case of 1969, in which it sustained the Federal Communication Commission's "fairness doctrine," which obliged radio and TV stations to provide coverage of public issues and to present both sides of an issue, including the provision of free reply time to individuals attacked on the air. The effect of the Court's holding was to broaden access to the airwaves in political contests (*Red Lion Broadcasting Co.* v. *FCC,* 1969). It extended protection to the press from an injunction sought by the federal government in the Pentagon Papers case (*New York Times Co.* v. *United States,* 1971), reaffirming a longstanding judicial hostility to prior restraints on publication. Finally, in *Cohen* v. *California* (1971), the Court carved a major exception to the *Chaplinsky* unprotected speech categories by reversing appellant's conviction on disturbing-the-peace charges for wearing a jacket bearing the words "Fuck the Draft" as a way of protesting American involvement in Vietnam. *Cohen* recognized a right to unruly, emotion-laden speech, not just reasoned, decorous, and socially acceptable communication. The effect of these various First Amendment decisions was to broaden access to the channels of political communication for all people, and to extend or assure access to groups that might otherwise not have had an adequate opportunity to participate in public dialogue.

Beginning in 1973, the Court modified this trend by either restricting the right-of-access cases or by creating new opportunities for access that would be meaningful only to those already possessed of ample economic power. In *CBS* v. *Democratic National Committee* (1973), for example, Chief Justice Burger rejected the claim of respondents (an antiwar group and the Democratic National Committee), whom he disparagingly characterized as "self-appointed editorial commentators," to run paid editorial ads on TV stations licensed by the FCC. In the same spirit, and inconsistently with *Red Lion,* he also held unconstitutional a state law requiring media to accord a "right of reply" to candidates they had criticized (*Miami Herald Publishing Co.* v. *Tornillo,* 1974).

While the Burger Court was thus cutting back on access, it displayed an unseemly solicitude for the free speech rights of the wealthy. It extended First Amendment protection to commercial speech in *Virginia Pharmacy Board* v. *Virginia Consumer Council* (1976) and protected the First Amendment rights of corporations in *First National Bank* v. *Bellotti* (1978). In *Bellotti,* Justice Powell rejected arguments that to accord corporations the same communication rights as natural persons would be to uphold "the special status of corporations [that] has placed them in a position to control vast amounts of economic power which may . . . dominate not only the economy but also the very heart of our democracy, the electoral process." (The source of this quotation was not some latter-day populist, but rather the usually conservative Justice Byron White, dissenting.) Instead, Powell formalistically declared that "the inherent worth of the speech . . . does not depend on the identity" of the speaker. The impact of his holding was acute because *Bellotti* involved a referendum, an electoral environment in which the voice of corporations carries particular weight.

The Court insisted that money should speak in politics by striking down limits on campaign expenditures (*Buckley* v. *Valeo,* 1976). In a per curiam opinion, the Court stated that "a restriction on the amount of money a person or group can spend on political communication during a campaign necessarily reduces the quantity of expression by restricting the number of issues discussed, the depth of their exploration, and the size of the audience reached." The wealth-favoring impact of this decision was made all the more vivid when the opinion rejected a comparison of the results in *Buckley* with the draft card–burning case of 1968, *United States* v. *O'Brien.* In the 1968 case the Supreme Court in effect authorized conviction of a war protester for a symbolic act of political communication. "The expenditure of money simply cannot be equated with such conduct as destruction of a draft card," the anonymous author of the per curiam insisted, but now ironically political communication by the rich was being protected, whereas symbolic communication by those more likely to be outside the purlieus of power was left within *Chaplinsky*'s nonprotected forms of communication. The Court restated its concern for speech rights of the powerful in *FEC* v. *National Conservative Political Action Committee* (1985), which struck down spending limits on political action committees.

The *Carolene Products'* third category, "when legislation appears on its face to be within a specific prohibition of the Constitution, such as those of the first ten Amendments," has proven to be an elusive grouping because it begs the essential question. Rarely if ever does a legislature enact a law that obviously flies in the face of an explicit constitutional command, so the categorization cannot be so self-evident as it appears at first glance. Instead, Chief Justice Stone meant to suggest that the Bill of Rights, specifically the First Amendment, and the Fourteenth Amendment, identify values supreme in the constitutional hierarchy, and because of this supremacy, legislation that intrudes on them should not be approached in a spirit of judicial self-restraint. Stone was not an absolutist; he favored a balancing approach, but for him the balance between individual freedom and governmental power always tilted in favor of freedom in the case of statutes falling within the scope of the Bill of Rights.

The Supreme Court in *Carolene Products'* half century has attempted to follow the path pointed out by Stone, but the results have been inconsistent and muddled. Four diverse subjects illustrate the difficulty of applying the Stone standard, even as he qualified it by the preferred freedoms gloss. These are the law of obscenity, the administration of criminal procedure, the First Amendment establishment and free-exercise cases, and the strange resurrection of the Tenth Amendment.

The law of obscenity has been aptly termed "a constitutional disaster area." *Chaplinsky* specifically excluded "the lewd and obscene," which presumably encompassed pornography, until the Court opened the controversy in 1957 by attempting a definition of obscenity in *Roth* v. *United States:* "Whether to the average person, applying contemporary community standards, the dominant theme of the material taken as a whole appeals to prurient interests." It was a well-meant attempt to enlighten judicial consideration of sexual censorship and move American courts away from absurdities of Victorian and Edwardian morality. But it had the unanticipated effect of confusing those charged with enforcement of pornography statutes. The Court nevertheless struggled along trying to make sense out of the various *Roth* elements, all the while being obliged to review lower-court determinations by the unwelcome technique of viewing smutty movies in its private theater. Justice Harlan noted the resultant confusion in the law a decade after *Roth,* when he observed that in the thirteen previous obscenity cases coming to the Court the justices had generated a total of fifty-five opinions—scarcely a reassuring commentary on the law's certainty, clarity, and predictability.

Almost in desperation, the Burger Court washed its hands of the whole thankless effort in *Miller* v. *California* (1973) by declaring that the relevant standards for obscenity are state rather than national, and by confining obscenity to materials depicting "patently offensive 'hard core' sexual conduct specifically defined by regulating state law." This ruling had the desirable effect of reducing (but not eliminating) the number of obscenity appeals the Court had to consider. Certainty still remained elusive, though, and the *Miller* definition did not provide much guidance for dealing with new varieties of constitutional confrontations with obscenity, such as that presented by an Indianapolis ordinance that redefined pornography in terms of the "subordination of women" and treated it as an equal protection rather than a First Amendment problem.

(A United States district court found the statute unconstitutional: *American Booksellers Association* v. *Hudnut,* 1984).

The Court fared no better in cases involving the administration of criminal justice. In one area, the death penalty, the Court's experience roughly parallels that in obscenity cases. In neither did the Bill of Rights provide much guidance to the Court in its effort to impose rationality and uniformity in the application of law. The constitutional difficulty posed by the death penalty was (and remains) twofold: its imposition is seemingly random, capricious, and arbitrary; and, if there is any pattern discernible at all, it is that the death penalty falls with undue frequency on racial minorities. (There are two other problems with executions that judicial intervention is not likely to resolve. First, is the infliction of death by the state, no matter by what means, in and of itself, so cruel as to be beyond the constitutional pale? Second, does it offend the Constitution that, in the nature of things, the victims of the death penalty are society's misfits and outcasts, its poor, uneducated, unemployed, and abused?)

The Court tried to deal with the problem of arbitrary imposition in *Furman* v. *Georgia* (1972), an opinion that condemned capriciousness so emphatically that some observers concluded that the Court would shortly outlaw the death penalty. It clearly had no intention of doing so, however, despite the hopeful proddings of Justices Brennan and Marshall, both of whom considered the death penalty in any form, inflicted for any reason, per se cruel and unusual. The years since *Furman* have been marked by persistent state efforts to achieve two seemingly inconsistent objectives, and by the Court's encouragement of them in that contradictory quest. The ends are jury discretion unimpeded by too much judicial oversight in imposing the death penalty, and avoidance of the appearance of arbitrariness. The result of this indecent pursuit of appearances has been, in the words of Robert Weisberg, that "the Court has reduced the law of the [death] penalty trial to almost a bare aesthetic exhortation that the states just do something—anything—to give the penalty trial a legal appearance. The new cases reveal the art of legal doctrine-making in a state of nervous breakdown" (Robert Weisberg, "Deregulating Death," *Supreme Court Review* [1983]: 305–95, quote on 306), and, he might have added, utter incoherence.

The Court has done better—at least in terms of achieving coherence—with the problem known as "incorporation," the process whereby the Supreme Court has determined that restrictions on the federal government contained in the Bill of Rights are restrictions on the states as well. This venture began offhandedly a century ago in Justice Stanley Matthews's opinion for the Court in *Hurtado* v. *California* (1884), which defined due process of law in a procedural sense as consisting not of any particular practices of Anglo-American courts, but instead of "principles of liberty and justice." Vague though this formulation was, the Court adhered to it in the earliest twentieth-century incorporation case, *Twining* v. *New Jersey* (1908), which inaugurated what legal observers have called the "selective incorporation" approach, whereby the Court picks and chooses which particular criminal procedure guarantees are incorporated and which are not.

This tradition was sanctioned by Justice Cardozo's eloquent formulas in *Palko* v. *Connecticut* (1937), in which he held that only those rights were incorporated that were "of the very essence of a scheme of ordered liberty." He defined these as derived from "a principle of justice so rooted in the traditions and conscience of our people as to be ranked as fundamental," so essential that "neither liberty nor justice would exist if they were sacrificed."

Justice Hugo Black attacked this tradition in a classic confrontation with his antagonist Justice Frankfurter in *Adamson* v. *California* (1947). Black rejected the Cardozo-Frankfurter position as a "natural law" approach to judging, by which the judges ratify their own personal views of what justice requires in the name of high-sounding but contentless principles. Frankfurter in rebuttal simply reiterated the standard as being "those canons of decency and fairness which express the notions of justice of English-speaking peoples."

This dispute sputtered along inconclusively until the 1960s, when the Court began incorporating specific guarantees one by one, with the result that by the end of Chief Justice Warren's tenure almost everything had been incorporated. Thus the Court reached Justice Black's result of total incorporation, but by a steady expansion of the selective incorporation formula derived from Cardozo and Frankfurter.

Chief Justice Stone's vision of preferred positions for First Amendment rights has, in some sense, been realized for the clauses prohibiting establishment of religion and securing its free exercise. The subject of religion does occupy a special, favored place in the American constitutional order. No other Bill of Rights subject, not even freedom of speech, requires of government such a heavy burden of justification for any action that either favors or hinders a religious group or practice. Yet there is not one religion clause, but two, the free-exercise and establishment clauses, and they potentially conflict with each other, posing a dilemma for the *Carolene Products'* paradigm. If the Court vigorously bars some form of establishment, someone can reasonably claim that its action intrudes on his or her free exercise, and vice versa. Literalism and logical extremes are out of place here.

Michael E. Smith has traced a suggestive pattern in the history of the Court's evolution of religion clause doctrine. Before 1937, few religion cases came before the Court, and when they did, the Court always upheld the power of government to regulate or inhibit religion (as, for example, by suppressing polygamy). Since 1937, a plethora of religion cases amply demonstrate the potential for inconsistency and conflict between the two clauses.

The cases have bunched in two clusters, one before 1962 and the other since 1968. These two periods have been dominated by quite different judicial attitudes toward the relations between government and religion. In the earlier cases, the strongly held views of Justices Douglas, Black, Frankfurter, and Rutledge placed the Court in a posture of near antagonism to large, mainline, organized denominations, especially the Roman Catholic Church, and of reflexive sympathy for dissenting and individual forms of religious expression. This attitude toward religion has long antecedents in American experience, tracing back to the free-church sectarianism of Roger Williams and the deism of so many of the Framers, particularly the Virginians. These values have been especially powerful because nearly all jurists have been uncomfortable with an explicit examination of their own prejudices in the area, and have thus been all the more vulnerable to being dominated by those unexamined values.

The biases of the earlier period have not exactly been reversed in the later, but they have undergone shadings of emphasis so strong that the Court of the 1980s clearly proceeds from radically different premises than it had four decades ago. The modern Court, led by Chief Justice Burger and Justices Stewart and Powell, has been sympathetic to organized, corporate churches, and, with Justice Rehnquist taking the lead, receptive to their demands for various forms of state aid and for state involvement in religious observance. At the same time, the sectarian and individualist are likely to encounter a less hospitable environment when they seek to defend some particular practice (conscientious exemption, for example) against the secular intrusion of the state.

Take, as an illustration, Justice Powell's 1977 complacent judgment that the dangers posed by state aid to parochial schools are "remote, and when viewed against the positive contributions of sectarian schools, any such risk seems entirely tolerable" (*Wolman* v. *Walter*, 1977). Such an attitude is unimaginable on the Court of the late 1940s which agonized over the released-time cases and in doing so exalted Jefferson's wall-of-separation metaphor into constitutional dogma. Similarly, the scarcely concealed anti-Catholicism of Justices Black and Douglas is unthinkable in the more tolerant atmosphere of the Burger Court.

Given these diverse attitudes, it should come as no surprise that the religion cases of the postwar Court do not display a consistent, unitary line of development, once again demonstrating the illusory quality of Stone's formulation, "on its face . . . within a specific prohibition." On only one religious subject, school prayer, has the Court spoken consistently. It has regularly rejected every attempt by the states to require that children in public schools recite a prayer in any form, whether it be the Lord's Prayer, a state-composed "nondenominational" prayer, or even a moment of silence in which the children are encouraged to formulate a private "voluntary prayer" (*Engel* v. *Vitale,* 1962; *Abington School District* v. *Schempp,* 1963; *Wallace* v. *Jaffree,* 1985). The Court has not been deterred in this course by vociferous political opposition, including proposed constitutional amendments that would permit school prayer. Apart from this topic, though, a tortuous line of development characterizes doctrine. Two problems are illustrative: aid to parochial schools and sabbath observance.

The matrix of modern establishment and free-exercise doctrine has been programs enacted by the states over the years that have provided various forms of assistance (textbooks, busing) to children in religious schools or that supplement instruction in religious schools by having public teachers or specialists (audiologists, for example) paid by the state spend a fraction of the school day teaching nonreligious subjects in parochial schools. The earliest decisions in this area, from the late 1940s, began the process of pricking out a line on a case-by-case basis distinguishing permissible forms of aid from those that are not (*Everson* v. *Board of Education,* 1947; *Zorach* v. *Clauson,* 1952). This line has been difficult to follow or explain, and it has produced bizarre results, such as that a state may lend textbooks to pupils in religious schools, but may not lend magazines to those schools. Justice Rehnquist and other critics of the Court insist that such anomalies are the product of a fundamentally misleading assumption in *Everson,* namely, that the meaning of the First Amendment's religious clauses was captured in Thomas Jefferson's wall-of-separation metaphor, producing a "separationist" doctrine that is easy to carry to extremes and difficult to apply sensibly. Critics have also pointed out, with ample justification, that the Court has strayed far from any discernible intent of the Framers or original meaning in this area.

Sensitive to such criticism, the Court has tried to fashion a definitive rule that would at least provide some guidance in establishment clause cases. In *Lemon* v. *Kurtzman* (1971), Chief Justice Burger articulated a three-part test to uphold challenged legislation, requiring a secular purpose, predominantly secular effect, and no excessive entanglement between state and church. He also suggested that the Court would frown on "politically divisive" measures. But the *Lemon* test has not weathered well; a minority of the post–1973 Court has called for its abandonment. The Court seems as much at sea as ever when it deals with problems of aid or released time.

The sabbath cases are no more susceptible of rationalization, perhaps because they above all others illustrate the potential for conflict between the two religion clauses. How far *must* a state go to accommodate variant religious practices under the free-exercise clause? How far *may* it go before it violates the establishment clause? Four companion cases in 1961 dashed the effort of sabbatarians to have Sunday-closing laws declared unconstitutional as applied to them (*McGowan* v. *Maryland* et al.). Yet in *Sherbert* v. *Verner* (1963), the Court required a state to pay unemployment benefits to a Seventh Day Adventist fired because she would not work on a Sunday. The decisions are probably irreconcilable, but for once that situation is not the fault of the Court. Instead it seems to be an inevitable price for a pair of constitutional commands that can hardly be implemented before they encroach on each other.

One last topic illustrates the difficulty of applying Stone's category: the clash between federal commerce regulatory power on the one hand and the Tenth Amendment on the other. Since 1937, this clash scarcely seemed to be a problem: Congress's power was seen to be plenary, while at the same time the Tenth Amendment lapsed into a condition of disuse and irrelevance. Or so it seemed until 1976, when Justice Rehnquist and four of his colleagues astonished the American bar with their decision in *National League of Cities* v. *Usery,* holding that the federal Fair Labor Standards Act could not be applied to force states to pay overtime wages to their employees because of the Tenth Amendment. The amendment, Rehnquist declared, protects "attributes of sovereignty attaching to every state government" and prevents the federal government from pursuing policies that would "interfere with the integral governmental functions of these bodies." This regressive holding threatened to raise the Tenth Amendment from its profound slumber and send it stalking through the United States code gutting an unknowable number of federal commerce regulatory statutes. The decision came under massive criticism, not least because Justice Rehnquist seemed to be manufacturing his Tenth Amendment criteria out of thin air, something he was not reticent about accusing his colleagues of doing in other cases.

No one was therefore surprised when the Court reversed itself less than a decade later in *Garcia* v. *San Antonio Metropolitan Transit Authority* (1985). With apparent relish, Justice Harry Blackmun discarded the *National League of Cities* criteria as unworkable and anachronistic, a threat to the workings of the federal system. Justice Rehnquist, now in dissent, smugly predicted that the Court would once again reverse itself in the future, thus coming around 360 degrees. This erratic performance has led many observers (few of whom regret the result of *Garcia*) to worry about the role of stare decisis in a constitutional system.

The day of *Carolene Products* is probably past. As a paradigm of law, it served well for a half century. It was the positive component of a two-part reorientation of American law which occurred in the crucible of the constitutional revolution of 1937. The negative part was the abandonment of economic substantive due process. Had the Court stopped there, it would have consigned itself to a much more withdrawn and reticent role in American life than the Framers envisioned. The *Carolene Products'* formula served as a guidepost to the future. It exalted trends already underway: incorporation of the Bill of Rights and a heightened concern for libertarian values. It provided a rationale, even if it was a simplistic one, for a new judicial role in the civil liberties realm. And it called on the Court to assume the role of conscience to the political order rather than to interpose itself as a roadblock to democracy. We should not expect more of judicial vision, and can hope only that the paradigm that succeeds it will serve us as well.

Chapter 8

"The very essence of judicial duty"

SUBSTANTIVE DUE PROCESS

DEBATE ABOUT the legitimacy of judicial activism on the modern Court invariably returns to the touchstone of judicial review, *Marbury* v. *Madison,* and its core ambiguity: does the United States Supreme Court exercise some special function of constitutional supervision? Or does it acquire its power to hold laws unconstitutional from its ordinary judicial function of deciding cases and having to choose from among conflicting laws? This unresolved ambiguity derives from Chief Justice Marshall's two basic postulates in *Marbury:* first, the Constitution is *law,* and second, "it is emphatically the province and duty of the judicial department to say what the law is." As with many of Marshall's grand aphorisms, these turn out on analysis to be Delphic. Did Marshall mean to say that the Court merely resolves constitutional controversies in a manner no different from that by which it resolves other litigation, namely, that it merely selects the governing law and applies it? Or did the Framers create the Court as a unique guardian of constitutionalism, indispensable for the maintenance of separation of powers? Are its opinions "the supreme Law of the Land"?

Such questions recur in periods of judicial activism because those whose oxen have been gored by a Court decision accuse the justices of usurpation, of short-circuiting the processes of democracy, of being an unelected and elite oligarchy that thwarts the will of the people and their representatives. The modern Court has once again provoked this stereotyped reaction by its decisions creating a modern doctrine of substantive due process. These decisions deal principally with individuals' rights of association, privacy, and personal autonomy, especially in family and sexual contexts.

The right to privacy achieved constitutional status in two cases of the

Lochner era, the only substantive due process decisions that survived the 1937 revolution. Each case was an easy one, striking down indefensible legislation. *Meyer* v. *Nebraska* (1923) voided a World War I statute that prohibited school instruction in any language but English, a misguided attempt to repel the Hun from America's heartland. *Pierce* v. *Society of Sisters* (1925) struck down an Oregon statute, enacted at the behest of the resurgent Ku Klux Klan, that outlawed parochial school education. Justice James C. McReynolds identified noneconomic substantive due process rights in *Meyer:* "to acquire useful knowledge, to marry, establish a home and bring up children, to worship God according to the dictates of his own conscience, and generally to enjoy those privileges long recognized at common law as essential to the orderly pursuit of happiness by free men."

McReynolds's conception of noneconomic substantive due process rights remained dormant until the post–World War II era. The idea resumed its place in constitutional discourse indirectly, after the Court recognized a constitutionally protected right of association in *NAACP* v. *Alabama* (1958), holding it to be a liberty protected by the Fourteenth Amendment. This newly acknowledged right then expanded dramatically in *Griswold* v. *Connecticut* (1965). Voiding a statute that prohibited giving birth control information to married couples, Justice Douglas for the Court imaginatively drew on a string of metaphors—"peripheral rights," "emanations," "zones of privacy"—to hold that "the First Amendment has a penumbra where privacy is protected from governmental intrusion." From this holding, he found a constitutionally protected right of association and a "right of privacy [that is] older than the Bill of Rights." He refused to specify which constitutional guarantee provided the core that this penumbral right surrounds, suggesting the First, Third, Fourth, Fifth, Ninth, and Fourteenth amendments.

Justice Arthur J. Goldberg found such lack of discrimination too loose, and in his concurring opinion specified the Ninth Amendment as the appropriate source. Justice Harlan, also concurring, drew instead on the Fourteenth Amendment, and insisted that the Court must balance interests, specifically, the tension between "liberty and the demands of organized society." He rejected a formulaic approach, suggesting instead that the liberty interest guaranteed by the Fourteenth Amendment is a "rational continuum" that "includes a freedom from all substantial arbitrary impositions and purposeless restraints." Seven years later, in *Eisenstadt* v. *Baird* (1972), the Court extended the *Griswold* privacy right to unmarried couples and individuals, as well as to all "childbearing" decisions.

The *Eisenstadt* extension proved to be a threshold to the preeminent substantive due process decision of the modern era, *Roe* v. *Wade* (1973), which restricted the powers of the states to regulate abortions. In this momentous case, Justice Harry A. Blackmun recognized the exceptionally sensitive impact his holding would have. He acknowledged opposing moral and legal positions, but avoided addressing questions he considered unanswerable by judges, such as when life begins. Instead, he created a legal time line, based, he thought, on the cycle of human pregnancy and divided into three roughly equal periods, to accommodate the conflicting interests of a woman seeking an abortion, the fetus, and the state attempting to restrict or regulate abortions.

Blackmun found the woman's right to obtain an abortion secured by the privacy/autonomy cases from *Meyer* on, but he rejected the claim that this right was absolute. Rather, it was offset by the states' interests in protecting maternal health and in guarding the "potentiality of human life" in the fetus. To reconcile the conflicting interests, he located them along the stages of pregnancy, holding that the woman's right is exclusive of the states' interest for the first third of her pregnancy (approximately twelve weeks); for the second third, the states may regulate the abortion process, but only to protect maternal health; and in the final third, the states may assert their interests in the fetus as well, and regulate fully, even prohibiting abortions if they choose (except when necessary to preserve the life of the mother). To identify the point at which the state might intervene to protect the interests of potential life, Justice Blackmun chose viability, the stage at which the fetus "presumably has the capability of meaningful life outside the mother's womb."

Roe became intensely controversial, more so than *Brown* v. *Board of Education,* and incomparably more than any of the activist Warren Court decisions. Perhaps for any other subject—search and seizure,for example, or pornography—arguments based on the right of privacy, the primary place of individual autonomy, and the fundamental claims of human dignity might have overcome political and ideological resistance. But abortion cut too deeply, and privacy/autonomy/dignity claims proved to be fragile barriers to the political hurricane that *Roe* called up. The Court found itself again buffeted by political controversy. Political attacks on the Court were abetted by persistent dissents. In *Roe,* Justices White and Rehnquist accused the Court of Lochnerizing, and their view commanded increasing support on the Court itself. The Court tended to become polarized in abortion cases, not only on the substance of the abortion question, but on the larger issues of judicial review, majoritarianism, federalism, and democracy in which the abortion controversy was embedded. This controversy, in turn, focused scholarly, popular, and political attention on the Court itself and its role in American society.

Meanwhile, *Roe* slowly eroded conceptually. Even Justice Blackmun conceded that the right to have an abortion was qualitatively different from all previously identified privacy rights. In a dissent to a 1980 decision, *Akron* v. *Akron Center for Reproductive Health,* Justice O'Connor pointed out that *Roe* "is on a collision course with itself." She maintained that viability was a completely arbitrary choice as a constitutional benchmark, and it has constantly been altered since by changes in medical technology that assure the survival of fetuses at ever earlier points in their development. What sort of a constitutional doctrine is it, she asked, that is determined by technological developments wholly outside the control of courts?

Justice Byron White, dissenting in a 1986 case, *Thornburgh* v. *American College of Obstetricians and Gynecologists,* carried O'Connor's point a step further: the state's interest in the life of the fetus is just as compelling before viability as after. There is no nonarbitrary line separating a fetus from a human being. The supposedly fundamental value identified in *Roe* cannot be reasonably inferred from any previously identified source: not from the "traditions and consensus of society," or from the logical implications of a system of ordered liberty, or from "the nation's history and traditions." The intense controversy itself over *Roe* was proof of that. The American people have not established an abortion right in the Constitution, White insisted, and *Roe* thwarts their opportunity to adopt a contrary value by legislation.

The Court nevertheless expanded the privacy/autonomy right after 1973 in cases not involving abortion. Though these decisions derived from *Roe,* they were not particularly controversial; in fact, several of them seemed more popular than not, suggesting that the vice of *Roe* was not the general principle of privacy or autonomy, but its specific application to the abortion decision. In *Moore* v. *East Cleveland* (1977), the Court drew on modern substantive due process as a basis of family privacy rights to void an ordinance that restricted residential households to the nuclear family. Substantive due process is tolerable, Justice Lewis Powell wrote for the majority, because it is limited by a "careful respect for the teachings of history [and] solid recognition of the basic values that underlie our society." In *Zablocki* v. *Redhail* (1978), the Court identified the right to marry as fundamental and therefore protected under the privacy/autonomy rubric. It struck down a Wisconsin statute that prohibited someone who was obliged to support minor children not in his or her custody from marrying without prior official permission.

Capping this trend, Justice William Brennan for a unanimous Court in *Roberts* v. *United States Jaycees* (1984) upheld a state prohibition of gender exclusion against a Jaycees' challenge that it infringed on their freedom of (male) association. He analyzed the sorts of association protected by privacy and autonomy, and he came up with these criteria: "personal bonds [that] have played a critical role in the culture and traditions of the Nation by cultivating and transmitting shared ideals and beliefs" and "emotional enrichment from close ties with others" that create and protect "the ability independently to define one's identity that is central to any concept of liberty." Such intimate associations, of which the family is a modal example, are secured from state intrusion. By this process of extrapolation, the Court created a new right, intimate association, grounded in the guarantee of liberty in the Fifth and Fourteenth amendments.

The surprising ease with which the Court evolved such new substantive rights, and the equally surprising candor by which it admitted that it was doing so on a substantive due process basis, led observers to wonder whether the Court had reentered a new *Lochner* era in the realm of personal liberty. That observation in turn raised questions about the legitimacy of the judicial enterprise, and Justice White responded in *Bowers* v. *Hardwick* (1986), a case challenging the constitutionality of a Georgia sodomy statute as applied to consensual adult homosexual activity. By a 5–4 majority, the Court upheld the statute. In a terse opinion, White curtailed the Court's tendency to expand substantive due process, in an effort to preserve the legitimacy of judicial review. Drawing on *Palko, Griswold,* and *Moore,* he stated that fundamental values included only those "implicit in the concept of ordered liberty" and those "deeply rooted in the nation's history and tradition." To go beyond these headlands and venture out into the open sea of nontextual fundamental rights makes the Court "most vulnerable and . . . nearest to illegitimacy when it deals with judge-made constitutional law having little or no cognizable roots in the language or design of the Constitution." White called for "great resistance" to any expansion of fundamental rights lest federal judges arrogate to themselves "further authority to govern the country without express constitutional authority." This blunt language suggested that the expansionist phase of fundamental rights jurisprudence had reached its limits, and that henceforth a cautious majority would labor within the constraints of legitimacy and the values clustered around majoritarian democracy.

In periods when decisions of the United States Supreme Court have been politically controversial, especially when proponents of state power saw those decisions as tipping the balance of federalism toward national power, legislative leaders in Congress and the states resorted to political maneuvers to restrict the powers of the Court. This political response has created an informal dialogue between the Court on the one hand and

Congress and the states on the other over the nature of judicial power and the restraints on it permitted by the Constitution.

In the early nineteenth century, disgruntled state power advocates proposed various ways of curbing the Court's power: a super–Supreme Court composed of the chief justices of all state supreme courts, constituting the United States Senate as a review panel for the Court's decisions, or permitting Congress to remove particular justices. This first phase of political reaction to the Court's perceived inroads on state power reached a climax in 1831 with a bill introduced in Congress that would have repealed section 25 of the 1789 Judiciary Act. The repeal bill ultimately failed, and with its failure the antebellum tide of anti-Court animus ebbed for a time. In reaction to the *Dred Scott* decision, some anti-Court rhetoric frothed up in Congress throughout the Civil War and into Reconstruction, but produced no significant results aside from the McCardle repealer act. Between 1895 and 1924, Populists and Progressives sought to restrict the Court's power to no effect. FDR's Court-packing initiative foundered on popular assumptions about the Court's inviolability.

The desegregation, internal security, reapportionment, school prayer, and substantive due process decisions of the Warren-Burger years provoked a fifth phase of political resistance to judicial power. Segregationists promoted the "Southern Manifesto," signed by nearly the entire southern congressional delegation in 1956, a declaration that *Brown* v. *Board of Education* was a judicial usurpation unwarranted by the Constitution. Conservatives of both parties deplored the decisions from 1957 on that curtailed internal security investigative power.

While the John Birch Society financed an "Impeach Earl Warren" billboard campaign, congressional conservatives promoted a wide array of Court-leashing devices. These included permitting Congress to override or reverse a Supreme Court decison; making the federal judiciary elective and reducing tenure from good behavior to a term of years; permitting recall of federal judges (an old Populist panacea); abolishing judicial review itself; requiring some sort of supermajority or unanimity for a Court decision holding a federal statute unconstitutional; reversing the effect of a decision by constitutional amendment (a technique that had produced the Eleventh, Fourteenth [section 1], Sixteenth, and Nineteenth amendments, as well as proposed amendments that had failed of ratification, such as the Child Labor Amendment); reversing the effect of a Court decision by statute (such as the ineffectual attempt to abolish the labor injunction in the Clayton Act). FDR had vaguely toyed with the idea of threatening to disregard a Supreme Court decision, as had Richard Nixon, but when confronted with a challenge, both presidents complied with judicial rulings, Nixon at the cost of being forced from office for doing so.

The Court sailed through the turbulence of these attacks on its power, taking no official notice of them and even expanding the reach of *Marbury* v. *Madison* beyond the scope of Chief Justice Marshall's opinion. Confronted with massive southern resistance to desegregation, the Court handed down an opinion in *Cooper* v. *Aaron* (1957) unique in form in that it was signed by each of the justices individually; it held that *Marbury* laid down "the basic principle that the federal judiciary is supreme in the exposition of the law of the Constitution." "It follows," the justices went on, that the Court's interpretation of the Constitution "is the supreme law of the land," a position the Court had not previously claimed so bluntly. Five years later, in *Baker* v. *Carr,* Justice Brennan stated in passing that the Court was the "ultimate interpreter of the Constitution," again a view that went beyond *Marbury.*

Finding the justices intransigent, opponents of judicial activism returned to an earlier means of preventing unwelcome decisions: curtailing the jurisdiction of the Supreme Court or lower federal courts. This idea was nothing new. The antebellum movement to repeal section 25 was just that. But modern efforts were backed by the authority of the ambiguous *McCardle* precedent, and they held out the promise of succeeding even though more drastic head-on attacks on the Court had failed. A narrowly focused 1958 proposal by Senators William Jenner and John M. Butler nearly succeeded. It would have withdrawn Supreme Court jurisdiction over appeals from state bar-admission decisions, an attempt to reverse two 1957 decisions that voided refusals to admit bar applicants on grounds of suspected disloyalty (*Schware* v. *Board of Bar Examiners; Konigsberg* v. *State Bar*). The Senate Judiciary Committee's 1968 Crime Control Bill contained a comparable provision that would prevent future *Miranda* decisions. (*Miranda* v. *Arizona* [1966] laid out guidelines for police to follow after taking suspects into custody, including informing them of their rights to remain silent and to consult counsel.) In the late 1970s and early 1980s, congressional conservatives promoted bills that would have withdrawn federal jurisdiction, including appellate jurisdiction of the Supreme Court, in cases involving school busing, school prayer, and abortions.

Proponents of jurisdiction stripping have the advantage of a simple argument. The text of the Constitution's Article III—"with such Exceptions, and under such Regulations as the Congress shall make"—is explicit and unqualified. It seems to confer absolute congressional power, just as Chief Justice Chase had implied in *McCardle.* Thus opponents of jurisdiction stripping are driven to find some kind of implicit limits on this congressional power in the Constitution. If no such limits exist, Congress could, in effect, "reverse" an unpopular Court decision by withdrawing jurisdiction over the subject matter. The search for this limiting principle takes the form of holding that no jurisdictional withdrawal can deprive the Court of its place in the structure of government under the Constitution, or deprive the Court of its "essential role," or prevent it from maintaining the supremacy of federal law and resolving inconsistent lower-court interpretations.

It is clear that *some* principled limitation must exist on Congress's power over the Court's jurisdiction. All concede that Congress could not deprive the Court of the power to take jurisdiction of appeals by blacks or Episcopalians or Democrats. But if that is so, it must be by reason of some implicit textual or structural constraint. This internal constraint has something to do with the idea that the exceptions and regulations clause cannot "trump" the rest of the Constitution, as, for example, by permitting Congress to withdraw jurisdiction in all appeals based on the equal protection clause. Further, opponents cite two insuperable practical arguments in favor of restraints on Congress. First, if Congress can strip the Supreme Court of appellate jurisdiction, then there will be no ultimate authority to reconcile conflicting lower-court interpretations. Second (and conclusively), withdrawal of appellate jurisdiction might have the perverse and unintended effect of leaving the objectionable decision and result not only intact but immune from reconsideration. Jurisdiction withdrawal, in other words, freezes into constitutional interpretation just what its proponents want to remove. Perhaps for this reason, perhaps because the Court is popularly considered to be inviolate from attacks of the Right as well as the Left, jurisdiction withdrawal has thus far had no success.

The structure of external constraints on Supreme Court discretion works problematically at best—leaving aside for the moment the question of whether it is desirable that it should work at all. Congress's ability to "discipline" the Court or divert its doctrinal trends is feeble, even when it enjoys popular support. Political intrusion must in its nature be crude and occasional; how many times can we ratify a Sixteenth Amendment to correct the Court? (This thought is even more sobering if we recall that passage of the Sixteenth Amendment in Congress was the product of a misfired, excessively clever conservative attempt to *defeat* an income tax measure rather than to assure the constitutionality of one.) Corrective intervention through the political processes confronts an impossibly high threshold of consistent popular veneration of the Constitution and the Supreme Court.

Only one external control on doctrinal development seems to work effectively: presidential appointment of Supreme Court justices. In this area, the president can intervene decisively to reshape doctrine, as, for example, Lincoln did in the nineteenth century. In the twentieth century, four presidents have used this power with dramatic success: William Howard Taft and Warren G. Harding, who together created the conservative Court of the 1920s; Franklin Delano Roosevelt, who clumsily but effectively ended the ride of the Four Horsemen; and Richard M. Nixon, whose determination to appoint what he called "strict constructionists" eventually curbed much of the Warren Court activism of the 1963–73 decade. The Senate can moderate the president's role in the appointment process by rejecting his nominees, and it has used this power often, but usually for crudely political ends.

Since all but one of the external political constraints on Court power have proved to be of dubious utility, students of the Court have turned their attention to "internal" checks on judicial discretion. They have sought legal criteria from some authority other than the will of the judges that would control, guide, and legitimate the exercise of judicial review. Scholars have identified five criteria of judgment that guide the justices when they ponder the constitutionality of a statute.

The first is the text of the Constitution itself. We no longer find plausible the simplistic "mechanical jurisprudence," as Roscoe Pound once called it, in which, as Chief Justice Marshall claimed in *Marbury* and Justice Roberts echoed in *Butler,* the judge merely lays the text of a statute next to the text of the Constitution, in a parallel-column comparison, and determines whether they square with each other. Yet the text does remain relevant, and all agree that it controls where it is applicable. But what of constitutional text that is vague ("the equal protection of the laws") or susceptible only of historical definition ("according to the rules of the common law") or obscure ("other High Crimes and Misdemeanors")?

The next obvious criterion is the Framers' intent. Some persons, including the Reagan administration's Attorney General Edwin Meese, believe that the constitutional text and Framers' intent exhaust the list of resources available to guide constitutional interpretation. The more sophisticated versions of this idea go by the awkward and misleading label of "interpretivism." But Justice White in his *Thornburgh* dissent correctly observed:

> As its prior cases clearly show, however, this Court does not subscribe to the simplistic view that constitutional interpretation can possibly be limited to the "plain meaning" of the Constitution's text or to the subjective intention of the Framers. . . . [The Constitution] is a document announcing fundamental principles in value-laden terms that leave ample

> scope for the exercise of normative judgment by those charged with interpreting and applying it.

Yet however simplistic and inadequate the demand for "intent-based constitutionalism" may be, it is clear that, when it can be known, the Framers' intent must always be one ingredient in the construction of constitutional meaning.

But intent poses daunting problems, too: for one, *whose* intent? After all, every provision of text and amendment must be ratified as well as drafted, and we must therefore look to the intent of the ratifiers as well as the drafters. How do we determine intent? Who speaks authoritatively for the Framers? Do we take into account only their known wishes, or do we go beyond to explore the intellectual and historical context of their thought? And if we push our inquiry into contextual research, what do we seek? Their vision of history (and what if their history was faulty, as it often was)? Their ideology? Can we truly look to the ideology of Alexander Hamilton, say, as reflective of the ideas of the American people or of the other Framers? Here the attempt to simplify truth quickly drives it into falsity and error.

A third criterion was suggested by Professor Charles Black, who emphasizes structure and relationship in the constitutional mechanism. Drawing heavily on checks and balances and separation of powers, Black argued that analysis of the way the Constitution works can tell us something about what it means. But structure-oriented inquiry is limited: it tells us little about the vaguely phrased values embedded in such terms as "due process" or "cruel and unusual punishments."

History, in several forms, provides a fourth criterion for judgment. The Supreme Court is at the apex of a system of common law courts, and thus one particularized kind of history, judicial precedent, plays a prominent but not conclusive role in its deliberations. How far should precedent be binding? How readily should the Court reverse itself when it considers a precedent to be wrong? Should it reverse itself more readily in constitutional cases than in nonconstitutional ones?

Justices Holmes and Cardozo were the foremost exponents of another form of history as a guide for judging: what Cardozo called "the traditions and conscience of our people" (*Snyder* v. *Massachusetts,* 1934). Throughout his career, Holmes emphasized that in appellate judging "a page of history is worth a volume of logic" (*New York Trust Co.* v. *Eisner,* 1921). Because "the law embodies the story of a nation's development through many centuries," as he wrote in *The Common Law* (1881), Holmes considered history to be an indispensable key to legal interpretation, and the surest guide to the subtle judicial intuition that his *Lochner* dissent offered as the alternative to the desiccated logic of formalism. But problems abound here, too. History is discovered, interpreted, and written by human beings, not by God, and is thus as fallible as any other source of constitutional interpretation. It has much to tell us, but it cannot be authoritative.

Justice Harlan identified a fifth criterion in his concurrence in *Griswold:* "the basic values that underlie our society." Some commentators suggest that the Court has the responsibility of identifying, articulating, and then applying the evolving fundamental values of the American people. Harry Wellington expressed the idea candidly: "The Court's task is to ascertain the weight of [a] principle in conventional morality and to convert the moral principle into a legal one by connecting it with the body of constitutional law" (Harry Wellington, "Common Law Rules and Constitutional Double Standards: Some Notes on Adjudication," *Yale Law Journal* 83 [1973]:284). This is often called a "consensus" approach, because the function of the justices is to identify and give effect to an evolving, modern, and widely shared value affirmation by the American people.

The search for an unassailable criterion of judgment, *the* authoritative touchstone of judicial review, has engendered a dialogue among judges and scholars that has persisted through most of this century. The roots of this debate are found in the *Lochner* era and assumptions then widely shared by lawyers and jurists, for modern juristic thought was formed in reaction to these now discredited assumptions. Formalist judges of the 1895–1937 period assumed that law was objective, unchanging, extrinsic to the social climate, and, above all, different from and superior to politics. Judges such as Rufus Peckham and legal thinkers such as Thomas Cooley were mesmerized by a fear of socialism. They did not repudiate democratic, majoritarian government, but they were alarmed by the tendency they detected in it to degenerate into a plunder of the rich minority by the poor majority, accompanied by the disintegration of republican government into tyranny. Thus their highest value was individual liberty, protected by a Constitution whose commands were unchanging and transcendent. In this view, judicial review was essential to the survival of constitutional government.

The Legal Realists of the 1920s and '30s, tutored by Holmes, Pound, and Cardozo, devastated these assumptions, but the momentum of their attack occasionally carried their arguments to extremes. They sought to weaken, if not dissolve, the law-politics dichotomy, by showing that the act of judging was not impersonal or mechanistic, but rather was necessarily infected by the judges' personal values. The problem this approach posed, however, was that if the law-politics distinction were destroyed, constitutionalism itself was meaningless and judicial review was illegitimate. The inevitable postwar reaction set the agenda for the modern debate. How to legitimate judicial review and set the proper bounds for its scope?

The earliest postwar approach has been called "Reasoned Elaboration." It was expounded by Henry Hart of the Harvard Law School, Herbert Wechsler of the Columbia Law School, and Alexander Bickel of the Yale Law School. Hart condemned result-oriented decision making, and was deeply concerned with judicial craftsmanship. By this he meant the technical quality and persuasive force of opinions (Henry M. Hart, "The Time Chart of the Justices," *Harvard Law Review* 73 [1959]:84). Hart and Wechsler were distressed that major decisions seemed to be ad hoc, written to achieve some particular result, such as destroying racial segregation, and lacking in both reasoning and the grounding in principles that would free them from the suspicion of being nothing more than a raw exercise of judicial will. Herbert Wechsler insisted that the substance of judgment must be guided by "neutral principles" outside of and prior to the policy preferences of the judges (Herbert Wechsler, "Toward Neutral Principles of Constitutional Law," *Harvard Law Review* 73 [1959]:1). Hence Reasoned Elaboration strongly reinforced the Marshall law–politics dichotomy and repudiated much of Legal Realism. Wechsler and others feared that if the Marshall distinction were abandoned, the rule of law itself would be threatened.

Alexander Bickel modified the Hart-Wechsler position significantly. In his 1962 book, *The Least Dangerous Branch,* he agreed that when the Court either upholds or strikes down a statute or executive action it must do so on the basis of transcendent principles. But he emphasized what he called "the passive virtues," the Court's ability to evade or defer action. These decisions need not be principled; they are expediential, returning the issue to the political realm to be further refined and perhaps resolved there. Bickel went beyond Hart and Wechsler, though, in accepting the idea that when the Court does choose to address an issue laden with substantive value choices it can go beyond consensus and a priori principles to anticipate emergent and changing values. Thus he supported the result in *Brown* v. *Board of Education,* which Wechsler had condemned as unprincipled.

The Reasoned Elaboration approach had been provoked by *Brown;* successive schools of thought would be responsive to the period of Warren Court activism inaugurated by the retirement of Justice Frankfurter in 1962 and his replacement with Arthur Goldberg, assuring a liberal and activist majority of five justices through the ensuing decade. Bickel, significantly, was one of the first to emerge as a critic of the new activism that his 1962 book had justified. In *The Supreme Court and the Idea of Progress* (1970) and *The Morality of Consent* (published posthumously in 1975), Bickel repudiated what he saw as the excessive intervention of the liberal Court in policy making which should more appropriately have been left to the political branches.

Bickel's disillusioned criticism was soon overtaken by an attack on liberal activism from the political Right. Robert Bork, at the time a Yale Law School professor and shortly to play a prominent role in the events of Watergate, demanded that judges apply only values identified by the Framers, uncontaminated by subsequent value preferences—whether of judges or of the American people was irrelevant (Robert H. Bork, "Neutral Principles and Some First Amendment Problems," *Indiana Law Journal* 47 [1971]: 1–35). Raoul Berger carried this view further in his tendentious but influential 1977 study, *Government by Judiciary.* Concentrating on the equal protection clause of the Fourteenth Amendment, Berger attempted to demonstrate that its drafters did not intend it to abolish school segregation. He therefore condemned *Brown* as wrong on principle, but stated that it had been too important in its time, and by then too much a part of America's social organization to be uprooted. Berger demanded that judges hew closely to the Framers' intent, subjectively defined, and that judges attempt to identify what result they would have sought in their own time. This view went back to Taney's hitherto discredited *Dred Scott* conception of a concrete Constitution set in meaning at the time its phrases were drafted.

These academic interpretivists, as they have been called—a better term might be "literalists"—were now seconded by a powerful voice on the Court itself, Justice Rehnquist, appointed by Nixon in 1972. On and off the Court, Rehnquist posed a radically different model of judicial review in a democracy. In a position smacking oddly of philosophical relativism, Rehnquist maintained that all value choices, whether made by judges or legislators, are inherently arbitrary. Beating yet another time the dead horse of natural law, Rehnquist and most other conservatives insisted that there was no objective criterion by which values could be authoritatively placed in a hierarchy. Thus, in a representative democracy, the selection of values is appropriately left to the democratic process, which he conceived of as functioning like a marketplace.

This strikingly contrasted with the position of Rehnquist's ideological forebears such as Justice Field. The *Lochner*-era judges squinted suspiciously at democracy and majoritarian government; Rehnquist confidently embraced majoritarianism. To today's neoconservatives, constitutional liberty is threatened not by the people, but by a nonelected judicial elite imposing its values on the representative branches of government. Rehnquist insisted that the only valid criteria for judging were text and Framers' intent. Judges could apply only those values identified and included in the Constitution by the Framers. Searching for noninterpretivist, consensual sources of values therefore threatened democratic government. Rehnquist remains deeply suspicious of talk about a "living Constitution." The Framers established the meaning of the words of the Constitution; judges cannot alter that meaning, but are limited to applying it in changing circumstances.

Repelled by this pseudo-populistic positivism, and seeking to defend the legitimacy of *Roe* v. *Wade* and Warren Court activism generally, liberal scholars of the 1970s in rebuttal developed theories aimed at restricting the power of majorities. Whereas conservatives exalted liberty, liberal theorists spoke of equality and dignity. Kenneth Karst, Michael J. Perry, and Harry Wellington insisted that values were not chosen arbitrarily (Kenneth Karst, "Why Equality Matters," *Georgia Law Review* 17 [1983]:245; Michael J. Perry, "Noninterpretive Review in Human Rights Cases: A Functional Justification," *New York University Law Review* 56 [1981]:278–352; Wellington, "Common Law Rules," *supra*). Rather, they maintained, a consensus among the American people on fundamental values could be identified by the application of reason, and this definition would be objective, in the sense that it was not merely a projection of the judges' personal values. These values change over time, and all branches of government are charged with responsibility for adapting the constitutional order to them. But it was inherent in a democratic form of government that majorities would define values,and impose their conception on minorities. Hence the courts were assigned the unique role of preserving the rights of all within a system of government that permits majorities to rule.

Preeminent among those academics defending the possibility of objectively identifying fundamental values is John Hart Ely, who at the time of publication of his influential book *Democracy and Distrust* (1980) was a professor of law at Yale. The power of Ely's argument derived from his pursuit of process-oriented values, not substantive ones. He maintained that judicial review legitimately functioned to remove barriers that restricted access to political power, such as limitations on political speech or dilutions of the vote. He also supported an interventionist role for the Court in assuring that majorities would always consider the interests of minorities. He called this a "representation-reinforcing" mode of review.

The coherence of constitutional theory disintegrated in the 1980s, partly because of a breakdown in agreement on the fundamental terms of the debate. Scholars on the political Left, who called themselves the

Conference on Critical Legal Studies, attacked fundamental presuppositions about the purposes of judicial review. Under the slogan "law is politics," they dissolved the Marshallian dichotomy, and generally skewered the notion of the rule of law as a sham meant to perpetuate the hegemony of ruling elites. More moderate constitutional authorities, such as Owen Fiss, decried this approach as nihilism, and insisted that constraint and objectivity in law were possible (Owen M. Fiss, "Objectivity and Interpretation," *Stanford Law Review* 34 [1982]:739). But no single school of thought dominated debate or even set the terms of argument.

The essentials of debate over the place of judicial review in American democracy, as that debate had been refined through the mid-1980s, center around the problem of legitimacy. All agree that judicial review, to be legitimate, must consist of something more than judges simply imposing their own values, especially when they thwart the will of democratic majorities. Thus the act of judging must be objective; that is, it must proceed by criteria other than the judges' personal political, religious, and social beliefs. These external and objective criteria are bundled together in the concept of the rule of law. Thus the task becomes one of maintaining the rule of law, "to the end that it may be a government of laws and not of men." The formulation is John Adams's, embodied in Article XXX of the Massachusetts Declaration of Rights. As a formula, it has not been improved upon in two hundred years.

In American constitutional experience, the rule of law has been approximated in several ways. First, American courts have generally respected the distinction between rules of law on the one hand and religion, morality, and policy objectives on the other. This distinction has kept courts from enforcing religious or political programs. It is easy to think of failures, of course: Taney's blind and willful promotion of slavery or the Four Horsemen's obstinate attachment to a formalistic fantasy world that abhorred democracy. Though these exceptions are shocking, their existence proves the rule: The Court normally and usually does not plant itself athwart the direction of majority rule. Taney and the Four Horsemen are memorable precisely because they were exceptional. Were they the norm, the political process would have long ago performed major corrective surgery on the Court, by constitutional amendment if necessary. Law is secular and apolitical. As Hamilton insisted, it is an exercise of judgment rather than will, will being the domain of the legislative and executive branches.

A second component of the rule of law is the process of common law development itself. Because judges are bound by precedent (unless they overrule or distinguish it), the evolution and development of legal rules take place through a dialogue that refines concepts, often over long periods of time. The history of the clear-and-present-danger test is illustrative. From its original formulation in Holmes's *Schenck* opinion, through its attenuation in the 1920s over Holmes's and Brandeis's protests, to its current refinement in *Brandenburg,* clear and present danger as a rule of law has sometimes served to constrain the power of government to suppress speech and sometimes to restrict the bounds of communication. Its development has been partly autonomous, as lawyers and judges strove to find some inherent and enduring meaning in the verbal formula, and partly instrumental, as the formula was adapted to serve the needs of society (as the judges perceived them). But it is the process of refinement, rather than the state of the rule at any particular time, that moves the law toward justice.

Third, common law courts over the past several centuries have evolved procedural ground rules that function to keep certain kinds of cases—those improper for adjudication—out of courts, leaving them to be resolved in the political process. One of the most important of these rules at the constitutional level is that federal courts under the Constitution cannot take jurisdiction over collusive suits: feigned or simulated legal quarrels made up to get a point of law before the courts. Collusive suits have produced some of the worst specimens of judicial decision making in the nearly two centuries' history of the Court. Other procedural exclusionary devices include the rules of standing, which operate in a rough way to exclude parties who have no real and personal interest in the subject matter or outcome of litigation, or whose interest is purely ideological; and the political question doctrine, a discretionary device that permits courts to decline to decide cases that are not justiciable. The effect of the procedural limitations on judicial authority is to filter out many cases whose resolution belongs in the political arenas. That filtering out does not guarantee principled decision making in every case, of course. No verbal formula can, and it is self-deluding to search for such a will-o'-the-wisp.

Finally, law is autonomous because its evolution is so closely tied to history. In the hands of a judge open to history's potentials, such as Cardozo or the second Harlan, law unfolds out of its own past. The legislature is free to reject or ignore the past at will, or to consult it solely as a catalog of mistakes; courts are not. Granted, judicial history is notoriously bad: Cardozo and Harlan were exceptions. Yet even done poorly, history serves as an anchor or constraint on judicial whim. The past remains a monitor and a criterion by which the judges' performance can be evaluated.

Two millennia ago, Juvenal asked: but who will guard the guardians?

Democracy is the precondition for the Supreme Court's legitimacy and creativity. Constrained by both internal restraints and exterior monitors, the Court checks the excesses of the political process while being bound by that very process itself. To Juvenal's challenge, we properly respond: Congress, the president, the states, and ultimately the American people themselves.

GLOSSARY

Technical subjects such as law necessarily employ their own specialized professional language, and it is impossible to discuss the subject without some use of its jargon. I have tried to keep jargon to a minimum, and here define those words or phrases that are not household words rather than breaking the text narrative.

ADMIRALTY Variously, a body of law distinct from the common law, or the courts that administer that law. It is the law of the sea, historically covering both civilian subjects (e.g., marine insurance, salvage, torts at sea, and so on) and military (prize and capture). Juries are not used in admiralty courts.

AMICUS CURIAE (*L.* "friend of the court"; pl. amici) Courts sometimes permit some nonparty (e.g., the federal government or the American Civil Liberties Union) to participate in the argument of a case in which it has both an interest and expertise. An amicus typically files a brief presenting the argument that it would have made if it had been a party to the original suit.

BILL OF EXCHANGE A form of commercial paper widely used in the eighteenth and nineteenth century. A orders B to pay a specified sum of money to C at a fixed future time.

CERTIORARI (*L.* "to be made more certain") Today, the principal means by which cases come for review to the United States Supreme Court. Its origin is a writ of common law by which a superior court orders an inferior court to send up a certified record of proceedings before it to determine whether there were errors below. Its principal characteristic is that it is discretionary, that is, the superior court can choose to issue it or not, as it wishes, in contrast with an appeal, which is allowed as of right.

COLLATERAL ATTACK This phrase describes an attempt by a party to one proceeding (or even someone who is not a party) to defeat, avoid, or reverse that proceeding in some other legal action that lies outside the established procedures for appellate review.

COLLUSIVE SUIT A suit in which the opposing parties do not have any genuine controversy or adversarial conflict between them. "Friendly parties," so called, bring collusive suits in order to create a test case to get an abstract ruling on a question of law. Collusive suits are a mischievous abuse of judicial power and have produced some of the Supreme Court's worst decisions.

COMMERCIAL PAPER Various forms of legally enforceable orders between private parties, such as promissory notes, checks on bank accounts, and other kinds of negotiable instruments.

COMMON LAW The system of law derived from judicial decisions, developed by judges who follow precedent and adhere to the principle of stare decisis (q.v.). In theory, the common law grows out of usage and custom. It is contrasted with the civil law systems of the continental nations, based on codes and derived remotely from Roman law; in this sense, England and the former members of the British Empire, including the American states, are common law jurisdictions. It is also contrasted with statutory law, which consists of statutes enacted by legislatures.

CONTEMPT A willful disregard of a court's or legislature's order or dignity by a party to a proceeding before it or by some other person within its jurisdiction. The court or legislature has power to punish contempts by fine and imprisonment.

DICTUM See obiter dictum.

DISTRESS (from L. *distrahere,* "to pull apart") A right recognized at common law whereby a creditor, such as a landlord, can seize a debtor's chattels (thereby pulling the debtor apart from his property) without recourse to judicial process.

DIVERSITY JURISDICTION Jurisdiction of federal courts conferred by Article III, section 2, over suits between citizens of two different states. The parties are said to be "diverse."

EQUITY A body of Anglo-American law parallel to the common law. Historically, it developed in England out of the need to provide discretion in the application of common law rules. In England it came to have its own courts and proceedings, but in the United States since the nineteenth century it has been merged with common law in many jurisdictions. However, it survives in the law of remedies (e.g., injunctions).

EX PARTE (*L.* "on the side of") A judicial proceeding or order that is undertaken on behalf of one party only, with either no opposing party or the opposing party absent from the proceeding. Ex parte actions provide opposing parties no notice or opportunity to be heard.

FEDERAL QUESTIONS Cases within the jurisdiction of federal courts that involve questions of interpretation of the United States Constitution, laws, or treaties.

HABEAS CORPUS (*L.* "you should have the body") A generic name for a group of writs that command someone restraining an individual to produce the detainee before a judge so that the cause and legality of the detention can be reviewed. The most important of these writs, technically known as habeas corpus ad subjiciendum but more popularly and justly termed "the great writ of liberty," is the fundamental guarantor of personal freedom and limited government in common law jurisdictions.

IN CHAMBERS (*L. in camera*) When a judge disposes of business in his or her private office, rather than in open court, the hearing is said to be in chambers.

INDICTMENT A way to begin criminal proceedings in common law jurisdictions. A grand jury returns an indictment, which signifies its determination that the prosecutor has demonstrated sufficient probable cause to justify placing a defendant on trial.

INJUNCTION (v. to enjoin) A judicial order, originating in equity rather than in the common law courts, which commands an individual to do an act, or prohibits him or her from doing some act, that is either illegal or injurious to the petitioner seeking the injunction. Like all equitable remedies, it can be issued only when there is no adequate remedy at law (i.e., when money damages will not satisfactorily prevent or redress the threatened injury).

IPSE DIXIT (*L.* "he himself said") An assertion resting on nothing more than the authority of the individual making it.

JUDICIAL REVIEW The power of courts to hold a statute or an act of the executive in violation of the Constitution, and therefore to refuse to enforce it.

JUSTICIABILITY A case is justiciable if it presents a question judges are capable of resolving, in contrast with, for example, a political question, which only the legislative or executive branches can resolve.

MANDAMUS (*L.* "we command") One of the so-called extraordinary writs at common law by which a court commands an officer of government to perform some act required by law.

MILITARY COMMISSION A panel of military officers and/or civilians that functions as a tribunal to determine and punish violations of martial law. It functions as a court martial, but is used to try civilians. Its existence is antithetical to the jurisdiction of regular civil courts.

NEGOTIABILITY A legal characteristic by which an instrument (that is, a written document such as a bank check, a note evidencing indebtedness, or some other form of commercial paper) can be transferred from A to B by being endorsed or simply delivered by A. If the instrument is negotiable, B succeeds to all or most of the rights of A.

OBITER DICTUM (*L.* "said in passing"; sometimes simply obiter or dictum [pl. dicta]) A statement by a judge in a judicial opinion that is not necessary to the decision of the case. The remark is incidental to the principal line of reasoning. As a gratuitous expression of opinion, it is not binding as precedent. Sometimes, especially in modern cases, the line between dicta and holdings is unclear.

ON CIRCUIT When a judge is on circuit, he or she is traveling to locations away from the place where his or her court normally sits to do judicial business. Justices of the United States Supreme Court have always been assigned a circuit; in the eighteenth and nineteenth centuries, they actually traveled to their circuits to sit as circuit judges.

PER CURIAM (*L.* "by the court") Designates an opinion by the court as a body rather than by an individual judge. In the past, it has been used for summary dispositions of appeals with only the briefest of explanations; in recent times, it has sometimes been as lengthy and substantive as a conventional opinion. Individual judges may dissent from it by opinion if they choose.

PLURALITY OPINION An opinion by less than a majority of the judges of a court, but announcing the result for the judges composing the majority.

PREROGATIVE COURTS Certain non–common law English courts, such as Star Chamber or High Commission, which sometimes became instruments of royal power and, in a Whiggish historical view, endangered the liberty of the subject.

QUESTION OF FIRST INSTANCE When a case involves an entirely new question for judicial decision, never before addressed by the court, it is said to be a question of first instance.

QUO WARRANTO (*L.* "by what warrant?") One of the extraordinary writs at common law, by which a court inquires into the exercise of authority alleged to be unlawful or not conferred. Historically, quo warranto reached both public officials and private entities such as corporations.

RECUSE Judges recuse themselves, in effect disqualifying or excusing themselves from hearing a particular case, because they have an interest (financial, familial) in the outcome of the case or because they suspect that their decision would be tainted by bias.

REMOVAL JURISDICTION The jurisdiction of federal courts, conferred by statute, whereby cases may be taken out of state courts and tried in federal courts.

SERIATIM OPINIONS (*L.* "separately") Before the nineteenth century, English and American courts followed the practice of rendering opinions seriatim, whereby all the judges would deliver an opinion in the case, with none purporting to speak for the whole bench. Attorneys were left to their own devices to figure out which opinion, if any, reflected the collective opinion of the court.

STARE DECISIS (*L.* "to stand by a decided [case]") The policy of common law courts to follow precedent in cases presenting essentially the same facts. The principle dictates courts follow settled questions of law and principles as found in earlier decisions. Courts, of course, can overrule their own prior decisions if they believe the earlier case was wrongly decided or no longer persuasive, but until they do so, stare decisis assures continuity in common law adjudication. The principle does not exist in civil law jurisdictions.

SUBPOENA DUCES TECUM (*L.* "bring with you under penalty") A court order requiring an individual to produce a document in a hearing.

ULTRA VIRES (*L.* "beyond the power [of]") A doctrine of corporate law by which a court determines that some corporate act was beyond the lawful authority of the corporation as defined by its charter.

WRIT OF PROHIBITION An extraordinary writ issued by a superior court to an inferior, commanding the latter to relinquish jurisdiction over the parties and cause of action of a case before it on the ground that the inferior court lacks authority to hear the cause.

RECOMMENDED READINGS

The literature on the United States Supreme Court and American constitutional history is vast. The reading list that follows suggests some of the best of it and offers the reader a guide to more detailed explorations of the topics covered in the Introduction and each of the chapters.

Introduction: The United States Supreme Court and American Constitutionalism

There are numerous historical studies of the United States Supreme Court. Charles Warren, *The Supreme Court in United States History,* 2 vols., rev. ed. (Boston, 1932), is *the* classic study, astonishingly relevant more than a half century after its publication; it is conservative and nationalist in its orientation. Alfred H. Kelly, Winfred A. Harbison, and Herman Belz, *The American Constitution: Its Origin and Development,* 6th ed. (New York, 1983), is a general text covering American constitutional history. Its latest edition, completely rewritten by Professor Belz, surpasses the high standards set by the senior authors. David P. Currie, *The Constitution in the Supreme Court: The First Hundred Years, 1789–1888* (Chicago, 1985), is constitutional history in a lawyer's doctrinal mode. G. Edward White, *The American Judicial Tradition: Profiles of Leading American Judges* (New York, 1976), consists of chapter-length evaluations of America's most prominent jurists, many of them justices of the United States Supreme Court. Allison Dunham and Philip B. Kurland, eds., *Mr. Justice,* rev. ed. (Chicago, 1964), also comprises biographical sketches of selected justices. Leon Friedman and Fred L. Israel, eds., *The Justices of the United States Supreme Court, 1789–1969,* 4 vols. (New York, 1969–78), contains comprehensive biographical sketches, plus reproductions of each jurist's principal opinions. Lawrence M. Friedman, *A History of American Law,* 2d ed. (New York, 1985), a path-breaking survey of American legal history, includes much constitutional material, but concentrates principally on the nineteenth century. Leonard W. Levy et al., eds., *Encyclopedia of the American Constitution,* 4 vols. (New York, 1986), is a magisterial encyclopedic treatment of topics and figures in American constitutional history, prepared by historians, lawyers, and political scientists. The Holmes Devise *History of the Supreme Court of the United States* to date includes the following volumes in print: volume 1, *Antecedents and Beginnings to 1801,* by Julius Goebel, Jr. (New York, 1971); volume 2, part 1, *Foundations of Power: John Marshall, 1801–1815,* by George L. Haskins and Herbert A. Johnson (New York, 1981); volume 5, *The Taney Period, 1836–1864,* by Carl B. Swisher (New York, 1971); volume 6, part 1, *Reconstruction and Reunion, 1864–1888,* by Charles Fairman (New York, 1971); and volume 9, *The Judiciary and Responsible Government, 1910–1921,* by Alexander M. Bickel and Benno C. Schmidt, Jr. (New York, 1984).

The most useful bibliographies available to guide the reader to the literature on the Court and its history are the one in Kelly, Harbison, and Belz, *The American Constitution* (74 pp., annotated), and Kermit L. Hall, comp., *A Comprehensive Bibliography of American Constitutional and Legal History, 1896–1979,* 5 vols. (Millwood, N.Y., 1984), an incredibly complete collection of virtually everything written on the subject in the last century.

Several interpretive studies of the Supreme Court stand out. Paul A. Freund, *The Supreme Court of the United States: Its Business, Purposes, and Performance* (Cleveland, 1961), is a model of balanced judgment. Robert G. McCloskey, *The American Supreme Court* (Chicago, 1960), was for a generation the leading interpretive history of the Court. Laurence H. Tribe, *American Constitutional Law* (Mineola, N.Y., 1978, plus 1979 supplement), is a lawyer's handbook organized around the author's bold and imaginative effort to rethink the whole of American constitutional law, limited unfortunately to the traditional legal sources the lawyer is trained to work with. Alexander M. Bickel, *The Least Dangerous Branch: The Supreme Court at the Bar of Politics* (Indianapolis, 1962), is an imaginative justification for judicial review and a landmark in the interpretive tradition.

The serious reader will want to get into the primary sources. These of course begin with the official reports of the Court's decisions, the *United States Reports,* also reprinted in two commercial series: *The Supreme Court Reporter* and *United States Supreme Court Reports: Lawyers' Edition.* Stanley I. Kutler, ed., *The Supreme Court and the Constitution: Readings in American Constitutional History,* 3d ed. (New York, 1984), is a collection of excerpts of Supreme Court opinions, historically arranged. Two of the best topical arrangements in law school casebooks are Gerald Gunther, ed., *Constitutional Law,* 11th ed. (Mineola, N.Y., 1985), and Geoffrey R.

Stone et al., eds., *Constitutional Law* (Boston, 1986). James M. Smith and Paul L. Murphy, comps., *Liberty and Justice,* 2 vols. (New York, 1965), is an excellent selection of constitutional documents; regrettably it is now out of print.

Chapter 1. The Origins of American Constitutionalism

Philip B. Kurland and Ralph Lerner compiled a remarkably complete collection of documents embodying the origins of American constitutionalism, from 1603 through 1835: *The Founders' Constitution,* 5 vols. (Chicago, 1987). There is no convenient one-volume survey of the English background to American constitutionalism, but Arthur E. Sutherland, *Constitutionalism in America: Origin and Evolution of Its Fundamental Ideas* (New York, 1965), provides a brief introduction integrated with later American developments. Catherine D. Bowen, *The Lion and the Throne* (Boston, 1957), is a pleasurable and illuminating biography of Sir Edward Coke. Theodore Plucknett, "*Bonham's Case* and Judicial Review," *Harvard Law Review* 40 (1926): 30–70, corrects extravagant readings of that landmark. Despite the richness of studies in early American legal history (see David H. Flaherty, ed., *Essays in the History of Early American Law* [Chapel Hill, N.C., 1969], a collection of some of the best secondary work), we suffer from a dearth of comparable work in pre-Independence constitutional history. This lack is partly due to a pernicious tradition originating early in the twentieth century and ratified by the immense authority of Roscoe Pound, *The Formative Era of American Law* (Boston, 1938), that presumed no significant legal and constitutional development in America existed before 1776. Stanley N. Katz considers this question in "The Problem of a Colonial Legal History," in Jack P. Greene and J. R. Pole, eds., *Colonial British America: Essays in the New History of the Early Modern Era* (Baltimore, 1984). The late Stephen Botein sketched the beginnings of a useful survey in *Early American Law and Society* (New York, 1983), but his larger work in this direction was brought to an end by his untimely death. George Dargo, *Roots of the Republic: A New Perspective on Early American Constitutionalism* (New York, 1974), is a welcome essay in the field. See also Michael Kammen, *Deputyes and Libertyes: The Origins of Representative Government in Colonial America* (New York, 1969); Bernard Bailyn, *The Origin of American Politics* (New York, 1968); and the essays collected in George A. Billias, ed., *Law and Authority in Colonial America* (Barre, Mass., 1965). Some of the best work in the field is now quite old though still valuable; see, for example, Andrew C. McLaughlin, *The Foundations of American Constitutionalism* (New York, 1932).

Studies of American republican thought are rich and instructive. Gordon Wood, *The Creation of the American Republic* (Chapel Hill, N.C., 1969), is a massive survey. Bernard Bailyn, *The Ideological Origins of the American Revolution* (Cambridge, Mass., 1967), complements it nicely. This work, now twenty years old, has stimulated lawyers to undertake reconsideration of early constitutional development; see, for example, Thomas C. Grey, "Origins of the Unwritten Constitution: Fundamental Law in American Revolutionary Thought," *Stanford Law Review* 30 (1978): 843–93. The actual fruits of republican thought, the first American constitutions, are collected in William F. Swindler's *Sources and Documents of United States Constitutions,* 10 vols. (Dobbs Ferry, N.Y., 1973–79).

The history of the earliest American courts is traced in Roscoe Pound, *Organization of Courts* (Boston, 1940); Peter S. Onuf, *The Origins of the Federal Republic: Jurisdictional Controversies in the United States, 1775–1787* (Philadelphia, 1983); Henry J. Bourguignon, *The First Federal Court: The Federal Appellate Prize Court of the American Revolution, 1775–1787* (Philadelphia, 1977); and John P. Frank, "Historical Bases of the Federal Judicial System," *Law and Contemporary Problems* 13 (1948): 3–28. For the United States Supreme Court itself, in addition to the general studies noted earlier, especially those of Goebel, Warren, and Currie, see Richard B. Morris, *John Jay, the Nation and the Court* (Boston, 1967), and Stephen B. Presser, "A Tale of Two Judges: Richard Peters, Samuel Chase, and the Broken Promise of Federalist Jurisprudence," *Northwestern University Law Review* 73 (1978): 26–111.

Chapter 2. The Court under Chief Justice Marshall

Differing interpretations of the work of the Marshall Court can be found in George L. Haskins and Herbert A. Johnson, *Foundations of Power: John Marshall, 1801–1815* (New York, 1981) (the first of three Marshall volumes in the Holmes Devise *History of the Supreme Court*); Kent Newmyer, *The Supreme Court under Marshall and Taney* (New York, 1968); Charles G. Haines, *The Role of the Supreme Court in American Government and Politics, 1789–1935* (Berkeley, 1944); and the essays in W. Melville Jones, ed., *Chief Justice Marshall: A Reappraisal* (Ithaca, N.Y., 1956).

Several excellent biographies of Marshall and his brethren provide a valuable analytical perspective on the Court. Kent Newmyer, *Supreme Court Justice Joseph Story* (Chapel Hill, N.C., 1985), is outstanding. James McClellan provides a contrast in his *Joseph Story and the American Constitution* (Norman, Okla., 1971), a presentist effort to depict Story as being even more conservative than he was. On Marshall, Francis N. Stites, *John*

Marshall: Defender of the Constitution (Boston, 1981), is a brief modern biography. Albert J. Beveridge, *The Life of John Marshall,* 4 vols. (Boston, 1929), was the pioneer of the interpretive school that views Marshall as a conservative nationalist. Supplementing biographical approaches are several studies that consider the jurisprudential approaches of the Court. These include Robert K. Faulkner, *The Jurisprudence of John Marshall* (Princeton, 1968), and William Nelson, "The Eighteenth Century Background of John Marshall's Jurisprudence," *Michigan Law Review* 76 (1978): 893–960.

The subject of judicial review has a body of literature all to itself. Its classics include James B. Thayer, "The Origin and Scope of the American Doctrine of Constitutional Law," *Harvard Law Review* 7 (1893): 129–56, still worth reading; Edward S. Corwin, "The 'Higher Law' Background of American Constitutional Law," *Harvard Law Review* 42 (1928): 145–85; Corwin, *The Doctrine of Judicial Review* (Princeton, 1914); and Corwin, "The Basic Doctrine of American Constitutional Law," *Michigan Law Review* 12 (1914): 247–76. William W. Crosskey, *Politics and the Constitution in the History of the United States,* 3 vols. (Chicago, 1953–80), attacks the legitimacy of judicial review, whereas Raoul Berger, *Congress and the Supreme Court* (Cambridge, Mass., 1969) defends it. Kermit L. Hall provides a concise modern survey of the subject in *The Supreme Court and Judicial Review in American History* (Washington, 1985). William E. Nelson studied the emergence of judicial review at the state level in "Changing Conceptions of Judicial Review: The Evolution of Constitutional Theory in the States, 1790–1860," *University of Pennsylvania Law Review* 120 (1972): 1166–85. A valuable historiographic survey of the controversy over judicial review is provided by Alan Westin's introduction to the modern reprint of Charles A. Beard, *The Supreme Court and the Constitution* (Englewood Cliffs, N.J., 1962).

Given the importance of the landmark decisions of the Marshall Court, it is no surprise that some of them have entire volumes devoted to them alone. One of the most wide-ranging is Maurice G. Baxter, *The Steamboat Monopoly: Gibbons v. Ogden, 1824* (New York, 1972). See also William Van Alstyne, "A Critical Guide to Marbury v. Madison," *Duke Law Journal* (1969): 1–47; Donald Dewey, *Marshall v. Jefferson: The Political Background of Marbury v. Madison* (New York, 1970); C. Peter Magrath, *Yazoo: Law and Politics in the New Republic: The Case of Fletcher v. Peck* (Providence, 1966); Francis N. Stites, *Private Interest & Public Gain: The Dartmouth College Case, 1819* (Amherst, Mass., 1972); Gerald Gunther, ed., *John Marshall's Defense of McCulloch v. Maryland* (Stanford, 1969). Two older but still valuable studies of lines of decisions, rather than specific cases, are Felix Frankfurter, *The Commerce Clause under Marshall,*

Taney, and Waite (Chapel Hill, N.C., 1937) and Benjamin F. Wright, *The Contract Clause of the Constitution* (rpt., Westport, Conn., 1982).

Informative studies of specific issues that rose to prominence in the Marshall years include Richard Ellis, *Jeffersonian Crisis: Courts and Politics in the Young Republic* (New York, 1971); Charles Warren, "New Light on the Judiciary Act of 1789," *Harvard Law Review* 37 (1933): 49–132; and Warren, "Legislative and Judicial Attacks on the Supreme Court of the United States—A History of the Twenty-fifth Section of the Judiciary Act," *American Law Review* 47 (1913): 161–89.

Chapter 3. Democracy, Slavery, and Capitalism before the Taney Court

The Taney Court is not so richly served by general studies and biographies as its predecessor, perhaps a consequence of the long shadow still cast by John Marshall. In addition to studies noted earlier, see Charles G. Haines and Foster H. Sherwood, *The Role of the Supreme Court in American Government and Politics, 1835–1864* (Berkeley, 1957). Useful biographical studies include Swisher, *Roger B. Taney* (New York, 1936) (a comparison of this biography, written early in Professor Swisher's illustrious career, with his posthumously published Holmes Devise study of the Taney Court, is instructive, demonstrating how a scholar's evaluation of the subject of his life's work can evolve as his thought matures and the times change). Leonard W. Levy, *The Law of the Commonwealth and Chief Justice Shaw* (Cambridge, Mass., 1957), remains superb a generation after its appearance. Gerald T. Dunne, *Justice Joseph Story and the Rise of the Supreme Court* (New York, 1970), complements the Story biographies noted previously. Robert J. Harris, "Chief Justice Taney: Prophet of Reform and Reaction," *Vanderbilt Law Review* 10 (1957): 227–57, was the earliest study to capture the shadows as well as the light in Taney's achievements. John P. Frank, *Justice Daniel Dissenting: A Biography of Peter V. Daniel* (Cambridge, Mass., 1964), is good on that unique jurist, and Maurice G. Baxter ably traces the influence of the leading advocate before the Court in *Daniel Webster and the Supreme Court* (Amherst, Mass., 1966).

The era of the Taney Court is illuminated by several studies that provide the economic and political background in which the Court did its work. Harold M. Hyman and William M. Wiecek, *Equal Justice under Law: Constitutional Development, 1835–1875* (New York, 1982), surveys the political and constitutional trends of the middle period. Morton J. Horwitz, *The Transformation of American Law, 1780–1860* (Cambridge, Mass., 1977), is a provocative analysis of private law developments. J. Willard Hurst, *Law and the Conditions of Freedom* (Madison, 1956), is legal history elevated to jurisprudence; its insights on the Taney era are profound and have shaped the thinking of the present generation of legal and constitutional historians.

Unlike its predecessor, the Taney Court was dominated by concerns over slavery. Numerous works trace linkages between slavery and constitutional development. David M. Potter, *The Impending Crisis, 1848–1861* (New York, 1976), provides insightful background. On slavery itself, Arthur E. Bestor, Jr., "State Sovereignty and Slavery: A Reinterpretation of Proslavery Constitutional Doctrine, 1846–1860," *Journal of the Illinois State Historical Society* 54 (1961): 117–80, is profound in its reconceptualization of proslavery ideology and constitutional processes. The constitutional struggle over slavery is surveyed in William M. Wiecek, *The Sources of Antislavery Constitutionalism in America, 1760–1848* (Ithaca, N.Y., 1972); Paul Finkelman, *An Imperfect Union: Slavery, Federalism, and Comity* (Chapel Hill, N.C., 1980); and Louis S. Gerteis, *Morality and Utility in American Antislavery Reform* (Chapel Hill, N.C., 1987). Slavery cases coming before the Supreme Court are reviewed in Don Fehrenbacher, *The Dred Scott Case: Its Significance in American Law and Politics* (New York, 1978), and in William M. Wiecek, "Slavery and Abolition before the United States Supreme Court, 1820–1860," *Journal of American History* 65 (1978): 34–59.

There have been several specialized studies of cases before the Taney Court (in addition to Fehrenbacher's). Outstanding among these is Stanley I. Kutler, *Privilege and Creative Destruction: The Charles River Bridge Case* (Philadelphia, 1971). On the same topic, see R. Kent Newmyer, "Justice Joseph Story, the Charles River Bridge Case and the Crisis of Republicanism," *American Journal of Legal History* 17 (1973): 232–45. Tony Freyer places *Swift* in its larger context in *Harmony & Dissonance: The Swift & Erie Cases in American Federalism* (New York, 1981). The Dorr Rebellion constitutional background to the *Luther* case is well surveyed in Patrick T. Conley, *Democracy in Decline: Rhode Island's Constitutional Development, 1776–1841* (Providence, 1977), and in George M. Dennison, *The Dorr War: Republicanism on Trial, 1831–1861* (Lexington, Ky., 1976).

Chapter 4. Civil War, Reconstruction, and the Rights of Black People

Two excellent article-length studies place the constitutional struggles of the Civil War in a large perspective: Arthur E. Bestor, Jr., "The American Civil War as a Constitutional Crisis," *American Historical Review* 69 (1964): 327–52; and Philip S. Paludan, "The American Civil War Considered as a Crisis in Law and Order," *American Historical Review* 77

(1972): 1013–34. A valuable modern survey of the war and its constitutional aftermath may be found in Harold M. Hyman, *A More Perfect Union: The Impact of the Civil War and Reconstruction on the Constitution* (New York, 1973). Several older studies retain their value. Premier among them is James G. Randall, *Constitutional Problems under Lincoln,* rev. ed. (New York, 1951); see also Robert M. Spector, "Lincoln and Taney: A Study in Constitutional Polarization," *American Journal of Legal History* 15 (1971): 19–214; and David M. Silver, *Lincoln's Supreme Court* (Urbana, Ill., 1956) (the title is a misnomer: the author refers to the Court in the war years, which was anything but "Lincoln's Court").

In the 1960s, scholars again turned their interest to Reconstruction, a field largely abandoned for a generation and hence dominated by outdated interpretations. The result was a fresh look at old problems and assumptions. Stanley I. Kutler led the way with *Judicial Power and Reconstruction Politics* (Chicago, 1968). Herman Belz extended our conception of Reconstruction backward in time in his prize-winning *Reconstructing the Union: Theory and Policy during the Civil War* (Ithaca, N.Y., 1969). Michael Les Benedict produced a synthesis of politics and constitutional issues in *A Compromise of Principle: Congressional Republicans and Reconstruction, 1863–1969* (New York, 1974). Benedict offers an interpretive survey of the work of the Waite Court in "Preserving Federalism: Reconstruction and the Waite Court," *Supreme Court Review* (1978): 39–79. Charles Fairman's contribution to the Holmes Devise *History of the Supreme Court* has resulted to date in one massive volume, *Reconstruction and Reunion, 1864–1888* (New York, 1971); the second is in preparation. C. Peter Magrath studied the life of the chief justice in *Morrison R. Waite: The Triumph of Character* (New York, 1963). William M. Wiecek surveys the important subject of the growth of the Court's power in "The Reconstruction of Federal Judicial Power," *American Journal of Legal History* 13 (1969): 333–59.

The literature on the Reconstruction amendments is as controversial as it is vast. The following titles are only suggestive. G. Sidney Buchanan's *The Quest for Freedom* (Houston, 1976), delivers what its subtitle promises: *A Legal History of the Thirteenth Amendment.* Raoul Berger's tendentious *Government by Judiciary: The Transformation of the Fourteenth Amendment* (Cambridge, Mass., 1977) stimulated a flood of debate on the intentions of the drafters of the Reconstruction amendments. Two men who participated in *Brown* v. *Board of Education* produced distillations of their own differing research involvement: see Alexander M. Bickel, "The Original Understanding and the Segregation Decision," *Harvard Law Review* 69 (1955): 1–65; and Alfred H. Kelly,

"The Fourteenth Amendment Reconsidered: The Segregation Question," *Michigan Law Review* 54 (1956): 1049–86.

The generation since *Brown* has witnessed an outpouring of work on the constitutional status and rights of black people. Two collections of primary source materials are useful: Derrick Bell, *Race, Racism and American Law,* 2d ed. (Boston, 1980), plus 1984 supplement (a law school casebook); and Richard Bardolph, ed., *The Civil Rights Record: Black Americans and the Law, 1849–1970* (New York, 1970; unfortunately, now out of print). Two valuable studies by Herman Belz provide overviews: *Emancipation and Equal Rights: Politics and Constitutionalism in the Civil War Era* (New York, 1978), and *A New Birth of Freedom: The Republican Party and Freedmen's Rights, 1861 to 1866* (Westport, Conn., 1976). William Cohen provides a preliminary analysis of the legal systems that replaced slavery in "Negro Involuntary Servitude in the South, 1865–1940," *Journal of Southern History* 42 (1976): 31–60. See also Pete Daniel, *Shadow of Slavery: Peonage in the South, 1901–1969* (Urbana, Ill., 1972), and Daniel, "The Metamorphosis of Slavery, 1855–1900," *Journal of American History* 66 (1979): 88–99.

Chapter 5. The Formalist Era, 1873–1937

In contrast with the relative paucity of materials on the Taney Court, the period from 1870 to 1940 has been well served by historical scholarship. Among the best background surveys are Morton Keller, *Affairs of State: Public Life in Late-Nineteenth-Century America* (Cambridge, Mass., 1977); Loren Beth, *The Development of the American Constitution, 1877–1917* (New York, 1971); Sidney Fine, *Laissez-Faire and the General-Welfare State: A Study of Conflict in American Thought, 1865–1901* (Ann Arbor, 1956), a work typical of the Progressive–New Deal liberal tradition that until recently had dominated interpretations of the era; Robert McCloskey, *American Conservatism in the Age of Enterprise, 1865–1910* (Cambridge, Mass., 1951), a work in the same tradition. Calvin Woodward, "Reality and Social Reform: The Transition from Laissez-Faire to the Welfare State," *Yale Law Journal* 72 (1962): 287–328, is an excellent survey that goes beyond liberal assumptions.

The rise of the administrative state has captured scholarly attention. Some of the best recent work includes Stephen Skowronek, *Building a New American State: The Expansion of National Administrative Capacities, 1877–1920* (Cambridge, Mass., 1982); William E. Nelson, *The Roots of American Bureaucracy, 1830–1900* (Cambridge, Mass., 1982); and studies by Thomas K. McCraw, including the prize-winning *Prophets of Regula-*

tion: Charles Francis Adams, Louis Dembitz Brandeis, James A. Landis, Alfred E. Kahn (Cambridge, Mass., 1984); "Regulation in America: A Review Article," *Business History Review* 49 (1975): 159–83; and *Regulation in Perspective: Historical Essays* (Cambridge, Mass., 1981). Wallace D. Farnham, "The Weakened Spring of Government: A Study in Nineteenth-Century American History," *American Historical Review* 68 (1963): 662–80, retains its relevance.

Studies of the Court that survey the era are William F. Swindler, *Court and Constitution in the Twentieth Century: The Old Legality, 1889–1932* (Indianapolis, 1969), and its successor volume, *Court and Constitution in the Twentieth Century: The New Legality, 1932–1968* (Indianapolis, 1972). See also John Semonche, *Charting the Future: The Supreme Court Responds to a Changing Society, 1890–1920* (Westport, Conn., 1978); the Holmes Devise volume, Alexander M. Bickel and Benno C. Schmidt, Jr., *The Judiciary and Responsible Government: 1910–1921* (New York, 1984); and John Johnson, *American Legal Culture, 1909–1940* (Westport, Conn., 1981). Two specialized studies of the Court's more conservative phases are illuminating: Alan Westin, "The Supreme Court, the Populist Movement, and the Campaign of 1896," *Journal of Politics* 15 (1953): 3–41, and Stanley I. Kutler, "Chief Justice Taft, National Regulation and the Commerce Clause," *Journal of American History* 51 (1965): 651–68, an evaluation that revises traditional Progressive assumptions. Two still useful studies in the older tradition are Benjamin Twiss, *Lawyers and the Constitution: How Laissez-Faire Came to the Supreme Court* (Princeton, 1942), and Clyde Jacobs, *Law Writers and the Courts* (New York, 1954).

Judicial biographies are plentiful and of high quality. See Charles Fairman, *Mr. Justice Miller and the Supreme Court, 1862–1890* (Cambridge, Mass., 1939) and Carl B. Swisher, *Stephen J. Field: Craftsman of the Law* (Chicago, 1963), a work that will be largely supplanted when Charles McCurdy's work-in-progress on Justice Field is published. Until it is, McCurdy's various revisionist articles on phases of Field's career will have to do; see particularly "Justice Field and the Jurisprudence of Government-Business Relations: Some Parameters of Laissez-Faire Constitutionalism, 1863–1897," *Journal of American History* 61 (1975): 970–1005. Willard L. King tried to make something out of *Melville Weston Fuller, Chief Justice of the United States* (Chicago, 1950), a hopeless task. Mark De Wolfe Howe's magnum opus, a multivolume biography of Justice Holmes, was interrupted by the author's untimely death after publication of the second volume: *Justice Oliver Wendell Holmes,* 2 vols. (Cambridge, Mass., 1957). Justice Holmes has not been treated kindly by historians of the last generation: see the historiographic survey of G. Edward White, "The Rise and Fall of Justice Holmes," *University of*

Chicago Law Review 39 (1971): 51–77. Joel F. Paschal, *Mr. Justice Sutherland: A Man against the State* (Princeton, 1951), does justice to that conservative giant and limns a surprisingly sympathetic figure. On an influential jurist and legal authority of the period who was not elevated to the Supreme Court, see Alan Jones, "Thomas M. Cooley and 'Laissez-Faire Constitutionalism': A Reconsideration," *Journal of American History* 53 (1967): 751–71.

Legal and historical scholars have been fascinated by substantive due process, and have explored it exhaustively. Two massive contemporary studies retain their pertinence: Rodney L. Mott, *Due Process of Law,* rpt. (New York, 1973), and Ernst Freund, *The Police Power, Public Policy and Constitutional Rights* (Chicago, 1904). The Progressive liberal tradition is well represented by Arnold M. Paul, *Conservative Crisis and the Rule of Law: Attitudes of Bar and Bench, 1885–1895* (Ithaca, N.Y., 1960). Edward A. Purcell, Jr., masterfully sketches the thought of the era that witnessed the disintegration of formalism in *Crisis of Democratic Theory: Scientific Naturalism and the Problem of Value* (Lexington, Ky., 1973).

The following evaluative essays are illuminating: Duncan Kennedy, "Toward an Historical Understanding of Legal Consciousness: The Case of Classical Legal Thought in America, 1850–1940" in S. Spitzer, ed., *Research in Law and Sociology* 3 (1960): 3–35; Robert W. Gordon, "Legal Thought and Legal Practice in the Age of Enterprise, 1870–1920," in Gerald L. Geison, ed., *Professions and Professional Ideologies in America* (Chapel Hill, N.C., 1983), 82–97; Michael Les Benedict, "Laissez-Faire and Liberty: A Re-evaluation of the Meaning and Origins of Laissez-Faire Constitutionalism," *Law and History Review* 3 (1985): 293–331; Janet Lindgren, "Beyond Cases: Reconsidering Judicial Review," *Wisconsin Law Review* (1983): 583–638. Studies in a revisionist direction (that is, away from the Progressive liberal assumptions) began with Charles Warren, "The Progressiveness of the United States Supreme Court," *Columbia Law Review* 13 (1913): 294–313. Among the best of the modern revisionist essays is Mary C. Porter, "That Commerce Shall Be Free: A New Look at the Old Laissez-Faire Court," *Supreme Court Review* (1976): 135–59. Amazingly, two modern scholars argue that *Lochner* was rightly decided, surely the *ne plus ultra* of revisionism: Bernard H. Siegan, *Economic Liberties and the Constitution* (Chicago, 1980), and Richard Epstein, *Takings: Private Property and the Power of Eminent Domain* (Cambridge, Mass., 1985). See also Epstein's defense of this position in "Self-Interest and the Constitution," *Journal of Legal Education* 37 (1987): 153–61.

There have not been many studies of individual cases in the formalist era; however, two excellent ones are Harry N. Scheiber, "The Road to

Munn: Eminent Domain and the Concept of Public Purpose in the State Courts," *Perspectives in American History* 5 (1971): 329–404, and Charles W. McCurdy, "The *Knight* Sugar Decision of 1895 and the Modernization of American Corporation Law, 1869–1903," *Business History Review* 53 (1979): 301–42.

Chapter 6. Foreign Affairs, Executive Authority, and the Court

Basic general surveys of the subject of presidential power include Edward S. Corwin, *The President: Office and Powers,* 4th ed. (New York, 1957), and Louis Henkin, *Foreign Affairs and the Constitution* (Mineola, N.Y., 1972). Charles A. Lofgren reexamined *Curtiss-Wright* in "United States v. Curtiss-Wright Export Corporation: An Historical Assessment," *Yale Law Journal* 83 (1973): 1–32, and found little support for the doctrine Sutherland formulated in that case. Peter Irons has written a comprehensive study of wartime treatment of the Japanese in *Justice at War* (New York, 1983). J. Willard Hurst's *Law of Treason in the United States* (Madison, 1982) is thorough. Maeva Marcus reviewed the *Youngstown* case in *Truman and the Steel Seizure Case: The Limits of Presidential Power* (New York, 1977). Before the Vietnam War, liberal scholars confidently supported an expansion of presidential power. See Clinton Rossiter, *Constitutional Dictatorship: Crisis Government in the Modern Democracies* (Ithaca, N.Y., 1948); Rossiter, *The Supreme Court and the Commander-in-Chief* (Ithaca, N.Y., 1951); Richard Neustadt, *Presidential Power: The Politics of Leadership* (New York, 1956); James MacGregor Burns, *Presidential Government: The Crucible of Leadership* (Boston, 1965). Arthur Schlesinger, Jr., came to a more chastened view in *The Imperial Presidency* (Boston, 1973).

The body of writings on the First Amendment is extensive. Modern approaches derive from John Stuart Mill's essay "On Liberty." An able survey of the origins of First Amendment problems in the era of World War I is found in Paul L. Murphy, *World War I and the Origin of Civil Liberties in the United States* (New York, 1979), written from a liberal perspective. William Preston, Jr., *Aliens and Dissenters: Federal Suppression of Radicals, 1903–1933* (Cambridge, Mass., 1963), and Richard Polenberg's soon-to-be-published *Fighting Faiths* provide more detailed studies of specific problems from the same perspective. Gerald Gunther reviewed Hand's contributions in "Learned Hand and the Origins of Modern First Amendment Theory: Some Fragments of History," *Stanford Law Review* 27 (1975): 719–73. Gunther's work-in-progress of a biography of Hand should further illuminate the topic. Wallace Mendelson traced the subsequent history of First Amendment doctrine to the Cold War in "Clear and Present Danger: From *Schenck* to *Dennis,*" *Columbia Law Review* 52 (1952): 313–33.

First Amendment issues in the Cold War are studied in Henry Steele Commager, *Freedom, Loyalty, Dissent* (New York, 1954); Stanley I. Kutler, *The American Inquisition: Justice and Injustice in the Cold War* (New York, 1982); Michal R. Belknap, *Cold War Political Justice: The Smith Act, the Communist Party, and American Civil Liberties* (Westport, Conn., 1977); Harold M. Hyman, *To Try Men's Souls: Loyalty Oaths in American History* (Berkeley, 1959); and Walter Goodman, *The Committee: The Extraordinary Career of the House Committee on Un-American Activities* (New York, 1968). The propriety of balancing competing individual and governmental interests in First Amendment issues is debated by Laurent B. Frantz, "The First Amendment in the Balance," *Yale Law Journal* 71 (1962): 1424–50, and Wallace Mendelson, "On the Meaning of the First Amendment: Absolutes in the Balance," *California Law Review* 50 (1962): 821–28. A survey of the whole topic is in Frank E. Strong, "Fifty Years of Clear and Present Danger: From Schenck to Brandenburg and Beyond," *Supreme Court Review* (1969): 41–80.

Richard Nixon's contributions to American constitutional history are considered in Philip S. Kurland, *Watergate and the Constitution* (Chicago, 1978); Alexander M. Bickel, "Watergate and the Legal Order," *Commentary* 57 (1974): 19–25; and Bernard Schwartz, "Bad Presidents Make Hard Law: Richard M. Nixon in the Supreme Court," *Rutgers Law Review* 31 (1977): 22–38. Raoul Berger's *Impeachment: The Constitutional Problems* (Cambridge, Mass., 1973), could not have been more timely.

Chapter 7. Substantive Equal Protection

Overviews of Warren Court activism from varying perspectives include J. Skelly Wright, "The Role of the Supreme Court in a Democratic Society: Judicial Activism or Restraint," *Cornell Law Review* 54 (1968): 1–28; Arthur J. Goldberg, *Equal Justice: The Supreme Court in the Warren Era* (Evanston, Ill., 1971); Philip B. Kurland, *Politics, the Constitution, and the Warren Court* (Chicago, 1970); and Alexander M. Bickel, *The Supreme Court and the Idea of Progress* (New York, 1970). The controversy stirred by *Carolene Products* is considered in Louis Lusky, "Footnote Redux: A Carolene Products Reminiscence," *Columbia Law Review* 82 (1982): 1093–1109; Alpheus T. Mason, "The Core of Free Government, 1938–1940: Mr. Chief Justice Stone and 'Preferred Freedoms,'" *Yale Law Journal* 65 (1956): 597–628; and Wallace Mendelson, *Justices Black and Frankfurter: Conflict on the Court* (Chicago, 1961). For a post–*Carolene*

Products future, see Bruce A. Ackerman, "Beyond Carolene Products," *Harvard Law Review* 98 (1985): 713–46.

On the new era of equal protection, see the truly seminal article by Joseph Tussman and Jacobus ten Broek, "The Equal Protection of the Laws," *California Law Review* 37 (1949): 341–81; Philip B. Kurland, "Egalitarianism and the Warren Court," *Michigan Law Review* 68 (1970): 629–82; Gerald Gunther, "In Search of Evolving Doctrine on a Changing Court: A Model for a Newer Equal Protection," *Harvard Law Review* 86 (1972): 1–48; Wallace Mendelson, "From Warren to Burger: The Rise and Decline of Substantive Equal Protection," *American Political Science Review* 66 (1972): 1226–33; J. R. Pole, *The Pursuit of Equality in American History* (Berkeley, 1978); and Judith A. Baer, *Equality under the Constitution: Reclaiming the Fourteenth Amendment* (Ithaca, N.Y., 1983).

An immense body of scholarly writing has illuminated the problem of civil rights in the modern era. Richard Kluger, *Simple Justice: The History of Brown v. Board of Education and Black Americans' Struggle for Equality* (New York, 1976) is a detailed study of *Brown.* To single out any one item from the large body of controversial writing on that decision's legitimacy is invidious, but Charles L. Black, Jr., "The Lawfulness of the Segregation Decisions," *Yale Law Journal* 69 (1960): 421–30, is of particular interest because it combines scholarly analysis with illumination from the author's personal perspective. The aftermath of *Brown* has come under sharper criticism than the decision itself. Even when racist condemnations are put aside as unworthy of notice, the extent of criticism is surprising. See Lino Graglia, *Disaster by Decree: The Supreme Court Decisions on Race and the Schools* (Ithaca, N.Y., 1976); J. Harvie Wilkinson, *From Boston to Bakke: The Supreme Court and School Integration, 1954–1978* (New York, 1979); Terry Eastland and William J. Bennett, *Counting by Race: Equality from the Founding Fathers to Bakke and Weber* (New York, 1979). There are other views, however: John H. Ely, "The Constitutionality of Reverse Race Discrimination," *University of Chicago Law Review* 41 (1974): 723–41; Laurence H. Tribe, "Perspectives on Bakke: Equal Protection, Procedural Fairness, or Structural Justice?" *Harvard Law Review* 92 (1979): 864–77. On extrapolations of substantive equal protection beyond race, see Charles Reich, "The New Property," *Yale Law Journal* 73 (1964): 733–87; Frank I. Michelman, "On Protecting the Poor through the Fourteenth Amendment," *Harvard Law Review* 83 (1969): 7–59; and Kenneth Karst, "Woman's Constitution," *Duke Law Journal* (1984): 447.

On other subjects realizing the ambiguous promise of *Carolene Products*: Thomas Emerson, "Toward a General Theory of the First Amendment," *Yale Law Journal* 72 (1963): 877–956; Harry Kalven, Jr., " 'Uninhibited, Robust, and Wide-Open'—A Note on Free Speech and the Warren Court," *Michigan Law Review* 67 (1968): 289–302; Robert Weisberg, "Deregulating Death," *Supreme Court Review* (1983): 305–95; Richard Cortner, *The Supreme Court and the Second Bill of Rights* (Madison, 1981) (on incorporation); Michael E. Smith, "The Special Place of Religion in the Constitution," *Supreme Court Review* (1983): 83–123; Leo Pfeffer, "Freedom and/or Separation: The Constitutional Dilemma of the First Amendment," *Minnesota Law Review* 64 (1980): 561–84; and William Van Alstyne, "Trends in the Supreme Court: Mr. Jefferson's Crumbling Wall: A Comment on Lynch v. Donnelly," *Duke Law Journal* (1984): 770–87.

Chapter 8. Substantive Due Process

Modern substantive due process in its extreme embodiment, *Roe* v. *Wade*, has not been treated kindly by critics. See, e.g., John H. Ely, "The Wages of Crying Wolf: A Comment on Roe v. Wade," *Yale Law Journal* 82 (1973): 920–49, and Richard E. Epstein, "Substantive Due Process by Any Other Name: The Abortion Cases," *Supreme Court Review* (1973): 159–86. But see a thoughtful recent defense: Andrew L. Kaufman, "Judges or Scholars: To Whom Shall We Look for Our Constitutional Law?" *Journal of Legal Education* 37 (1987): 184–202.

The success of differing methods of political assault on the substance of judging is evaluated in Laurence H. Tribe, *God Save This Honorable Court: How the Choice of Justices Can Change Our Lives* (Cambridge, Mass., 1986), and William M. Wiecek, "The 'Imperial Judiciary' in Historical Perspective," *Yearbook 1984* of the [U.S.] Supreme Court Historical Society, 61–89.

A good overview of the modern controversies in constitutional theory may be found in Erwin Chereminsky, "The Price of Asking the Wrong Question: An Essay on Constitutional Scholarship and Judicial Review," *Texas Law Review* 62 (1984): 1207–61. Charles L. Black's contribution is in *Structure and Relationship in Constitutional Law* (Baton Rouge, La., 1969). G. Edward White critiqued scholarly thought of the 1950s in "The Evolution of Reasoned Elaboration: Jurisprudential Criticism and Social Change," *Virginia Law Review* 59 (1973): 279–302. The members of the Reasoned Elaboration school of thought presented their views in Henry M. Hart, Jr., "The Time Chart of the Justices," *Harvard Law Review* 73 (1958): 84–125; Learned Hand, *The Bill of Rights* (New York, 1958) (an extreme demand for judicial restraint delivered in the 1958 Holmes lectures at the Harvard Law School); Herbert Wechsler, "Toward Neutral Principles of Constitutional Law," *Harvard Law Review* 73

(1960): 1–35 (the Holmes lectures of the following year, delivered as a rebuttal to Hand's views); Herbert Wechsler, "The Courts and the Constitution," *Columbia Law Review* 65 (1965): 1001–14. Alexander M. Bickel was a host unto himself; in addition to his *The Least Dangerous Branch,* see *The Supreme Court and the Idea of Progress* (New York, 1970); and *The Morality of Consent* (New York, 1975). Raoul Berger may justly be considered to have detonated the avalanche of current controversies with his *Government by Judiciary,* but interpretivist views were already in the air at the time he wrote, as, for example, in Robert Bork, "Neutral Principles and Some First Amendment Problems," *Indiana Law Journal* (1971): 1–35. Justice Rehnquist put forth his views in "Observation: The Notion of a Living Constitution," *Texas Law Review* 54 (1976): 693–706. John Hart Ely attempted an end run around the intractable problem of judge-defined substantive values in *Democracy and Distrust: A Theory of Judicial Review* (Cambridge, Mass., 1980), a book influenced by Robert H. Jackson's *The Struggle for Judicial Supremacy: A Study in American Power Politics* (New York, 1941). Dismayed (or other) reactions to the seeming disintegration of constitutional theory appear in Robert Gordon, "Historicism in Legal Scholarship," *Yale Law Journal* 90 (1981): 1017–56; Paul Brest, "The Fundamental Rights Controversy: The Essential Contradictions of Normative Constitutional Scholarship," *Yale Law Journal* 90 (1981): 1063–1109; Richard D. Parker, "The Past of Constitutional Theory—and Its Future," *Ohio State Law Journal* 42 (1981): 223–59; and Owen M. Fiss, "Objectivity and Interpretation," *Stanford Law Review* 34 (1982): 739–63.

INDEX